GRASSROOTS LAW IN PAPUA NEW GUINEA

GRASSROOTS LAW IN PAPUA NEW GUINEA

EDITED BY MELISSA DEMIAN

Australian
National
University

ANU PRESS

MONOGRAPHS IN
ANTHROPOLOGY SERIES

Australian National University

ANU PRESS

Published by ANU Press
The Australian National University
Canberra ACT 2600, Australia
Email: anupress@anu.edu.au

Available to download for free at press.anu.edu.au

ISBN (print): 9781760466114
ISBN (online): 9781760466121

WorldCat (print): 1397089446
WorldCat (online): 1397089079

DOI: 10.22459/GLPNG.2023

Cover design and layout by ANU Press. Cover photograph by Melissa Demian.

This book is published under the aegis of the Anthropology in Pacific and Asian Studies editorial board of ANU Press.

Contents

Acknowledgements

Deepest thanks go to the original team whose work on various parts of the *Legal Innovations in Papua New Guinea* project formed the inspiration for this book: Michael D. Fischer, Eve Houghton, Fiona Hukula, Michael Goddard and the late Kritoe Keleba, whose dedication as a researcher and insights shared at the project workshops are to be found throughout the questions and challenges posed in this collection. He is much missed by friends and colleagues alike.

That project was funded by the UK Economic and Social Research Council, grant no. ES/J012300/1. The present volume stands as evidence of how the effects of research funding can often outlast the specific projects for which it is awarded, and it is critical to acknowledge the points at which these effects are materialised, even—or especially—years after a funded project has concluded.

Thank you to Camila F. Marinelli for the stellar transcription work that brought one of our chapters to fruition.

Especial thanks to Matt Tomlinson, Chair of the Editorial Board for Pacific and Asian Studies at ANU Press, for his support, patience and sound advice in shepherding the book through the ups and downs of the road to publication.

Thanks also to the two reviewers for this volume, whose close attention to the chapters offered here transformed the book in many ways. One reviewer helped to make it stronger; the other helped to make it longer.

Melissa Demian
September 2022

Introduction: The magic of the court

Melissa Demian

> It is law that defines everything we see and hear going on around us.
>   – Former Chief Justice of PNG Sir Salamo Injia,
>   speaking in Canberra, 2015

What does it mean to speak of a law of the grassroots in Papua New Guinea (PNG)? Does it refer to what a legal observer of the newly independent nation called 'a true people's law' (Fitzpatrick, 1975: 284), which he hoped would emerge to serve the whole population and not just metropolitan elites? Or is it something even more diffuse, an atmosphere of law generated by the sometimes fraught relationship between a citizenry and a state that can appear to have little interest in interacting with them other than generating laws to constrain the flow of everyday life? These questions and a host of related ones form the backbone of this book, as they address how Papua New Guineans who are not metropolitans engage with the part of the legal system that was 'designed' for them—that is, the village courts—as well as with any number of court-like forums and other legal sensibilities that exist in dialogue with the formal legal system without necessarily being part of it.

To talk about non-metropolitan law in contemporary PNG poses some risks, given that the very idea of a metropole in relation to a periphery has such a long and contested history in the social sciences and humanities. It dates at least to the spatial metaphor of centre and periphery offered by postwar sociology to describe the concentration of political, economic and cultural influence in particular physical spaces and institutions, usually although not always located in cities (Shils, 1975). This urban inflection of the concept was later adopted by other disciplines such as history, geography and anthropology to theorise the ways that colonising states and their capitals, the metropoles, existed in an interdependent relationship with the colonised periphery (Slater, 2004; Stoler & Cooper, 1997). For my purposes, a salient observation about this relationship from Connell (2010) underscores the way law in formerly colonised countries like PNG has been studied in the past. As she notes:

> The distinction of metropole from colony is also a distinction of function in the making of scientific knowledge. Theory-making was located in the metropole; data-gathering, and some applications of science at the end of the process, occurred in the colonies. (2010, p. 74)

This one-way directionality is no longer quite so straightforward in the era of the postcolony, but Connell usefully highlights the way that the metropole–periphery relationship in colonialism was a set of knowledge practices as much as it was a system of political and economic domination.

If law was a component of that domination, the way law was studied in colonised societies also became a way for metropoles using data gathered in the periphery to speak to themselves about their own theories. In Merry's (1991) consideration of the relationship between colonial-era law and socio-legal studies, she notes that this created a doubling effect in colonial legal regimes, often with one set of courts (and regulations governing them) for the colonial metropole and another for the colonised periphery. Combining her observation with Connell's, one could say that these dual legal regimes also gave rise to a kind of double vision in late colonial-era work in the anthropology of law. Case studies of the ways that colonised people resolved their disputes, from indigenous North America (Llewellyn & Hoebel, 1941) to sub-Saharan Africa (Bohannan, 1957; Gluckman, 1955; Schapera, 1955) to Melanesia (Epstein, 1974), all contributed to the development of a legal anthropology informed by precisely this aspect of the metropole–periphery relationship. Practices and concepts gathered among peripheral peoples were meant to inform theory in the metropole, but more than that, they subtly enforced the distinction between the two sides of colonial legal systems even as politically engaged scholars such as Gluckman sought to undermine the divide between them. But as important as this emergent legal anthropology was in arguing that there was something law-like in the disputing practices of colonised peoples, its very premise—the ethnographic study of something analogous to European jurisprudence—maintained the duality of a metropolitan versus a peripheral set of legal sensibilities and courts intended to serve those dual sensibilities.

A double system of this kind always holds the relationship between metropole and periphery in productive tension. Among the aims of this book is to ask how this uneasy relationship between metropolitan law and a law of the grassroots has informed the other's concepts of what law is, what it is for and *whom* it is for. To acknowledge this phenomenon and investigate it ethnographically, it has become necessary to treat 'actually legal' and 'nonlegal but law-adjacent' practices in PNG as part of the same social repertoire, as they have indeed been treated since the beginnings of a robust legal anthropology in the country just prior to its independence in 1975 (e.g. Epstein, 1971; Lawrence, 1969; Strathern, 1972). In other words, this is a collection of observations conceived of deliberately as offering the perspectives not of specialists in the field of legal scholarship, but of social scientists and the populations of ordinary Papua New Guineans with whom we have worked. While formal law for the purposes of state-building and the institutions created to support it are generated in the metropole, people can and must find ways to make these institutions work for them, which often starts with disregarding any distinction between institutional and non-institutional forms. This then becomes part of a people's 'legal consciousness', to employ the useful term once coined by Merry (1990) to describe the processes whereby people arrive at such a consciousness in their dealings with a particular legal system. They deal with the law that defines everything they see and hear going on around them not only through metropolitan institutional forms, but also through the entire set of values, experiences and expectations they bring to the category of law and legal action. This collection aims to expand that category accordingly, in an effort at ethnographic commitment to the future of the 'underlying law' of PNG—a concept enshrined in the country's constitution and elaborated further through the *Underlying Law Act 2000*. If the underlying law, with its metaphoric suggestion of a bedrock-like stratum lying just beneath the conduct of everyday life, is to be found in what people are already doing, then it cannot be 'developed' from the metropole: it must come from the grassroots.

Who do we mean by the grassroots, and can the slightly problematic class implications of that term be turned to an advantage? Most of the people consulted for the studies in this book—although by no means all—are either rural people or those on the economic and physical peripheries of PNG's towns and cities. They are, for the most part, not metropolitans. They have substantially varying levels of educational attainment, experience of different parts of the country besides their own and, critically for our purposes, access to formal legal mechanisms and the social class necessary to being able to use those mechanisms skilfully. Village courts were created precisely for this majority population in PNG to use, and to formalise in some way their modes of seeking redress from each other under conditions of conflict.

Having said this, it is important to note that the concept of customary law was not an organising principle for this project, nor is it central to most of the chapters collected here. This concept does formally ride in tandem with that of 'underlying law' due to the way the latter is articulated in the Underlying Law Act (Demian, 2011; Zorn & Care, 2002), and it is also meant to form the basis for most village court decisions according to the *Village Courts Act 1989*. But as the chapters to follow will demonstrate, what happens in reality is far more complex. Some village courts explicitly position themselves as dispensing state law and, in so doing, they claim a direct relationship to the metropole, in blithe disregard for the metropolitan perspective of the Village Courts Act, which establishes exactly the kind of dual system (one legal body for the centre, another for the periphery) described by Merry (1991). Other courts appear to combine what they regard as the law of the state with practices or relationships that could, conceivably, come under the rubric of customary law. But even this concept, as a wealth of scholarship has shown, is itself an artefact of the metropole–colony relationship, wherein the intersecting interests of colonial and indigenous elites produce the 'discovery' of a body of law-like principles that are in fact synthesised out of the far more contingent and relational decisions that emerge from local disputing practices (see e.g. Chanock, 1985; Fitzpatrick, 1989; Lev, 1985; Moore, 1986; Vincent, 1989). As I have argued elsewhere (Demian, 2014a), this process of 'recognising' customary law is simultaneously a project of holding it at bay, in order to control and circumscribe those practices placed under the category of custom that metropolitans do not wish to see becoming part of the law in the modern liberal state they are building.

If the present collection is not yet another evaluation of the place of customary law in Papua New Guinean legal practices, what is its remit? The germ of this book formed with a research project entitled *Legal Innovation in Papua New Guinea*, which ran from 2012 to 2015 and involved a team of researchers from the United Kingdom, Australia and PNG, who conducted work with village courts in different parts of the country. Among our objectives for that project was to investigate the widespread sentiment, expressed by legal practitioners in Port Moresby and other urban centres, that the activities of village courts had become uncontrolled or even chaotic, and that they were certainly exceeding their jurisdiction on a number of fronts. The 'unlawfulness' of village courts seemed a timely subject at a time when the Village Courts Secretariat was exerting additional efforts to appoint and train women as magistrates, and to come to grips with the often stark differences between who was officially gazetted in their records and who else was out there in the provinces, acting in a magisterial capacity without any knowledge on the part of the secretariat in its offices in Port Moresby.

What we found in the course of the project was far more interesting, as our research was required to encompass the workings not only of the courts themselves but also of the wider social fields of which they were a part. As Moore (1973) once observed, the social field inhabited by local courts in the postcolony is 'semi-autonomous' in that it is defined not by an institutional structure so much as by 'a processual characteristic, the fact that it can generate rules and coerce or induce compliance to them' (1973, p. 722). Other anthropological observers of law as a social field such as Greenhouse (1982) and Strathern (1985) emphasised even more strongly this processual and relational characteristic of local disputing practices, and asked whether there was even anything as stable or identifiable as rules, control or coercion in the picture. For our own project this meant, among other things, attending to the ways in which the formal constraints upon village courts in the context of the everyday lives of people they were trying to help all but *required* them to go 'off script' to do their job of keeping the peace. Several of the chapters in this book will show precisely this improvisational mode of dispute management in action.

In principle, village courts in PNG are meant to execute their functions within the parameters of the Village Courts Act, which are operationalised in the handbook provided to some magistrates, and whose provisions are also the foundation for any training they may have received. Training and remuneration of village court magistrates can be patchy at best and, in some parts of the country, have not occurred for years (Demian, 2014b; Howley, 2005). Additionally, magistrates themselves may have little or no formal education, as it was always the intention that village court magistrates should be local men—and these days, women—acknowledged by their communities to be persons of note and repositories of local or 'customary' knowledge. Formal advocacy is specifically excluded from village courts under the terms of the Village Courts Act; these courts were always intended as forums in which people should be able to represent themselves, in line with the courts' purpose of providing access to justice for all Papua New Guineans. So, while village court magistrates make every effort to operate within the bounds of the law as they understand it, it is precisely this 'as they understand it' that is at issue. Their lines of communication with Port Moresby and even their own provincial capital may be tenuous to nonexistent, especially if they are not literate in English, and their grasp of the latest legislative decisions of parliament similarly partial in nature. The communication infrastructure— and this is not a technological or transportation infrastructure so much as a political and economic one—between Port Moresby and the provinces, or even between the urban centres of Moresby, Lae, Goroka and so on, and their settlement peripheries, has not been able to support the range of needs that village courts must serve. The courts are, in many cases, effectively on their own, attempting to fulfil their obligations to a state to which they are functionally invisible much of the time.

As a consequence, that original project became one that was about much more than village courts and how well they 'functioned', as this book has also become. The social conventions and performative modes of the court have exerted their own influence over other ways of doing things and become part of the wider social imaginary in PNG—part of the 'magic' in the title of this introduction. I will return to that presently. The point is that it is no longer sufficient to ask 'Is X type of court executing Y element of its jurisdiction correctly?'. Arguably that was never the right question. One of the intentions of the present volume is to shift the conversation about how Papua New Guineans who are not legal specialists conceive of their relationship to the law. By now there has been exhaustive documentation not only of what village courts do and how they work, but also of non-court events and social forms that draw upon the blueprint of the court to serve a host of purposes, ranging from playful experimentation to the purposive appropriation of state authority. They may appropriate and emulate the style of court proceedings in order to have entirely different kinds of social effects (Lipset, 2004), they may claim the title of courts and government sanction in the demonstrable absence of either (Schwoerer, 2018) or the anticipation of one's actual day in court may serve as a means of hopeful future-formation for incarcerated Papua New Guineans (Reed, 2011). Courts in PNG have generated their own spaces of anticipation and anxiety, as have other modes of disputing and dispute management that may borrow some, but not all, of the ways of doing this that the village courts offer.

The chapters in this book grapple with both how the village courts create such spaces, in the technical sense of their actual practices and the ways in which they interpret the legal remit handed to them, and how these in turn indicate some of the ways that people in PNG imagine what law and the state from which it emanates are. As such, this collection may be thought of as a contribution to the new legal realism (NLR), which advocates for:

> A bottom-up approach [that] takes an expansive and open-minded view of the impact of law, and also includes within its purview a wide range of socio-economic classes and interests. Indeed, at times, this approach will reach outside of the boundaries of formal legal processes and institutions altogether to examine other forms of regulation and ordering. (Erlanger et al., 2005, p. 339)

The 'other forms of regulation and ordering' component of this approach is critical both to the project of NLR and to this book, particularly as the authors collected here investigate social forms that may appear to legal practitioners to be disorderly, unregulated or wrongheaded. Among the efforts of scholars interested in NLR is that of 'translating' between the work of legal scholarship and scholarship in social sciences such as anthropology. While this translation work is largely happening in law schools disposed to critical reflection on the actual effects of law (Klug & Merry, 2016), there remains an entire repertoire of action in relation to the changing landscape of law that is difficult to encompass without recourse to ethnographic work of the kind represented in this book.

Some examples may serve to illustrate the challenge. In many countries there are particular social phenomena or issues with which the law is felt perpetually to struggle; in PNG, those issues include gender-based violence and violence arising from sorcery accusations. In terms of the former, despite a decade of rigorous scholarship on gender violence in PNG and elsewhere in Melanesia (Biersack et al., 2016; Jolly et al., 2012; Rooney et al., 2022), the nongovernmental organisation (NGO) discourse has not moved far beyond the 'worst place in the world to be a woman' idea (Human Rights Watch, 2015; Médecins Sans Frontières, 2016). Many Papua New Guinean women would find this picture of their country difficult to recognise. At the same time, the very high prevalence of gender-based violence in the country is undeniable, and is undeniably an issue with which the formal legal system has struggled to keep up. Despite the passing of the *Family Protection Act 2013*, no resources have been devoted to enforcing its provisions and few cases are prosecuted in the district or national courts. The result is that gender-based violence persists almost entirely outside the domain of the law and has instead become a matter for NGOs, churches and community initiatives to manage as best they can.

Sorcery-related violence is another issue that has resisted becoming 'domained' as a legal matter. Until 2013, the *Sorcery Act 1971* provided the main toolkit for courts to deal with cases involving an accusation of sorcery and those involving violence arising from a sorcery accusation. This dual remit for a single piece of legislation was complicated further by an extraordinary attempt to reconcile sorcery's existence and non-existence in the same breath:

> Even though this Act may speak as if powers of sorcery really exist (which is necessary if the law is to deal adequately with all the legal problems of sorcery and the traditional belief in the powers of sorcerers), nevertheless nothing in this Act recognises the existence or effectiveness of powers of sorcery in any factual sense. (*Sorcery Act 1971*, s. 3)

This language attempted to satisfy an official nonrecognition of sorcery consistent throughout Commonwealth jurisdictions with the issue of 'belief' that courts would need periodically to confront. The legal fiction it generated in this way—sorcery does not exist, but courts are permitted to reach decisions as though it does—never quite did the work it was perhaps intended to do. As Riles observes, courts and lawmakers rely explicitly upon

> the particular character of the legal fiction as an assertion of what is understood always already to be false … [I]t is an *explicit instrument*, a device with a clearly defined purpose, *a means to an end*. (2016, p. 132, emphasis in original)

Riles notes, in her survey of a body of theory about legal fictions, that they can have the effect of allowing or obliging judges to reach decisions that reveal disharmonies in the law that the fiction concealed—say, that sorcery is not real but courts may act as though it is—and these decisions inherently reflect the political positions of the judges. The legal realist implications of this effect is a topic to which I will return shortly. My point for now is that the legal fiction at the heart of the Sorcery Act had precisely this effect. It generated a body of case law in which courts in PNG vacillated for decades between decisions reached as though an accusation of sorcery provided a mitigating defence for killings or other violence, and those refusing to recognise any such defence. Both these types of decisions were potentially reachable through the provisions of the Act, leading to the unavoidable conclusion that judges who came down on one side or the other were making decisions in accordance with the aspects of the Act they found more compelling. In 2013 the National Parliament of PNG finally repealed the Act, with the proposing Member of Parliament (MP), Kerenga Kua, declaring that 'the Sorcery Act belongs to another era' and also noting the way in which it had pulled the courts in two directions, although he was focused more on a distinction in the Act between 'innocent' and 'forbidden' sorcery than on its reliance on a legal fiction to enable different kinds of outcomes (Papua New Guinea, 2013). The concern of this MP was to foreclose on any possibility of the Act being used to mount a defence in cases of violence arising from sorcery accusations. The ontological status of sorcery was not an element of his proposed bill, nor did it have to be. Repealing the Act removed the necessity to talk about what kind of sorcery courts were dealing with, and about whether or not sorcery is real, in the same legislative move. This move transferred any violence committed in the name of a sorcery accusation unambiguously into the remit of the Criminal Code, disallowing any possibility of a defence on the grounds of a 'belief' that sorcery had occurred or might occur.

So much for parliamentary concerns in 2013. Whether or not a given village court has the decade-old repeal of the Sorcery Act on its radar, village courts continue to be confronted with sorcery accusations on a regular basis and must deal with them in their capacity as the institution charged with keeping the peace in their communities. Village courts are supremely pragmatic institutions and their officers—magistrates, peace officers and clerks—are committed to maintaining that bundled concept so beloved of the PNG Government and foreign donor agencies alike: 'law and order'. This very commitment to law and order means that their interpretation of jurisdiction can be quite flexible at times, which is often precisely what allows village courts to keep the peace. The courts' pragmatism can, at the same time, exacerbate problems with any assumptions about the efficacy of changes to the law beyond the metropole. There can be no presumption that laws enacted, repealed or amended in Port Moresby will be either communicated effectively or accepted by village courts as having any bearing on how they deal with sorcery accusations, because of the flexibility required of them.

This is because some people in PNG might interpret decisions like the repeal of the Sorcery Act as evidence that the law and the state are not on the side of the angels, as it were. Ethnographic reports of sorcery narratives that encompass the state itself indicate how ordinary people may deny the legitimacy of law as soon as it is perceived to serve the interests of a world inhabited not by themselves, but by other kinds of beings hostile to human lives and human flourishing.[1] The legal establishment is in a genuine bind vis-à-vis fears about sorcery in communities throughout the country. If sorcery were treated as a real phenomenon meriting a defence in cases of violence arising from a sorcery accusation, lawmakers in PNG risk denunciation for opening the door to human rights abuses by the agents of liberal humanism ranging from donor governments to NGOs and international development agencies. If, on the other hand, people's concerns about sorcery are not taken seriously, and are granted no status in law, the government risks further alienation from some groups of its citizens—the uncomfortable 'real' in any version of legal realism that might be applied to this situation. As one legal colleague in Port Moresby observed to me, law governs human affairs, but not the spiritual dimension inherent in sorcery accusations. Further legislation would not solve the problem, in his view. 'Law has reached its limit', he said, and suggested that the law had reached an impermeable border where law and spirituality meet (D. Gonol, pers. comm. 2015). Another colleague at the same meeting suggested that law is a technique of both measurement and standardisation for human action, but the spiritual domain by its very nature cannot be measured. He was effecting an analytical removal of the category of the spiritual from any question of human agency or human institutions being able to act upon it. In the absence of such agency (or indeed of structure), the potential of the spiritual to cause trouble is potentially limitless, which contributes in no small part to the anxieties produced through and around sorcery discourses in some parts of PNG. How can one exercise any kind of realism, legal or otherwise, under these conditions?

Some readers will have noted already that the title of this introduction is a reference to Taussig's *The Magic of the State* (1997), a trippy work of ethnographic fiction that I used to inflict on students when I taught classes on anthropological assessments of magical systems of thought. Taussig's book is not an assessment, though, so much as an attempt to reproduce in the reader the sense of disorientation experienced frequently by ethnographers whenever magical systems and political systems are found to be inextricable from each other—when one is always the 'behind' of the other, as he describes it throughout the book. Another way to describe this way of apprehending both magic and politics is as merographic forms, in that,

---

1   I am grateful to the unpublished work of Kritoe Keleba on Western Province, and Thomas Strong on Eastern Highlands Province, for drawing my attention to this particularly challenging aspect of sorcery discourses in some parts of PNG.

> although they precipitate a plural world of analogous contexts and domains, these domains are never sustained as exhaustive or total analogies. That is precisely because the domains are regarded as overlapping in certain 'places', in certain areas or institutions or persons, where they must appear only as parts (of other domains). (Strathern, 1992, p. 84)

My use of Strathern to parse Taussig is itself a merographic move: their ways of describing systems appear to be analogues of each other, but only in 'certain places' do they have this effect. They are not aiming at quite the same descriptive outcomes for the way institutions, persons and so on can appear as parts or sides of each other, but it is possible to discern a fleeting analogy in the way they both try to hold this phenomenon still long enough to make it visible.

'Certain places' can apply not only to conceptual meeting points, but also actual places, actual localities and the way people in these localities use one system to describe or measure the other; sorcery can be used to assess law, and law used to assess sorcery—but only in certain places. What would a realism applied to this particular legal system suggest for, say, attempting to reconcile a domain such as law with a domain such as the spiritual? Elsewhere law may be used to assess familial relationships between spouses, or between parents and children, but the same effect of temporary or partial analogy obtains, wherein Acts of parliament may be made to appear as the mode of measurement for a community meeting or a mediation. But these modes of measurement are themselves subject to assessment insofar as they appear to look towards an international audience rather than one residing within PNG, and as such they index a field of relationships in which many Papua New Guineans do not feel they participate.

Another way to put this is that Taussig's intervention, however dizzying in its literary effects, suggests some reasons for the way village courts and other non-court institutions exert so much effort in invoking both the symbols and the laws of the state in the face of the state's almost complete lack of interest in what they are actually doing. One might go so far as to suggest that the state itself can be invoked in a spiritual capacity, such as when a peace officer says that the law has two parts, the church side and the government side (Demian, 2021, p. 151), or when the rituals of district and national courts are followed, such as erecting the PNG flag next to the magistrates and bowing at the start and close of a village court sitting. But I also have Taussig in mind because there has been a concern in the PNG metropoles for many years that although what village courts are doing has the *form* of law, it lacks the content. In some respects they were engineered this way: early plans for the village courts explicitly envisioned them as adapting to local conditions, within the limits of their jurisdiction. It would not be too much of an exaggeration at this point to say that they have adapted so well to local conditions that they have entirely outgrown their jurisdiction and are operating as a system almost entirely independent of the rest of the legal apparatus of PNG. The only time village courts have any institutional relationship with the formal court system is when cases are appealed to the district courts, which is considered a highly undesirable option for many people. So the aim is to invoke the state as a source of symbolic—dare one say magical—authority, but actually involving that authority in local disputes is to be avoided if at all possible. One could pose a more theoretical question in regard to village courts and their adjacent conflict mediation forums: what exactly is the form that they appear to be reproducing? Law changes its form too, all the time. If village courts are trying to appear in the form of some other system, what and where is that system? Is it the law of the Papua New Guinean state and its legal infrastructures, or a law of the grassroots, or a manifestation of the relationship between them?

The chapters in this book have been organised in such a way as to attempt to answer these questions. In the first half, the 'bottom-up' approach championed by NLR and socio-legal studies more broadly is taken with the practices of village courts and non-court disputing forums in four regions of PNG. These chapters demonstrate that an ethnographic examination of the ways in which disputes are conducted and, more critically, the meanings that people make of their disputing by means of these forums offers particular insights into how 'the law' becomes translated through institutions that are only incompletely connected to a formal legal system.

This sets the stage for the second half of the book, which takes up both ethnographic and theoretical issues suggested by the relationship between citizens and the Papua New Guinean state that the law is meant to instantiate. Again, the 'real' of realism is challenged by the activities of people who may understand their participation in a state legal regime as being any mixture of education, capitulation, support or outright enmity. The effects of law are felt unevenly, as these chapters demonstrate, and can also have unintended consequences the more distanced people feel from decisions made in the metropole. This too speaks to the realism of the approach taken here: some of the interpretations and actions to which people turn in their relationship to the state may constitute a direct challenge to the moral authority of the state and its abilities to make laws that can or should affect people's relationships with one another.

Hiroki Fukagawa opens Part 1 by inviting a consideration of the way that village courts in Enga Province took their cues from the total authority of *kiap* courts during the colonial era as the model for how village courts should be run, and how village court magistrates in the present day should engage with the people who bring disputes to them. In his chapter, the 'external' authority of the Papua New Guinean state has been 'internalised' by the activities of village courts in Enga. This has the effect of consolidating the political influence of clan leaders, who frequently use their appointment as magistrates to steer court decisions in favour of their kin. People who bring their disputes to the village court rather than to the alternative forum of village-level mediations know and to a certain extent accept that this kind of self-dealing will occur, and that it is a normal part both of local politics in Enga and of the state authority that magistrates arrogate to themselves. This does not prevent people from imagining, as Fukagawa argues, how a court more properly connected to the state might operate, and whether its operations might deliver something less thoroughly entangled with the politics of local kinship formations.

Juliane Neuhaus employs a close analysis of an adultery complaint in Morobe Province to show how a single 'case' can move through multiple forums for redress, activated by the actors involved, their degree of involvement in these forums and their hopes for a particular outcome to the grievance. The accusation of adultery brings into view an entire range of moral, spiritual and legal concerns stemming from interpretations of international human rights discourses, from Christian ideas of fidelity and from the kinship implications of multiple partnerships. As a single complainant takes her accusation through a series of different forums, both legal and nonlegal in nature, Neuhaus shows how the pursuit of a grievance at the local level is not necessarily sequential in nature, is often taken to several forums at the same time and never kept solely within the purview of the law. Instead, even very localised and intimate issues around the nature of marriage in PNG allow people to engage with a set of cosmopolitan ideas of what it means to be an actor asserting a set of 'rights'.

Tomi Bartole then takes us to East Sepik Province to discuss the spectral nature of the presence of the village court: it is known as an institutional form but is avoided in practice, in favour of local dispute resolution forms such as the 'handshake'. The village court is not instantiated, Bartole argues, because it remains an unfinished or negatively evaluated 'gift' from the PNG state. The power of the court system is compared to the shells once exchanged in this part of the Sepik region for peacemaking purposes, wherein the threat of the shell to punish those who break a truce is analogous to the threat of violence from the police in the present day. But police and district courts cannot be integrated into productive local exchange the way that shells were, so the analogy remains incomplete, and the village court is avoided for its hazardous connections to those other institutions of the law. Law itself, as Tok Pisin *lo*, is then located as an uneasy—because still incomplete—supplement to *kastam*, which is itself rendered incomplete by the presence of *lo*.

Concluding this half of the book, Eve Houghton's chapter asks us to consider how village courts and their alternatives can coexist in the same space and even during the same dispute. Using the example of how courts are 'unmade' in West New Britain Province when magistrates determine that the issue at hand cannot be handled appropriately in the context of a formal court sitting, she shows how the inherent multiplicity of disputing forms supports the ability of magistrates and community leaders to switch between forums for the benefit of the disputing parties. In Houghton's analysis, the spatial and material nature of the shift between court and non-court is key to this skilful way in which magistrates—recast as mediators—navigate between the constraints placed on the village courts and the relational demands of justice in PNG. Unmaking a court may be signalled by the removal of the physical paraphernalia of the village court in the midst of a sitting, but it is also the changed bodily and spatial dispositions of the magistrates-as-mediators and their disputants that allow a different kind of outcome to be reached than what the court would have made possible.

The book shifts from there into Part 2, which is opened by Michael Goddard's chapter investigating the history, development and contemporary challenges faced by village courts. The courts, he notes, have functioned better as improvised local conflict management forums than as institutions standardised to a set of national-level expectations without much in the way of concrete national-level support. These expectations have expanded further in recent years to encompass a suite of international human rights regimes and discourses that PNG has become obliged by donor agencies to integrate into its 'development' initiatives. Such regimes are often at odds with precisely the sensitivity to local concepts of justice and peacekeeping at which the village courts excel. These concepts include a widespread distinction between responsibility and liability, and a sociocentric approach to dispute management that depends on such a distinction. An over-emphasis on attempting to standardise the courts' practices and harmonise them with international rule-of-law regimes, he argues, may undermine the very particularism with which village courts have successfully done their job for decades, with very little attention or material support from the PNG state.

My own chapter takes up another aspect of these problems, which is the scaling or measuring effect of law when it is used by people to assess their own practices against the intentions of the PNG state as they are read off recent pieces of legislation or their repeal. Courts, village or otherwise, are in many of these instances not in the picture at all, as ordinary people make their own determinations as to how they ought to modify their own behaviour or demand different behaviour from others. They may do this in the context of community meetings and informal mediations, or of experiments in creating local organisations that imagine a direct relationship to national organisations, whether or not there is any 'actual' connection between them. The 'local' in all of these examples becomes a way of imagining the law as a means of connecting one's own locality to other localities, including the source of lawmaking in Port Moresby. But that source can be problematic, as the concerns of legislators do not always seem to match up with those of people elsewhere in the country, particularly with regard to the repeal of the Sorcery Act, wherein some citizens now feel compelled to act outside the law to seek redress against those they suspect of sorcerous attacks.

The book concludes with a set of reflections from Fiona Hukula on the current relationship between formal and informal modes of disputing in PNG, and how this relationship might better be recognised as one of the most important ways that grassroots people—including those living in cities—can access some form of justice that is acceptable to them. The nature of Port Moresby, in particular, as a 'big village' sees it emerge as a space in which creative uses of both courts and *komiti* meetings enable people living in the city's settlements to find a way to live together well. The broader needs of settlement communities, from the provision of utilities to public health concerns, feed into both the conflicts that emerge and the ways that *komiti* seek to resolve conflicts. Hukula points out some of the areas where future research on PNG's legal systems, from the prisons to the way village courts should or should not be regulated, might be of use, especially as systems for dispute management such as restorative justice continue to be introduced to the country. Although there is probably a need for more oversight of the village courts, she suggests, they must also be allowed to do what they have always done best, in tandem with all the informal systems of managing conflict: allow people the chance to maintain good relations among themselves.

References

Biersack, A., Jolly, M., & Macintyre, M., (eds). (2016). *Gender violence & human rights: Seeking justice in Fiji, Papua New Guinea and Vanuatu*. ANU Press. doi.org/ 10.22459/GVHR.12.2016.

Bohannan, P. (1957). *Justice and judgment among the Tiv*. Oxford University Press.

Chanock, M. (1985). *Law, custom, and social order: The colonial experience in Malawi and Zambia*. Cambridge University Press.

Connell, R. (2010). Periphery and metropole in the history of sociology. *Sociologisk Forskning, 47*(1), 72–86. doi.org/10.37062/sf.47.18449.

Demian, M. (2011). 'Hybrid custom' and legal description in Papua New Guinea. In J. Edwards and M. Petrović-Šteger (eds), *Recasting anthropological knowledge: Inspiration and social science* (pp. 49–69). Cambridge University Press. doi.org/ 10.1017/CBO9780511842092.004.

Demian, M. (2014a). On the repugnance of customary law. *Comparative Studies in Society and History, 56*(2), 508–536. doi.org/10.1017/S0010417514000127.

Demian, M. (2014b). *Overcoming operational constraints in Papua New Guinea's remote rural village courts: A case study* (In Brief 2014/52). State, Society and Governance in Melanesia, The Australian National University.

Demian, M. (2021). *In memory of times to come: Ironies of history in southeastern Papua New Guinea*. Berghahn. doi.org/10.2307/j.ctv2tsxj8h.

Epstein, A.L. (1971). Dispute settlement among the Tolai. *Oceania, 41*(3), 157–170. doi.org/10.1002/j.1834-4461.1971.tb01149.x.

Epstein, A.L., (ed.). (1974). *Contention and dispute: Aspects of law and social control in Melanesia*. The Australian National University Press.

Erlanger, H., Garth, B., Larson, J., Mertz, E., Nourse, V., & Wilkins, D. (2005). Is it time for a new legal realism? *Wisconsin Law Review 2*, 335–363.

Fitzpatrick, P. (1975). A new law for co-operatives. *Annals of Public and Cooperative Economics, 46*(3), 277–287. doi.org/10.1111/j.1467-8292.1975.tb00431.x.

Fitzpatrick, P. (1989). Custom as imperialism. In J.M. Abun-Nasr, U. Spellenberg, & U. Wanitzek (eds), *Law, society and national identity in Africa* (pp. 15–30). Helmut Buske Verlag.

Gluckman, M. (1955). *The judicial process among the Barotse of Northern Rhodesia.* Manchester University Press and Rhodes-Livingstone Institute.

Greenhouse, C.J. (1982). Looking at culture, looking for rules. *Man,* n.s., *17*(1), 58–73. doi.org/10.2307/2802101.

Howley, P. (2005). Rescue mission for village courts: Mediation on non payment of allowances to village courts. *Contemporary PNG Studies: DWU Research Journal, 3,* 47–66.

Human Rights Watch. (2015). *Bashed up: Family violence in Papua New Guinea.* www.hrw.org/report/2015/11/04/bashed/family-violence-papua-new-guinea.

Jolly, M., Stewart, C., & Brewer, C., (eds). (2012). *Engendering violence in Papua New Guinea.* ANU Press. doi.org/10.22459/EVPNG.07.2012.

Klug, H., & Merry, S.E. (2016). Introduction. In H. Klug & S.E. Merry (eds), *The new legal realism: Studying law globally* (pp. 1–9). Cambridge University Press. doi.org/10.1017/CBO9781139683432.002.

Lawrence, P. (1969). The state versus stateless societies in Papua and New Guinea. In B.J. Brown (ed.), *Fashion of law in New Guinea* (pp. 15–37). Butterworths.

Lev, D.S. (1985). Colonial law and the genesis of the Indonesian state. *Indonesia, 40,* 57–74. doi.org/10.2307/3350875.

Lipset, D. (2004). 'The trial': A parody of the law amid the mockery of men in post-colonial Papua New Guinea. *Journal of the Royal Anthropological Institute, 10*(1), 63–89. doi.org/10.1111/j.1467-9655.2004.00180.x.

Llewellyn, K.N., & Hoebel, E.A. (1941). *The Cheyenne way: Conflict and case law in primitive jurisprudence.* University of Oklahoma Press.

Médecins Sans Frontières. (2016). *Return to abuser: Gaps in services and a failure to protect survivors of family and sexual violence in Papua New Guinea.* www.msf.org/papua-new-guinea-new-msf-report-return-abuser-reveals-cycle-abuse-survivors-family-and-sexual.

Merry, S.E. (1990). *Getting justice and getting even: Legal consciousness among working-class Americans.* University of Chicago Press.

Merry, S.E. (1991). Law and colonialism. *Law & Society Review, 25*(4), 889–922. doi.org/10.2307/3053874.

Moore, S.F. (1973). Law and social change: The semi-autonomous social field as an appropriate subject of study. *Law & Society Review, 7*(4), 719–746. doi.org/10.2307/3052967.

Moore, S.F. (1986). *Social facts and fabrications: 'Customary' law on Kilimanjaro, 1880–1980.* Cambridge University Press.

Papua New Guinea. (2013). *Parliamentary debates,* National Parliament, 28 May 2013. (Kerenga Kua, MP). www.parliament.gov.pg/hansard/2013.

Reed, A. (2011). Hope on remand. *Journal of the Royal Anthropological Institute, 17*(3), 527–544. doi.org/10.1111/j.1467-9655.2011.01705.x.

Riles, A. (2016). Is the law hopeful? In H. Miyazaki and R. Swedberg (eds), *The economy of hope* (pp. 126–146). University of Pennsylvania Press. doi.org/10.9783/9780812293500-006.

Rooney, N.M., Forsyth, M., Goa, J., Lawihin, D., & Kuir-Ayius, D. (2022). Thinking incrementally about policy interventions on intimate partner violence in Papua New Guinea: Understanding 'popcorn' and 'blanket'. *Culture, Health & Sexuality,* 1–16. doi.org/10.1080/13691058.2022.2103736.

Schapera, I. (1955). *A handbook of Tswana law and custom.* Frank Cass & Co.

Schwoerer, T. (2018). *Mipela makim gavman*: Unofficial village courts and local perceptions of order in the Eastern Highlands of Papua New Guinea. *Anthropological Forum, 28*(4), 342–358. doi.org/10.1080/00664677.2018.1541786.

Shils, E. (1975). *Center and periphery: Essays in macrosociology.* University of Chicago Press.

Slater, D. (2004). *Geopolitics and the post-colonial: Rethinking North–South relations.* Blackwell. doi.org/10.1002/9780470756218.

Sorcery Act 1971, Papua New Guinea. (1971). www.paclii.org/pg/legis/consol_act/sa1971117/.

Stoler, A.L., & Cooper, F. (1997). Between metropole and colony: Rethinking a research agenda. In F. Cooper & A.L. Stoler (eds), *Tensions of empire: Colonial cultures in a bourgeois world* (pp. 1–56). University of California Press. doi.org/10.1525/california/9780520205406.003.0001.

Strathern, M. (1972). *Official and unofficial courts: Legal assumptions and expectations in a Highlands community* (New Guinea Research Bulletin No. 47). New Guinea Research Unit and The Australian National University.

Strathern, M. (1985). Discovering social control. *Journal of Law and Society, 12*(2), 111–134. doi.org/10.2307/1409963.

Strathern, M. (1992). *After nature: English kinship in the late twentieth century.* Cambridge University Press.

Taussig, M. (1997). *The magic of the state.* Routledge.

Vincent, J. (1989). Contours of change: Agrarian law in colonial Uganda, 1895–1962. In J. Starr & J.F. Collier (eds), *History and power in the study of law: New directions in legal anthropology* (pp. 153–167). Cornell University Press. doi.org/10.7591/9781501723322-009.

Zorn, J.G., & Care, J.C. (2002). Everything old is new again: The Underlying Law Act of Papua New Guinea. *Lawasia Journal, 2002*, 61–97.

Part I: Village courts and non-courts in action

1

Legal consciousness and the predicament of village courts in a 'weak state': Internalisation of external authority in the New Guinea Highlands

Hiroki Fukagawa

I. Legal consciousness and village court studies

Legal consciousness is the concept of awareness of the law and it explains why everyone, not just legal professionals, uses the courts[1] (Merry, 1990; Silbey, 2005). There are two characteristic approaches to legal consciousness research. The first is the broad definition of 'consciousness' as a social practice in everyday life, not limited to the domain of linguistic thought suggested by the phrase 'legal consciousness'. The subject is analysed from the perspective of an objective social structure and its internalisation (Silbey, 2005, p. 334). The second is the study of the legal consciousness of ordinary people in

---

1   Some of the data in this chapter overlap with a short thesis written in Japanese entitled 'Sonraku saiban no keishikika to senryakuteki riyo: Nyu Guinea kochi Enga shu ni okeru keni no kikyu' ['The formalisation and strategic use of village courts: Authority-seeking in Enga Province, New Guinea Highlands'] (Fukagawa, 2012). That thesis focuses on the 'strategic use' of village courts, whereas this chapter includes new data and considers the issue anew from a theoretical framework of legal consciousness.

relation to hegemony. Here, it helps to 'explain the practical determinacy of a legal system that is theoretically indeterminate' (Silbey, 2005, p. 330). Power relationships penetrate objective social structure. Legal consciousness contributes to the reproduction of existing social inequalities.

However, when using this perspective in trying to analyse village courts in the New Guinea Highlands, problems immediately arise. The theoretical framework of legal consciousness presupposes the existence of a powerful state. In Papua New Guinea, it is difficult to say that a solid system has been established about the monopoly of violence by the state and the justification of domination by the realisation of public interest (maintaining order, fairly sharing resources, guaranteeing rights, etc.). Papua New Guinea is even referred to as a 'weak state' (Dinnen, 2001). Thus, we must clarify how the ordinary people perceive a 'weak state' and what expectations they have when using the village courts.

Previous studies on village courts pointed out that, contrary to village court law stipulations, village courts are formalised to resemble modern courts rather than using an informal, custom-based process. The formalisation of village courts is a phenomenon widely seen throughout the country (Goddard, 2009, pp. 90–91). Regarding this phenomenon, previous research focused on magistrates, utilising the two-pronged approach of 'legal centralism' and 'legal pluralism' (Scaglion, 1990, p. 17).

Research based on 'legal centralism' regards the formalisation of the village courts as proof that a modern legal ideology encompasses regional communities. It asserts that village courts become tools for state control, supporting the existing hierarchy (Fitzpatrick, 1980; Paliwala, 1982). Therefore, these studies consider the public's legal consciousness to be no more than a reflection of the ideology of a strong state's rule of law. Furthermore, those studies have incorrectly perceived village court magistrates as dependent, passive beings in relation to the state.

In contrast, research based on 'legal pluralism' considers the formalisation of village courts to be a creative activity that blends traditional mediation methods with modern court procedures (Scaglion, 1979, 1990; Westermark, 1978, 1986, 1991; Zorn, 1990). Among these studies, the interesting point is that magistrates formalise village courts by imitating colonial administrator courts and superior courts, thereby vesting authority in themselves (Westermark, 1986, pp. 136–139). In other words, village court magistrates are not merely subordinate to ideology, but also they appropriate the authority of both the colonial government and the post-independence state according to their own interests, redefining themselves as active beings and elevating their own social standing (Westermark, 1991).

In this way, research based on 'legal pluralism' in the 1980s through the early 1990s succeeded in understanding the creativity of the magistrates that 'legal centralism' had overlooked. However, those studies were later criticised for assuming a dualistic framework of customary law and modern law and for failing to inquire into the formulation of that framework (Demian, 2003; Goddard, 1996). Moreover, they were criticised for focusing too narrowly on conflict resolution, disregarding various aspects such as the transformation of leadership and the narrative of nation as expressed through courts (Brison, 1999; Lipset, 2004). Such criticism is to some extent valid. However, it should be appreciated that 'legal pluralism' interpreted village court formalisation as the attainment of power by magistrates, and it provided a clear explanation for the gap between village court law—which supposedly respected customary law—informality and the actual practice of village courts.

Rather, the problem with those studies is that they rely on a magistrate-centred viewpoint and do not sufficiently describe how the ordinary people perceive the courts and their magistrates, as well as how they perceive the law and the state. The effectiveness of village courts was questioned early on because of the limited support of law enforcement agencies such as the police (Goddard, 2009, pp. 55–74; Gordon & Meggitt, 1985, pp. 230–236). When studying village courts, we must not overlook the significant question of whether or not the people accept the authority and legitimacy of the magistrates.

Research that analysed informal 'trials' conducted by government officials or police officers in the Highlands region identified that the authority of these institutions was not simply passed on to 'magistrates'. Rather, the people themselves demanded strong legal authority, and read it into government officials and police (officers serving as 'magistrates') (Kurita, 1998). To elaborate on this point, when studying the legal consciousness, it is necessary to focus not only on their view of the state, but also on how and why the ordinary people seek such authority. This chapter will use the cases of the Wapenamanda District in Enga Province in the New Guinea Highlands to ask and answer the following questions. While magistrates give authority to themselves, in what ways do the people seek that authority, approve or deny it, and in what ways do they use the village courts as related to their consciousness regarding the state and the law?[2]

II. Weakening of 'governmental law'

1. Localisation of the court system

The current village court system was introduced at the end of the colonial period in the New Guinea Highlands. Generally, the courts used by villagers were localised and separate from courts presided over by colonial officials.

The Australian colonial government established a full-fledged governing system from the mid-1940s to the 1950s. Colonial officials, known as *kiap* in Tok Pisin, were the main actors during colonial times. The *kiap* post was all-purpose, with authority in administration, justice and even policing. The *kiap* had physical power in the form of guns and suppressed inter-clan warfare in the Highlands. In the process, the Highlanders came to regard the *kiap* as an absolute authority who must be obeyed.

Thereafter, on the judicial front, the *kiap* became judges in the Courts of Native Affairs and were engaged in maintaining order in the region. The Courts of Native Affairs processed offences and heard civil suits according to summary jurisdiction. Moreover, the *kiap* also engaged in the extrajudicial arbitration of disputes over land borders (Gordon & Meggitt, 1985, pp. 44, 85, 162–163, 186; Hatanaka, 1975, pp. 24–25; Kurita, 1998, pp. 143–148, 157; Strathern, 1972, pp. 43–48).

What is of great interest here is that in Enga Province, *kiap* courts at this time were embedded in inter-clan rivalries. After the suppression of warfare, people filled the gap by quarrelling with other clans through *kiap* courts. Victory in court or arbitration concerning inter-clan land borders was equivalent to the acquisition of land through fighting (Meggitt, 1977,

---

2   This chapter is based on data collected from fieldwork in a village in the Wapenamanda District of Enga Province, Papua New Guinea Highlands, between May 2007 and January 2009. The population of Enga Province is 295,031; of Wapenamanda District, 53,547; and of the village studied, 1,303 (Papua New Guinea National Statistical Office, 2000). The language spoken in Enga Province, aside from Porgera in the west, is the Enga language.

pp. 153–159). In this period, clan rivalries were settled not with the bow and arrow but by making use of a powerful external authority, represented by the gun-wielding *kiap*.

Under these circumstances, beginning in the mid-1960s, the localisation of the government and the inclusion of Papua New Guineans in government agencies progressed. Then, in 1966, the *kiap* Courts of Native Affairs were replaced with local courts that employed magistrates who had undergone specialised training (Goddard, 2009, pp. 46–47; Gordon & Meggitt, 1985, pp. 79–83). Local courts, facing independence, began employing Papua New Guinean professionals as judges. However, their authority was not accepted as well as that of the former *kiaps*, and the villagers, having no familiarity with modern courts, rarely used the local courts on their own initiative (Hatanaka, 1975, pp. 25–27; Strathern, 1972, p. 55).

To break this trend, village courts were created. This made it easier for villagers to access the courts, and it allowed for conflict resolution in accordance with local conditions (Goddard, 2009, pp. 47–51). However, village courts, from the time of their establishment, faced financial issues and were constantly troubled by noncooperation from administrative organisations and other law enforcement agencies. These issues continue into the present and are considered the biggest flaw of the village court system (Goddard, 2009, pp. 55–74; Gordon & Meggitt, 1985, pp. 224–236). While village courts are easily accessible to anyone, they have limited support from the state and, in this respect, are a fragile institution.

2. Aspirations for power

The village courts were introduced as a court system easily accessible to villagers and able to uphold customary law. By definition, village courts were a system qualitatively different from the Courts of Native Affairs and the arbitration presided over by *kiaps*. Nevertheless, to the villagers of the Wapenamanda District in Enga Province, village courts are positioned as an extension of the courts controlled by *kiaps*.

When I interviewed men aged in their fifties to seventies about the colonial period, they referred to the 'strong law' (*lo keto*) of the colonial government. They said that when Australian colonial officials arrived suddenly in Enga with the overwhelming strength of firearms, they laid down a 'strong law' represented by guns, courts, police officers and prisons. This came as quite a shock to the local people. In an age when men used stone axes in Enga

Province, the *kiaps* gathered the people in village squares and made a display of using guns to shoot and kill pigs from a great distance. They said that during this shocking display, everyone was silent in stunned amazement.

In those days, because people feared the 'government' (*gavman*) as a result of their experience with the *kiaps*, those I interviewed told me that people were extremely afraid of the courts. A man in his seventies who actually went through the court system at that time spoke of his first experience facing a *kiap* in trial, how his body shook and he dripped with sweat as he made his plea. Once, the men in his clan defied the orders of the colonial government and fought against the men of another clan. The colonial officials used the police to arrest those men and, after bringing them to trial, incarcerated them for six months. In Enga Province, there was a practice of naming children after dramatic events such as this. Thus, there are men named 'Prison' (*Kalabus*) and 'Everyone [was arrested]' (*Pebete*) after events revealing the colonial administrators' tremendous power. These events are remembered clearly, even today.

In contrast to the colonial period, from the time of independence to the present day, the 'collapse of the law' (*lo koyapae*) is emphasised. Around the time of independence, inter-clan warfare that had been suppressed during the colonial period was revived (Gordon & Meggitt, 1985, p. 220). The villagers of the Wapenamanda District say that after independence, the state could not control inter-clan wars. Thus, they call the state a 'weak government' (*gavman injapae*). Moreover, Papua New Guinea was facing the problem of robbery, theft, rape and murder by young people in gangs referred to as *raskols* in Tok Pisin (Dinnen, 2001, pp. 55–110), and the cities (especially Mount Hagen) were dangerous for the people of Enga Province. Such incidents are referred to as evidence of the 'collapse of the law'.

In this way, the colonial period is idealised, addressing consciousness that takes a pessimistic view of the post-independence era. When I inquired about colonial-period courts, the majority of interviewees referred to post-independence village courts as well, extolling the strength of the former and disparaging the incompetence of the latter. For example, a man in his sixties stated that in colonial-officer courts, the orders of the judge were absolute and those who gave false testimony were always incarcerated. In contrast, he expressed his discontent with the village courthouse, where no police officers are present and few people follow the magistrates' orders.

Additionally, he said that the magistrates accept bribes and support their own relatives. The corruption and the incompetence of magistrates are considered examples of a 'weak government'.

Nevertheless, the condition of the post-independence state was caused in large part by the colonial situation in which the colony became independent while its foundation as a state was still weak. We cannot necessarily attribute the results to differences between Australian and Papua New Guinean people (Gordon & Meggitt, 1985, pp. 39–69). However, the Papua New Guinean people themselves apply the cultural construct that boils down to 'they [white people] are superior and we are inferior' (or possibly Papua New Guinean magistrates are inferior). They tend to substitute cross-national power relationships at the macro level for issues of morals and the abilities of persons at the micro level (Fukagawa, 2014; Lattas, 1992, pp. 28, 32).

Based on this type of consciousness, *kiaps* and village court magistrates are both considered to shoulder 'governmental law' (*gavmanya lo*), but post-independence village court magistrates are criticised as perpetuating a 'weak government' and are inferior to *kiaps*. That is, they are perceived as not fundamentally different, but village court magistrates are criticised for not having the power that *kiaps* had, and the people harbour serious discontent on that point. To rephrase, they want the magistrates to carry strong external authority.

III. Village courts as 'poison'

This section first gives an overview of how conflicts are dealt with in Enga Province. Next, I will discuss the contrasting narratives of Engan regarding the two methods of dealing with a dispute: mediation and village courts. From those narratives, it becomes clear that the village court is regarded as closer to the 'poison' than the 'arrow'.

1. Mediation and the village courts

Before continuing the discussion on the formalisation of village courts, I want to present a brief overview of how disputes are addressed in the area. In Enga Province, exogamic landownership units called *tata* are the largest unit with regards to warfare and payment of reparations for murder. *Tata* are patrilineal, with patrilocal residence, but they have the flexibility to actively include non-patrilineal members. This chapter translates *tata* as 'clan' and the subordinate segments called 'single ancestor' (*yunbange mendai*) as 'lineages'.

In the Enga language, the word for conflict is *pundu*, and this includes everything from a quarrel between married couples to inter-clan war. Conflicts arise in some cases by an infringement of rights or aggressive acts, and in other cases by customarily inappropriate conduct or attitudes. In many cases, when a conflict arises, the concerned parties or clan members will bring it to mediation or to the village court.

Mediation in the Enga language is literally translated as 'making words straight' (*pii tolesingi*). During mediation, the interested parties and many others will gather in the village square and a discussion will take place under the management of the clan leader (*lidaman*). Anyone can speak freely during the mediation and usually the speaker will face the crowd and make a speech in a loud voice. Those who make speeches during a mediation are called 'speech-making men' (*agali magu lenge*). Among them, men with excellent speaking abilities skilfully bring disputes to a close by reconciling the interests of the concerned parties. This can earn them fame (*kenge andaki*). They also bring wealth to the clan by drawing significant amounts of compensation from other clans. As a result, they are considered leaders by clan members.

Because leaders have a high reputation, people have a tendency to listen carefully to the things they say. However, the respect of leaders is limited and they do not have the power to coerce the behaviour of others. For that reason, during mediation, they are only fundamentally responsible for reconciling individual interests and summarising the results. Consequently, it is not uncommon for the concerned parties to not be persuaded by the leader and for the mediation to fail.

A village court is known as a *kot* in Tok Pisin.[3] It is said that village courts are used when mediation fails or when the parties are extremely angry or dissatisfied. As I will explain in detail in the next section, trials are conducted inside the courthouse with a small number of participants, the magistrate makes a decision and hands down an order. Magistrates are selected from the clan leaders. Therefore, the magistrates who run the village court are, in reality, the clan leaders who also lead the mediations. However, unlike the

---

3   The Enga language does not have a word for village court.

mediations, in the village court, the magistrates settle the conflict by issuing an order and, further, the parties expect a clear outcome in court. Although there are no 'formal rules', there are usually five or six magistrates, and there are no positions such as chairman or vice-chairman.

2. Negative assessment of the village courts

People talk about the two types of conflict resolution—mediation and village courts—in contrasting terms. What is frequently emphasised in their stories is that the goal of mediation is an amicable settlement, while the goal of the village court is to win the case. Originally, the Courts of Native Affairs and arbitrations by colonial officials were used as a substitute for the competition of inter-clan warfare. By extension, it is hardly surprising if village courts are perceived as a place for nonviolent competition. The village courts are perceived not as a deviation from the colonial courts but as their direct descendant, because both were imposed by the government.

For example, in the village court, it is said that the defendant and the plaintiff compete to win the case at trial with a 'combination of lies and truth' (*sanbo pii kine pii nyoo mende palipali pingi*). That is, the statements of interested parties as well as witnesses interweave both true statements and falsehoods in order to persuade the court. Not only that, they also say that it is possible to make the magistrates acknowledge a falsehood as truth by using bribes or connections. Consequently, statements that would be criticised as untrue by others during the mediations in the village square are, within the court, considered to be true and thus true statements are considered to be false.[4] As a result of this spin, village courts are considered to be places where one competes to win a lawsuit using dirty tricks.

People stress that deception in the courts and underhanded activities such as bribing magistrates are 'evil deeds' (*mana koo*). They divide 'evil deeds' into two categories. One category is for 'obvious' (*pana*) deeds. For example, face-to-face abuse in public or violence towards one's family would fall under this category. The other category is for 'hidden' (*yalopeta*) deeds such as malicious gossip and theft.

---

4   It is said that similar events occurred not only in the village court, but also in the superior courthouses. According to people's stories, the amounts of bribes rise as follows: at the village courthouse, 10, 20 or 50 kina; at the regional courthouse, 100, 500 or 1,000 kina; at the high court, 1,000 or 5,000 kina; and at the supreme court, as much as 10,000 or 50,000 kina.

While both are 'evil deeds', 'hidden' acts are considered more malicious than 'obvious' acts and elicit stronger reactions from the opponent. For example, rather than shooting an arrow during an inter-clan dispute, secretly using poison (*toma kai*) is a far worse 'evil deed'. The use of a village court is categorised as a 'hidden evil deed'. Consequently, the village courts are more likely to instil lasting anger and resentment. For these people, the village court is closer to the 'poison' than the 'arrow' (cf. Westermark, 1986).

In most cases, the complaints brought to the village court involve relatives or in-laws. The maliciously competitive acts between relatives or in-laws, over time, arouse shame and feelings of guilt in the parties involved. For that reason, in contrast to mediations in the village square, parties before the village court become unable to look at one another, greet one another or shake hands after the trial. Therefore, it is thought that the courts do not reconcile the interests of the parties but instead make relationships worse.

Finally, there is one more difference of which my interviewees spoke—that is, mediations are something that 'only we' (*naim tange*) conduct, while the village courts are conducted by 'the government'. In reality, village court magistrates are clan leaders. Furthermore, in most cases, the magistrates are the relatives or in-laws of the plaintiffs and the defendants. Under such circumstances, how can village courts as 'government' and the authority of the magistrates be established?

IV. The form and substance of authority

How are village courts as 'government' and the authority of the magistrate established? In this section, we first argue that village courts are 'formalised' by the imitation of colonial administrators' courts and post-independence superior courts, contrary to the provisions of the Village Court Law. Next, specific cases of village courts will be discussed. What becomes clear is the way in which village courts are based on a delicate balance between the perception of the state for Engan and the political conflicts of kinship.

1. The formalisation of village courts

In the stipulations of village court law, village courts are permitted to impose orders for reparations or penalties for civil cases and petty criminal cases. However, their foremost purpose is to peacefully resolve conflicts in accordance with mediation that follows traditional practices (Village Court

Law, Articles 52, 57, 58).[5] The distinction of that provision is that, unlike superior courts, the village court is based on informality and demands adoption of the customs of each local area (Village Court Law, Articles 16, 17, 57, 58; Goddard, 2009, pp. 1, 50–54, 73–74, 88–91). However, contrary to these provisions, the village courts are becoming formalised as they imitate colonial-officer courts or post-independence superior courts.

In the area that I surveyed, there are eight village courts. The clan uses the court in its own village and/or the court in the adjacent clan's village.[6] In each court, there were five to seven magistrates, one peace officer and a clerk.[7] The cases processed in the village courts are mostly land disputes, disputes regarding bride price reimbursement following divorce, disputes originating in theft, and so on. In addition, various disputes are brought to the court such as acts of violence, arson of pigsties, non-payment of remuneration for road maintenance, dismissal of teachers, and other causes.

Aside from processing land-ownership disputes, these generally conform to the provisions in the Village Court Law.[8] In comparison, it is obvious when it comes to the village courts' implementation of place, time and procedure, that there is a different form from that listed in the provisions. First, in the provisions of the Village Court Law, it is prescribed that court may be opened in any place each time it is conducted (Article 9). However, in reality, a courthouse has been built in the village. The courthouse is a one-storey wooden hut. Its roof is made with galvanised sheet iron, which is rare in the village and is only otherwise used on schools and shops. Buildings that use galvanised iron are called 'house covers' (*haus kaba*) in Tok Pisin, meaning modern structures such as urban administrative buildings or superior courts. Inside the courthouse hangs a large Papua New Guinea national flag.

Furthermore, regarding court proceedings, the Village Court Law states that any date and time are permissible and that trial can be commenced as necessary and at irregular times (Article 9) (Goddard, 2009, p. 54).

---

5   Village Court Law referred to in this chapter is based on the *Village Courts Act 1989* (Consolidated to No. 17 of 1995).

6   The village courthouse of the studied clan was used by two clans. Four magistrates were selected from one clan and two from another. On the other hand, the neighbouring village courthouse was used by four clans. From each clan, one magistrate was selected.

7   The peace officer's role is to pass on directions or orders from the magistrates and assist in reliable fulfillment of court orders. This role is different from that of a police officer.

8   Village courts are prohibited from handling land disputes by the stipulations of the Village Court Law (Articles 43, 58).

However, in practice, trials are commenced regularly every Monday and Tuesday afternoon. A magistrate or clerk will receive a person's complaint, determine the date and time for trial, and issue a summons. If the parties do not appear in court on the date and time specified, the trial is postponed. If this state of affairs continues, by decision of the magistrate, the concerned party will be charged a small fine. Until payment is made, even if the party appears at the courthouse, there is a tendency to not open the trial. These rules are not stipulated by the Village Court Law but are levied by the magistrates personally, and they keep the cash that they acquire for their own personal use.[9]

Moreover, rules for the method of the trial have been established that are difficult to consider as conforming to custom. Trial participants are few—limited to witnesses and a small audience, as well as the magistrate, plaintiff and defendant. When a trial is held, everyone who enters the courthouse must leave in custody the hatchets or bush knives they usually carry.[10] Furthermore, during the discussion, the magistrate sits on a bench overlooking the courtroom giving rapid-fire questions in a commanding tone from above while parties and witnesses are seated on the floor. At this point, conflicting parties and witnesses answer only the magistrate's questions and do not have the freedom to speak. Sometimes, if a person's story deviates from the magistrate's question, they are strictly reprimanded. It takes approximately one hour for a hearing, which is short when compared with a village square mediation (two to three hours), and the case is closed at the discretion of the magistrate.

Judicial sentences are not handed down on the day of trial but are announced one week after the trial. The magistrate stands in front of the village courthouse, reads the concise content of the court order aloud and hands the plaintiff and the defendant each a copy of the order. At that time, the magistrate gives absolutely no clarification of the basis or grounds for the decision. Because the reason for the verdict is not made clear, on the side of the concerned parties, there is a lack of information, making it difficult to question the validity of the sentence.

---

9   Regarding this point, several magistrates mentioned that the 'fines' belong to the magistrates.
10   This mostly, but not completely, complies with the regulations banning the carrying of weapons (Village Court Regulation 1974, Section 3).

Additionally, disputes that result in a sentence are rarely discussed again in a village square mediation. The reason is that the magistrates, who are also the leaders who run the mediations, dislike overruling their own decisions or participating in discussions that are capable of undermining their authority.[11] Related to this, if a dispute that has already been decided flares up again, and if the same complaint is brought to the village court, a large fine called 'buying a court' (*kot sanbenge*) will be imposed on the parties. The magistrate will not open court until that fine has been paid.

Methods such as those described above are contrary to the spirit of the Village Court Law, which requires village courts to hear cases with informality and to apply the local customs of each area. Nevertheless, villagers generally accept village court procedures, which are seldom the target of criticism.[12] If village courts are perceived as an extension of courts run by colonial officials or of superior courts, this is to be expected. Even now, the ideal type of court judge is a colonial administrator, *kiap*, someone who perfectly embodies the authority of the government.

Based on the above formalities, village court magistrates act as though they are the government itself. This point is apparent in the way magistrates tell their stories. Magistrates use the subject 'the government' when talking about their own actions and present them as the actions of the government. By overlapping themselves with the state, the magistrates emphasise that they embody the authority of the state. It corresponds to the fact that the people call past colonial administrators or present-day individual politicians and bureaucrats 'the government', and use the subject 'the government' when talking about their actions. Not only in Enga Province but also throughout Papua New Guinea, the state is thought of not as an abstract system but as a person. The social construction of such a collective subject is always accompanied by uncertainty (Foster, 2002, pp. 68–69; Golub, 2014, pp. 194–196). Seen from this point of view, the formalisation of village courts could be an attempt to make magistrates a suitable 'face' of the state or 'to make the human actors feasible representatives of leviathans' (Golub, 2014, p. 195).

---

11 If concerned parties are dissatisfied with the sentence, they can appeal to a higher district court. However, villagers who use the modern district courts are exceedingly few.

12 However, some voice criticism about the 'fines' imposed by the magistrates as based partly on their greed.

2. 'Government' or kinship?

Taking the formalisation of the village courts as fact, this section will use specific cases to discuss how people support or oppose the village courts and how magistrates behave. As mentioned above, from the time village courts were first established, their effectiveness has been seen as problematic. In Case 1 below, in spite of the fact that the plaintiff complains to the court about the defendant, the defendant ignores this and never shows up to the courthouse. The village court issues a summons or an order but in the village, that does not always have validity. Because there are no police stations in the villages, there are very few opportunities for a police officer to visit. Thus, the village court has no physical enforcement power. Therefore, instantaneous violence sometimes surpasses the orders of the village court. In this example, what becomes evident is the reality of the powerlessness of the court and the effectiveness of violence in the village.

Case 1: Disregarding a village courthouse summons

On 14 July 2008, a man brought a complaint to the village courthouse against another man in the same clan regarding a land dispute. He personally handed the other man the summons in the village square. However, the other party tore up the summons on the spot and said that he would not go to the courthouse. Later that day, angered, the plaintiff went alone to the disputed land and destroyed the majority of the crops in his opponent's field. Upon hearing this, on the same day, the other man took his two sons and several other younger male relatives (classificatory sons) to exact revenge and destroyed all of the crops in three different locations belonging to the man who accused him. After that, the man did not summons his opponent to the village court again. Another man from the same clan told me that while the accused man had significant fighting potential with his sons and other male relatives, the man who filed the complaint had almost no sons or classificatory sons. Thus, he had no choice but to withdraw from the contested land.

In this manner, the summonses and orders of village courts are not always obeyed. However, they are not completely disregarded. Rather, they are frequently used, and sometimes court orders are effective. In Case 2 below, the village courthouse is perceived as 'the government' while at the same time, it is considered to act under the logic of kinship. What is essential to understand here is that the magistrates and concerned parties have embedded kinship ties.

Case 2: A magistrate's speech in response to a breach of the rules

During a trial on 1 September 2008, in spite of a ban on carrying weapons, the defendant took a bush knife into the courthouse. The peace officer went to stop him but the defendant lashed out violently. This angered the magistrate, who stopped the trial, threw the defendant and plaintiff out of the courthouse, and gave a speech. While the magistrate criticised the defendant's violation, he emphasised that this village courthouse was recognised by the central government in the capital city and used this fact to persuade the people to follow the courthouse rules. Next, clan leaders (other than the magistrate) made speeches saying that the village courthouse and the police were 'the government', and that if anyone behaved violently toward the magistrates, the police would come to retaliate. Moreover, another magistrate addressed the crowd, saying that because he was a member of the clan, if anyone acted violently towards him, male clan members would retaliate.[13]

In this example, the village courthouse was discussed as though it were 'the government' with accompanying physical coercive power from the state, when in reality, there was no evidence to support that claim. Although there may be peace officers, they do not carry guns or handcuffs and are not different from the other villagers who carry bush knives or hatchets every day.

However, this does not mean that the village court is completely powerless. The magistrate emphasised that the village courthouse not only has the backing of the state, but also is supported through retaliation by clan members. In fact, it is only supported through retaliation by clan members. No support will come from the state. Nevertheless, the village court and its magistrates seek the authority of the state. As is discussed in Case 3 below, in village courts, the question of whether or not summonses and court orders are followed is closely linked to political rivalries inside and outside the clan.

---

13   In instances such as Case 2 here, there is a tendency to not reopen the trial until the defendant hindering the trial has paid his 'fine'.

Case 3: A trial involving a land dispute between maternal relatives

On 24 August 2008, a man brought a claim against one of his own maternal relatives to the village court. The claim involved a land dispute. The plaintiff was renting land from the defendant's brother. However, the defendant was cultivating a garden on the land without giving notice to the plaintiff, so the plaintiff filed a suit against the defendant. At this time, the defendant's brother, who owned the land, was residing away from the village in the capital city, working as a high school teacher. At a later date, a trial was held and it was made clear that the landowning defendant's brother had told the defendant that the plaintiff was prohibited from using the land. One week after the trial, the sentence was read aloud in front of the courthouse, and the plaintiff lost the case. The result was that the plaintiff was prohibited from using the disputed land.

Behind the scenes, there were circumstances not directly related to the land dispute. There were complaints from the defendant's clan against the plaintiff. For that reason, two magistrates belonging to the defendant's clan colluded with the defendant during the trial. According to the magistrate I interviewed, they were displeased with the plaintiff because he failed to present a proper gift to the members of their clan. According to the magistrate, in the past, when the plaintiff's brother died in the capital city, the plaintiff failed to present a funeral gift (*kuumanda*) to the defendant and his clan members.[14] The magistrate told me that, as revenge, he handed down a sentence in the village court prohibiting the plaintiff from using the land.

In Case 3, the plaintiff lost the case to the defendant who colluded with the magistrates regarding the plaintiff's failure to do his part in an inter-clan gift exchange. During the trial and in the sentence, there were inter-clan politics from outside the court that were not outwardly discussed. Hence, the plaintiff was helpless at trial and had no choice but to follow the court order. However, conversely, it would seem that the defendant had no need to comply with the village court in the first place. This is because with instruction from the landowner, the defendant could have prohibited the plaintiff from using the land without using the court at all. However, it would have been inconvenient for this issue to have been brought to

---

14 In Enga, a funeral payment comprising cash and pork must be given to the maternal kin of a dead man. In Case 3, the defendant and his clan members were the maternal kin of the plaintiff.

mediation in the village square. At a village square mediation, people with various other interests would attend and there was the possibility that some would be allies of the plaintiff. On the other hand, because the village court involved only the concerned parties and the magistrates, if the defendant could collude with the magistrates behind the scenes, he could prohibit land use with certainty. To that end, the defendant provoked the plaintiff into complaining to the village court by using the land without communication with the plaintiff.

In this way, village courts are inseparable from the village's political rivalries. In every case, the village court is used based on the interests of individuals and clans as well as by a variety of oppositional groups at various levels. It is not always the case of course that courts overwhelmingly win by clear superior power of one party over the other. However, it is safe to say that within the political relationships inside and outside the clan, the village court summonses have validity, trials are advanced and court orders can be effective.

V. Internalisation of external authority and the predicament of the village court

As a consideration of this chapter, the first thing that should be pointed out is the following. First, *kiap* courts were not as ever-present parts of people's lives as contemporary village courts are. Second, it is clear that contemporary forms of manipulation and use of intra-kin violence might well have been characteristic of the colonial era. In consciousness, there is a fantasy of absolute power to intervene at the same time as people have always pragmatically calculated the real nature of that power. The current form has a continuity with the limited nature of the colonial state. The dilution of the authority of magistrates in relation to *kiaps* was about the transition from colonial power to state power (cf. Strathern, 1972). However, what has been discussed in this chapter is not within such a framework, but the connection and disconnection of the fantasy of state power and village politics—that is, different kinds of power relations.

In the past, colonial officials were seen as an absolute authority. The post-independence state has been criticised in comparison with the colonial government for its relative powerlessness and village court magistrates are also becoming targets for that criticism. However, they are criticised because villagers demand a strong external authority. In short, not only the magistrates but also the ordinary people themselves are the ones who desire the state to be the strong authority outside the village.

This is consistent with the schema that after independence, the people themselves created a person that embodies the external authority based on colonial rule. In the early 1980s, according to a study by Kurita in Southern Highlands Province, villagers solicited government officials or police officers patrolling the region to hold informal trials. These were no more than imitations of superior court trials but the villagers saw them as formal trials. This is because people who had experienced trials by powerful colonial officials, even peripherally, respected the orders from an external authority with even the slightest connection to the government. Naturally, those officials or police officers did not follow local customs and were not able to hand down sentences that were satisfactory to the concerned parties. However, in the context of village disputes, people used the courts as a way to justify their own assertions (Kurita, 1998, pp. 147–149, 156–157).

Kurita's argument makes clear to what extent people demand an external authority stemming from colonial rule and how they confer that authority on specific persons based on their own expectations. The same scheme was seen in Enga Province. However, what I want to focus on here is that Engans confer external authority on persons within the village rather than those outside it (government officials, police officers living in cities).

The magistrates mimic the trials of colonial officials and attempt to frame themselves as having external authority by formalising the village courts. The other villagers use the village courts on the assumption that magistrates do embody some external power. Hence, the formalisation of village courts, which contributes to the authority of the magistrates, is not based solely on the magistrate's creative actions but is more broadly created by ordinary people.

However, the power embodied in the magistrates is not guaranteed by the state and the magistrates themselves are village insiders—namely, clan leaders. In Enga Province, the leaders are respected for their superior speaking abilities but they do not have the power to coerce the actions of others. In the same way, magistrates hand down sentences but the court order itself cannot be strictly enforced. Furthermore, as leaders, village court magistrates are coerced by their own relatives to act as their allies. On the one hand, by meeting these demands, they can maintain their positions as leaders and the village court receives support from their relatives. On the other hand, however, when the village court answers to political interests based on the logic of kinship and leadership, it deteriorates the magistrates' power, making them easily swayed. Because of this paradox, their attempt to embody external authority is only ever partially successful.

Furthermore, this point is also affected by the fact that the village court is not an equitable means such as the 'arrow'. Taking a conflict to the village court combines malicious and unjust means, as in the 'poison' case. Hence, the village court is evaluated negatively. Competition within clans or with maternal relatives is by no means a rarity. Furthermore, mediations in the village square are seen as political rivalries and behind-the-scenes bargaining is also utilised. However, in mediations, competition and underhanded activities are criticised. In contrast, the village court is a place first and foremost to compete with relatives or in-laws, and it is considered a matter of course that negative, unfair means will be used. Therefore, for them, the village court is not for 'justice' and the state is not the protector of the weak (cf. Merry, 1990, pp. 176–179). What is shown in the village court is the effect of one's own power to defeat the opponent, or the effect of one's own actions against others.

Related to this point, Meggitt, who conducted research in colonial-era Enga Province, reported an interesting case. In those days, regarding arbitrations on inter-clan borders, people attached importance to a judgement from a specific colonial administrator. If another colonial administrator took the appointment, they would file the appeal again and redirect the contest. Every time the colonial officials rotated, the clan that was previously defeated would file a claim against the rival clan, and there was a case in which one border dispute was arbitrated five times[15] (Meggitt, 1977, pp. 153–159). The time frame and setting of this chapter are different, but perhaps arbitrations by colonial officials were used as a powerful tool for expanding their own power (Harrison, 1995, p. 93) and, as such, the legitimacy of these arbitrations was maintained. What we can see in the village courts is also the expansion of their own power based on the logic of kinship, political relationships inside and outside the clan, wealth (including money), physical violence and so on. However, a decisive difference between those arbitrations and the village

---

15 Most colonial officials demarcated borders at the arbitrations, but not only were the details not recorded, but also personnel changes were frequent. As such, it was unclear whether a colonial officer's predecessor had arbitrated on specific borders and, if they had, what decision they had handed down (Meggitt, 1977, pp. 153–159).

courts is that it was quite difficult for them to successfully manipulate the arbitrations because the colonial administrators were genuine outsiders. In contrast, when external power was internalised and to the extent that took the form of a court, the village court could not help but become invisible 'poison', manipulated behind the scenes, rather than the 'arrow'.

This point cannot be adequately grasped by research based on 'legal centralism' that discusses subordination to the state nor by research based on 'legal pluralism' that advocates for magistrates' creativity. It is essential to understand the context of the post-independence New Guinea Highlands in that while there is no external authority based on the colonial government, such authority is desired. Magistrates are expected to embody external authority and, in the form of the village court, that authority is accepted. However, simultaneously, the magistrate's power is weakened with the use of the court. This paradoxical state of affairs is made visible for the first time through the legal consciousness of the ordinary people. It is certain that what is clarified here is not the hegemony of the legal system but the creativity of Engan. The creativity is aimed at their own power and the evidence of that power, rather than at the legislative system. What is truly sought after is an increase in their own power. It is in this area of indigenous power—different from the study of hegemony—that a new path may be opened in the study of legal consciousness in a 'weak state'.

References

Brison, K. (1999). Imaging a nation in Kwanga village courts, East Sepik Province, Papua New Guinea. *Anthropological Quarterly, 72*(2), 74–85. doi.org/10.2307/3317965.

Demian, M. (2003). Custom in the courtroom, law in the village: Legal transformations in Papua New Guinea. *Journal of the Royal Anthropological Institute, 9*(1), 97–115. doi.org/10.1111/1467-9655.t01-2-00006.

Dinnen, S. (2001). *Law and order in a weak state: Crime and politics in Papua New Guinea*. Center for Pacific Islands Studies, School of Hawaiian, Asian, and Pacific Studies, University of Hawai'i Press.

Fitzpatrick, P. (1980). *Law and state in Papua New Guinea*. Academic Press.

Foster, R. (2002). Bargains with modernity in Papua New Guinea and elsewhere. In B. Knauft (ed.), *Critically modern: Alternatives, alterities, anthropology* (pp. 57–81). University of Indiana Press.

Fukugawa, H. (2012). Sonraku saiban no keishikika to senryakuteki riyo: New Guinea kochi Enga shu ni okeru keni no kikyu [The formalisation and strategic use of village courts: Authority-seeking in Enga Province, New Guinea Highlands]. *Kunitachi jinrui kenkyu [Kunitachi Anthropological Research]*, 7, 49–65.

Fukugawa, H. (2014). Constructing self and other in the New Guinea Highlands: Whiteness and inter-clan competition in the postcolonial period. In H.W. Wong & K. Maegawa (eds), *Revisiting colonial and postcolonial* (pp. 73–96). Bridge21 Publications.

Goddard, M. (1996). The snake bone case: Law, custom, and justice in a Papua New Guinea village court. *Oceania, 67*(1), 50–63. doi.org/10.1002/j.1834-4461.1996.tb02571.x.

Goddard, M. (2009). *Substantial justice: An anthropology of village courts in Papua New Guinea.* Berghahn Books.

Golub, A. (2014). *Leviathans at the gold mine: Creating indigenous and corporate actors in Papua New Guinea.* Duke University Press. doi.org/10.1515/97808 22377399.

Gordon, R., & Meggitt, M. (1985). *Law and order in the New Guinea Highlands: Encounters with Enga.* University Press of New England.

Harrison, S. (1995). Transformation of identity in Sepik warfare. In M. Strathern (ed.), *Shifting contexts: Transformations in anthropological knowledge* (pp. 81–98). Routledge. doi.org/10.4324/9780203450901_chapter_4.

Hatanaka, S. (1975). Choteisha ha dare ka: New Guinea kochi ni okeru bunka henyo no kenkyu. [Kot Bilong Husat: A study of the cultural change in a New Guinea Highlands society]. *Minzoku kenkyu [Ethnological Research]*, 40(1), 16–34.

Kurita, H. (1998). Who manages disputes? Introduced courts among the Fasu, Papua New Guinea. In S. Yoshida & Y. Toyoda (eds), *Fringe area of Highlands in Papua New Guinea* (pp. 139–161). National Museum of Ethnology.

Lattas, A. (1992). Skin, personhood and redemption: The double self in West New Britain cargo cults. *Oceania, 63*(1), 27–54. doi.org/10.1002/j.1834-4461.1992.tb00366.x.

Lipset, D. (2004). 'The trial': A parody of the law amid the mockery of men in post-colonial Papua New Guinea. *Journal of the Royal Anthropological Institute, 10*(1), 63–89. doi.org/10.1111/j.1467-9655.2004.00180.x.

Meggitt, M. (1977). *Blood is their argument: Warfare among the Mae Enga tribesmen of the New Guinea Highlands.* Mayfield Publishing.

Merry, S.E. (1990). *Getting justice and getting even: Legal consciousness among working-class Americans*. University of Chicago Press.

Paliwala, A. (1982). Law and order in the village: The village courts. In D. Weisbrot, A. Paliwala, & A. Sawyerr (eds), *Law and social change in Papua New Guinea* (pp. 191–217). Butterworth.

Papua New Guinea National Statistical Office. (2000). National census. Census Unit Register, Enga Province. National Statistical Office.

Scaglion, R. (1979). Formal and informal operation of a village court in Maprik. *Melanesian Law Journal, 7*, 116–129.

Scaglion, R. (1990). Legal adaptation in a Papua New Guinea village court. *Ethnology, 29*(1), 17–33. doi.org/10.2307/3773479.

Silbey, S.S. (2005). After legal consciousness. *Annual Review of Law and Social Science, 1*, 323–368. doi.org/10.1146/annurev.lawsocsci.1.041604.115938.

Strathern, M. (1972). *Official and unofficial courts* (New Guinea Research Unit Bulletin No. 61). New Guinea Research Unit, The Australian National University.

Village Courts Act 1989, No. 37 of 1989, Papua New Guinea. (1989). www.paclii.org/pg/legis/consol_act/vca1989172/.

Westermark, G. (1978). Village courts in question: The nature of court procedure. *Melanesian Law Journal, 6*, 70–96.

Westermark, G. (1986). Court is an arrow: Legal pluralism in Papua New Guinea. *Ethnology, 25*: 131–149. doi.org/10.2307/3773665.

Westermark, G. (1991). Controlling custom: Ideology and pluralism in the Papua New Guinea village courts. *Legal Studies Forum, 15*(2), 89–102.

Zorn, J. (1990). Customary law in the Papua New Guinea village courts. *Contemporary Pacific, 2*(2), 279–311.

2

Following an adultery case beyond the court: The making of legal consciousness in and around Nadzab Village Court, Markham River Valley

Juliane Neuhaus

Introduction[1]

If we assume that people's conceptions of law are different from states' or lawyers' perspectives, it is helpful to use the concept of legal consciousness. It addresses the gap between 'law in the books' and 'law in practice'. 'Legal consciousness' is a concept from socio-legal studies in 'law and society', reaching back to the early twentieth century. It has been in use as well as debated ever since (see Biersack et al., 2016; Silbey, 2005; Zorn, 2016). The way I use legal consciousness here critically reflects that of Sally Engle Merry (2006a, pp. 179–181). For her, it means the complex and competing perspectives one has on one's rights, obligations and relationships. It includes knowledge about legal institutions and one's willingness to become a legal actor. It is a helpful concept for thinking about people's conceptions of law,

---

1 I would like to thank several reviewers for their critical and encouraging comments, which were good to think with: series editor Matt Tomlinson, book editor Melissa Demian, two anonymous reviewers, as well as my dear colleagues at the University of Zürich—namely Sandra Bärnreuther, Olivia Killias, Esther Leemann and Irina Wenk. Any remaining mistakes are, of course, mine.

and their striving for justice and the relevance of feeling acknowledged by legal institutions. In the course of dealing with a dispute, actors broaden their legal consciousness, which enables them to act efficaciously. As the legal becomes better legible, legal actors gain a better understanding of processes of dispute management, the role they may play and how they contribute to a settlement.

Legal consciousness is vital to Merry's conception of legal vernacularisation[2] (see Merry, 2006a, pp. 136–137). She seeks to understand how international human rights law, especially women's human rights, is translated into local legal consciousness. Translation into local legal consciousness has three dimensions: framing, adaptation and a redefinition of the target group. Such a translation—or vernacularisation—of law aims to indigenise international law to fit local contexts. In various works, Merry and others look at social movements promoting a human rights package or a good governance package and at the processes translating these packages.[3] The main actors of these processes—so-called vernacularisers—are 'national political elites, human rights lawyers, feminist activists and movement leaders, social workers and other social service providers, and academics' (Merry, 2006a, p. 134). Targets of the translation process are grassroots groups who are 'not typically the translators' (p. 134). In an article further elaborating on the concept of vernacularisation, a whole chain of main actors is more clearly defined (Levitt & Merry, 2009). Vernacularisers most connected to the local level—the grassroots Papua New Guineans, in our case—are

> both the beneficiaries and enactors of vernacularization. Because they are locally based and relatively untravelled, they acquire new ideas and practices by interacting with fellow staff members and movement activists. They learn from the cosmopolitan elites and

---

2 Other than its wide use in socio-legal studies, the concept of 'vernacularisation' in social sciences is recent. To my knowledge, it first appeared in anthropology in 1996 (Merry) and 1997 (Comaroff & Comaroff). It was further developed by Merry (2006a) and during a larger research project in 2006–2009 (Merry et al., 2010). Other scholars from different disciplines discussed cultural circulation and translation in the 1990s and early 2000s, too (Levitt & Merry, 2009, pp. 443–444), but they initially did not use the concept of vernacularisation. The use of vernacularisation as a keyword only spread to the political sciences in the beginning of the twenty-first century (see, for example, Michelutti, 2007, 2008), after Merry's publication (2006a). For anthropologists, it remained in use only in the context of human rights discourse. It has not been taken up by legal anthropologists who focus on problems so far summarised under 'legal pluralism'.
3 There are in-depth studies about such social movements from several parts of the world. See, for example, the publications of a long-term collaborative project: Alayza Mujica & Crisóstomo Meza (2009); Levitt & Merry (2009); Liu, Hu & Liao (2009); Rajaram & Zararia (2009); Serban & Yoon (2009). Sally Engle Merry is the main actor in this field; see also Merry (1996, 2006a, 2006b); Merry et al. (2010).

perform a second level of vernacularization for the clients or fellow volunteers with whom they, in turn, interact. (Levitt & Merry, 2009, pp. 449–450)

My example from the Markham River Valley in Morobe Province shows that vernacularisers are part of a village's population themselves as they are part of the group of beneficiaries of vernacularisation. They may have become more external to the local level, living in the nearby town of Lae in Morobe Province, having travelled and had contact with persons whom Merry would call 'national or cosmopolitan elites'. They may also be strangers to the villagers they address, being from a different language group.

Unlike the authors mentioned above, I am not concerned with a social movement promoting 'a human rights package' or 'a good governance package'. Instead, I mainly look at the local legal scenery such vernacularisers may face when entering villages in the Markham River Valley. I analyse how the 'targets' of vernacularisation—those at the grassroots in rural Papua New Guinea who are 'not typically the translators' (Merry, 2006a, p. 134)— actually engage in the process of vernacularisation of law at the village level. Their legal consciousness is shaped within the multifaceted legal scenery in the realm of Nadzab Village Court—a scenery made up by ideas about state law, one's ancestors' way of doing things, kin and congregational belongings, and moral obligations rooted in Christian belief.

Nadzab Village Court[4] came into being in the Markham River Valley, Morobe Province, in 1992. It oversees an area of roughly 2,800 square kilometres, settled mainly by the Wampar language group of approximately 10,000 speakers.[5] It operates in several villages near Nadzab airport, the airport of the town of Lae, which is the second-largest town in Papua New Guinea. Figure 2.1 illustrates the multifaceted legal scenery in the realm of Nadzab Village Court and which forums may be employed to have one's dispute settled.

---

4   Nadzab Village Court was one of 87 village courts with a total of 960 members in Morobe Province in 2009, and one of roughly 1,500 village courts in Papua New Guinea overall in 2015.
5   There is, and has been for a long time, in-migration into the area from other parts of Papua New Guinea, mostly through marriages between foreign males and Wampar women (see Beer, 2006). On the recent increase of interethnic marriages in the area, see Beer and Schroedter (2014). I do not elaborate here on issues arising through different legal traditions within the country.

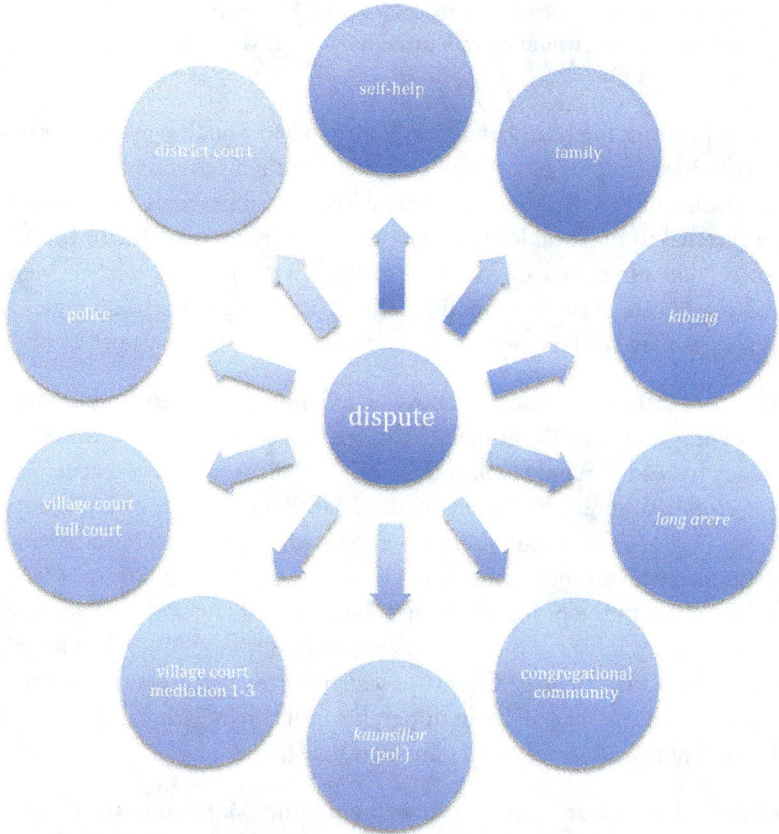

Figure 2.1. Forums for dispute management available in Wampar villages.
Source: Author's representation.

These forums are clearly distinctive but closely interrelated. A dispute arising in a Wampar village might be managed with the help of any of these since '[t]he fields of jurisdiction of these institutions overlap' (von Benda-Beckmann, 1981, p. 117). The main challenge posed to an in-depth analysis of non–village court procedures is their non-accessibility: non–village court procedures happen unofficially and remain invisible to outsiders to a dispute. They take place in ad hoc arrangements known only to the persons involved and on private premises, usually at night. They are hard to track and difficult to observe, and there are no written records available. I faced these challenges, too, when doing research in the area of Nadzab Village Court for six months in 2002 and for five weeks in 2009.[6]

---

6   Funding has been provided by the German Research Council (DFG) and by the Swiss National Science Foundations (SNF).

For several decades, studies on local law in Papua New Guinea mostly focused on state-imposed village courts. Hence, other forums of dispute resolution that are part of local legal life but without state support tended to remain unexamined. Focusing on village courts procedures has advantages in that research can be based on written accounts of cases. Court hearings and court personnel are accessible for observations and interviews. But it downplays the importance of all other possibilities for dispute resolution open to the rural population.

Treatment and settlement of a dispute by any of the existing forums in the realm of Nadzab Village Court do not always suffice to find an enduring solution. Disputes often linger for long periods; they may take the same paths as the dispute that makes up the main corpus of this chapter, or they may take other looped paths. Some of them end, somehow; others don't. I argue that to reach an enduring settlement of a dispute, it is important to integrate several forums of dispute management at the local level, belonging to different realms of dispute management. This approach goes beyond a mere study of courts and court records by including other forums and realms (see also von Benda-Beckmann 1981, 2003).

Disputants as well as mediators actively 'shop' for forums to find an enduring solution. To come to a better understanding of how disputes end, I look at the process of disputing and the outcomes of disputes as they are proposed in different forums. To be enduring, a settlement must be understood as just—it must relate to local conceptions of justice (see Podolefsky, 1978, pp. 215–237, 1986, pp. 35–36; Scaglion, 1981, p. 37). I thus ask what is needed—in local conceptions of justice—to find a just solution. My example of a woman's struggles to have her marital dispute settled enduringly is just one of many such cases. Rebeka, as I will call her, has had her case treated in village court as well as in non–village court forums. The complex interplay of legal actors' choices of forums and their respective procedures within such a 'semi-autonomous social field' (Moore, 1973) becomes better understandable in the light of Robbins's (2004) contradicting paramount values.[7] He differentiates three main paramount value systems: a) people following the paramount value of holism, 'where value is placed on the cultural whole' (Robbins, 2004, pp. 13–14), and where individuals understand themselves in relation to that whole; b) people

---

7   Robbins's 'paramount values' are close to John Barker's 'key value orientations' (2007, p. 1), Felstiner et al.'s 'prevailing ideologies' (1980/1981) and Podolefsky's 'basic underlying goals for justice' (1978). I further discuss the issue of moral values and disputing in Neuhaus (2020).

adhering to individualism, 'where value is placed on the individual and its development' (Robbins, 2004, p. 13), such as in Christianity; and c) peoples such as those in Melanesian societies, who place 'primary value ... rather on the relationship and hence might be called "relationist"' (Robbins, 2004, pp. 12–13). In relationist cultures, what guides people to be good—and what they aim for when settling disputes—is the maintenance of relations (Robbins, 2004, pp. 290–294). I argue that Wampar follow both relationist and individualistic value orientations. Compromises and contradictions they experience between these (sometimes) conflicting orientations become especially apparent in difficult situations, disputes and their management, 'in which moral assumptions are tested, affirmed or changed' (Barker, 2007, p. 2). To better understand how and why a dispute meanders between forums, and how this is connected to legal consciousness, I thus look at the moral orientations of the Wampar, and how these orientations guide and limit legal actors' choices.

That such choices are made by dispute settlers as well as disputants is distinguished by using the concepts of 'forum shopping' and 'shopping forums', first employed by Keebet von Benda-Beckman (1981) in her seminal article about disputing in an Indonesian village. The term 'shopping forums' means that persons engaged in managing disputes in a forum act as gatekeepers to that forum. Gatekeepers do or do not grant access to their forum by choosing whether to treat a case that is brought to them. When introduced by von Benda-Beckmann (1981), the term 'shopping forums' indicated that dispute processing forums (as she called them) 'shop' for cases in the sense that they are 'engaged in trying to acquire and manipulate disputes for their own, mainly local political ends, or to fend off disputes which they fear will threaten their interests' (p. 117). The way I use the term here is adapted to local circumstances in my area of research. Rather than implying political motivations for gatekeeping and trying to get hold of disputes for political interests, in the case of Wampar dispute settlement, I would rather propose that gatekeepers have other interests: their intake or denial is based on ideas about and criteria for the kinds of disputes they feel appropriate for their forum to handle. Another of their interests is to keep forums apart: once a dispute has entered one forum, other forums usually deny any further treatment. This resonates with Melissa Demian's studies in Western Suau Village Court. Under the heading 'legal transformations', she asks in which ways 'distinct legal forms have fared in each other's company since 1975' (Demian, 2003, p. 97). She also shows how different legal sources (customary law and state law) are kept apart by legal actors such as village court and state law officials.

Another interest relates to an ideal hierarchical use of dispute forums: the forum most closely linked to the disputant parties is considered appropriate as a start, such as self-help, and discussions within one's family and with close kin. At the next level up, at the level of one's village, there are congregational mediators, the mediation of a village magistrate and, further away in a spatial and metaphorical sense, the village court, the district court or the police. If a dispute is presented at a forum which considers itself inappropriate, its gatekeeper will deny access and redirect the dispute elsewhere. In this way, forums regularly 'shop' cases between them. Dispute managers in the forums within the vicinity of Nadzab Village Court advise disputants about which forum they deem appropriate and, in case of denial, they sometimes indicate reasons.

Aggrieved parties may follow the advice given to them when manoeuvring their dispute between different legal forums, framing their dispute accordingly to reach their goals. They develop their legal consciousness in the course of handling a dispute, often either ignoring or being unconscious of 'the state' and its intentions for local-level law. They do what von Benda-Beckman called 'forum shopping' (2001, p. 29), indicating that

> disputants have a choice between different institutions, and they base their choice on what they hope the outcome of the dispute will be, however vague or ill-founded their expectations may be. (1981, p. 117)

Thus, forum shopping is a complex situation in which an individual chooses consciously between legal forums. On the one hand, one's choices are oriented by what one has learned about the legal process and how this relates to a moral framework. On the other hand, one becomes more conscious about one's own moral values and what is necessary to reach an outcome conceived of as just. Forum shopping reveals contradictions between ideals and practices, as different aspects of a dispute become more important and aggrieved parties as well as mediators choose between possible outcomes.

Chapter outline

Following a brief introduction of the case under consideration, the main body of this chapter describes and analyses how an aggrieved person manoeuvres her dispute between several forums until its final settlement. The extended case material presented here integrates different approaches to the study of law: it looks at different institutions handling the dispute and how they are interrelated; it looks at sources of law and the moral frames to which mediators, as well as disputants, are oriented; it looks at mediators in managing the dispute and at disputants when manoeuvring the dispute between forums, as well as at individual choices in doing so; it describes the dispute's wider context and the subsequent history of the relationship between the parties; and it looks at the outcome of the dispute and its meaning for those aggrieved. In my conclusions, I summarise important aspects that may generally lead to an enduring settlement of disputes occurring in the realm of a village court. I also address the questions raised in the introduction.

The dispute

What I present here is the reconstruction of a marital dispute concerning adultery that at first glance seemed simple but showed itself to be quite difficult to settle. In this it is exemplary for many other cases I observed in various forums and found in Nadzab Village Court records. It occurred in the year 2000 and had been settled briefly before I conducted fieldwork in 2002. In reconstructing and analysing it, I was able to carefully triangulate differing individuals' standpoints about it as well as written accounts from village court records. I spoke at length with parties to the dispute and with many different persons involved in its settlement, both in 2002 and in 2009. As family life had proceeded without any new looped paths until 2009, and the dispute really seemed to be settled enduringly, I decided to use it as an example. Even though I mainly follow Rebeka, the deceived partner, in my account, I include information from interviews with several other actors involved in the settlement of the dispute. I begin with a brief overview of the dispute, emphasising the forums involved. Not all the forums displayed in Figure 2.1 were involved. Then I analyse in detail the steps taken by the aggrieved party, Rebeka, and discuss how Rebeka's legal consciousness became more complex. I also discuss how forums shopped the case between them and for what reasons. I analyse how the dispute was framed within different forums as well as how the final settlement was framed.

Dispute summary

Tomas (m.) and Rebeka (f.) had married at the age of 22, and were married for five years with one child when a dispute concerning adultery challenged their marriage for nearly a year. The dispute evolved when, over about two months, Tomas only transferred 50 kina to Rebeka instead of the usual sum of 270 kina as the main part of his fortnightly pay. During the same time, he unexpectedly and without explanation did not always come home on weekends. Rebeka learned from a relative that Tomas dated another woman from their village, Susan, in Lae. Rebeka first tried to mobilise her *family* and *church* support. Failing to draw support to her difficult situation, she approached *Nadzab Village Court*. The magistrate summonsed the husband and his lover to a court hearing, where they admitted guilt. Tomas and Susan were directed by the village court to stop seeing each other and were ordered to pay 350 kina each within two months.

Tomas complied but Susan did not. Later, it became known that Tomas and Susan had continued their extramarital affair. This time, Rebeka first used *self-help*. She also involved her *family*. She then tried to involve the Lutheran *church* of her village for a second time, but access was again refused. Rebeka informed the village magistrate, and the dispute was back at *Nadzab Village Court*. The former village court order was repeated. Susan still did not comply. Later that year, Rebeka abandoned dispute settlement with the village court. She instead organised a reconciliation ceremony *long arere* (in the unseen). Through this ceremony, the dispute was finally settled.

What struck me most while reconstructing this dispute was Rebeka's agency. She broadened her legal consciousness by actively manoeuvring her dispute through the different forums, making choices and adapting to changing circumstances. For nearly a year, Rebeka tried hard to get her dispute resolved enduringly by 'forum shopping'.

When recounting this process, she remembered single steps taken, still became emotional when talking about it and was still relieved that it was done. When talking to her and many others about this dispute, what became apparent was what has repeatedly been stated in the literature about concrete norms and substantial law in Papua New Guinean societies: '"Rules" are abstractions by the ethnographer' (Scaglion, 1981, p. 34). Talking about a concrete dispute, individuals gave their opinions and expressed valuation or discontent with Nadzab Village Court's decision and compared it with the past—be it before the installation of Nadzab Village Court or long before (*taim bilong bipo*). Without effort, they explained valuated behaviour as well as conduct considered morally bad. Contrary to the clear references to values and virtues exhibited in the discussion of a real case, it had been all but impossible to unearth any information about general norms when it came to abstractions. Scaglion also referred to 'impossible abstractions', saying 'Abelam rarely make generalizations about trouble' (Scaglion, 1981, pp. 29–30; Scaglion, 1983, p. 260). This is due to the fact that norms do not exist as abstract rules as such, but only in relation to persons and in relation to the relationships between aggrieved persons and their families.

In the following section, I analyse Rebeka's steps as they occurred through the case. To facilitate following Rebeka in how she manoeuvred her dispute through the different forums, I have divided the dispute into two phases. I analyse in detail Rebeka's expectations about the different legal forums, and I elaborate on moral framings of the dispute. I discuss how a young woman from rural Papua New Guinea attempts to use her understanding of the law as a type of efficacious action to gain justice.

Shopping for settlement

Even if Rebeka already had some suspicions about Tomas's behaviour, she was desperate when informed by a female relative about her husband dating another woman from the village in town. Rebeka remembered how she felt: 'She talks to me. She talks to me. And I, I cannot talk. She talks and I cry a lot. I produce a flood of tears.'[8] Rebeka knew the other woman, Susan: she worked in Lae, as did Tomas. And Rebeka knew about Susan's reputation for dating men. Tomas and Susan had been seen dancing in a bar. Rebecca did not explain why she immediately related the information she received to adultery. Details of what it meant to 'do adultery' were not the subject of any forum involved in this dispute, as far as I was able to reconstruct it. In my understanding, it seems sufficient to assume that adultery has 'happened', if it was possible—in terms of time and space—to imagine sexual intercourse. Tomas's and Susan's absences from home and the village, their dancing together in town and the missing money made sexual intercourse imaginable and this was sufficient to assume adultery.

Rebeka explained to me that it was immediately clear to her that she should contact both her in-laws and the pastor of her congregation about Tomas's adultery. In its first phase, the process of dispute settlement entered several forums in these steps (Figure 2.2).

---

8   '*Em stori long mi. Em stori long mi. Na mi, mi no gat tok. Em stori na mi kirai kirai olsem. Aiwora bilong mi wok long kapsait.*' (Rebeka, 3 July 2002).

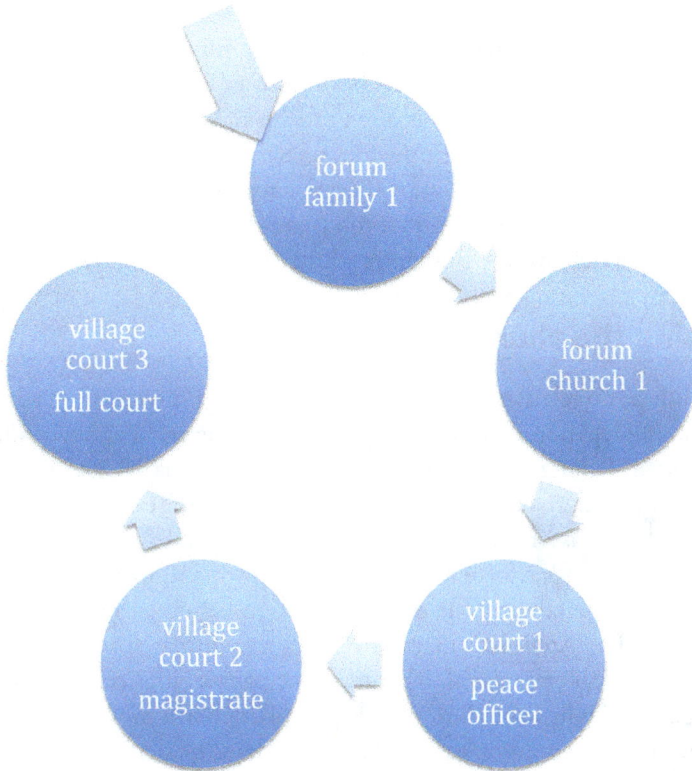

Figure 2.2. Rebeka's dispute, phase 1.

Source: Author's representation.

Involving the family I

At night, when Rebeka came back to the village after having learned about her husband's adultery, no *in-laws* were around to discuss the matter. Rebeka and Tomas lived on the premises of his family with several households nearby. She recalled: 'And I went to inform them about … I went there, but nobody was there. They must all have left to sleep on the other side.'[9] This rather unusual event—no relatives around at night and no information left for her—goes unexplained. Probably, her husband's kin had collectively gone to the other side of Markham River where some of their gardens lay. What did Rebeka expect from her family? For a long time, women in Papua New Guinea had to tolerate not only their husbands' adultery but

---

9   *'Na mi kam toksave long – mi kam, na ol nogat. Na olgeta, ol mas go slip long arasait.'* (Rebeka, 3 July 2002).

also polygamy. With Christianity, polygamy became less prevalent but still existed in isolated cases in the area, as census data from different villages show. Fidelity in marriage is a norm deeply rooted in Christian belief and morality; it is an important rule but is often broken and regularly contested, not only in Papua New Guinea. Both sides of Rebeka's family—especially her in-laws and Rebeka herself—are believers and active members of the Lutheran congregation. When she tried to address her family, she was sure to get their support against her husband's adultery.

Addressing the church I

In vain, and since no relatives were around, Rebeka went directly to see the *pastor* of her congregation that same night. Both Rebeka and her husband, as most Wampar, belong to the Lutheran Church of Papua New Guinea, whose intensive proselytisation in the region dates back to the early twentieth century. Their local pastor resembled the officials of Nadzab Village Court, for he was male and in his forties, had studied in town and had worked in different places in the country for the congregation before he returned to his natal village. The *pastor* had married Rebeka and Tomas. To Rebeka it seemed clear that problems related to her marriage, such as adultery (or *pasin pamuk*, as she called it in Tok Pisin), were to be mediated in a congregational forum, either by the *pastor* or by *ngaeng tsaru* (church elders). This idea may be based on the fact that her marriage had been consecrated in the Lutheran Church, and therefore it was a matter of the church's forums to treat marriage problems. When Rebeka told her story to the *pastor*, she knew what to expect from a church representative and she knew the remedies in which her congregation usually engaged. As mentioned above, there were several ways the church could engage in dispute mediation. One way of discussing the issue would involve a congregational mediator, the three adults concerned together with their families *long arere* (elsewhere). Generally, outcomes of such mediations are reconciliation ceremonies, healing affected relationships. Another possible remedy of the church in such cases was public and had a different effect. As Rebeka explained to me, and as I knew from gossip about similar disputes, persons involved in adultery may temporarily be excluded from church service. Those conducting immoral behaviour cannot attend church service and social pressure is directed at them to encourage them to let go, confess their fault and afterwards become reintegrated into the congregational community. A focus is thus put on individual wrong and its correction instead of healing relations, even though reconciliation between those affected might also happen later. Exclusion from church service usually happened when a severe issue such as adultery was already well known to the village public and the persons involved did not stop committing it. Exclusion from church service was a strong remedy. I understood it as an assimilation of Christian practice into traditional practices:[10] it publicly put shame upon a person (or two) for a moral wrong (such as adultery) and public shaming has traditionally been part of dispute management. Second, it was a sign for cutting relations between those who did wrong and the group to which they belonged. To be excluded from one's group meant that all bonds were cut and one no longer had any relationships in both a material and a metaphorical sense. One was not only without relations to people but also without relations to land and ancestors. Congregational exclusion from church service was not as severe: it was usually limited in time (three months) and it was ended by a reconciliation ceremony re-including the excluded into the congregational community.

The *pastor* listened to Rebeka, kept calm and—unexpectedly for Rebeka— sent her on to the village court: '*Na yu go na kotim ol.*' (Tok Pisin, 'You take them all to court!'). When using the term *kot* or *kotim*, the pastor referred to Nadzab Village Court. Villagers very well knew about the existence of Nadzab Village Court, even though their knowledge about its procedures remained rather nebulous. It was unclear whether the *pastor* referred to *kot* as a mediation within the village by a court official or whether he referred to a *ful kot* hearing of Nadzab Village Court, usually taking place elsewhere. To *kot* somebody generally meant to inform a village court official about a grievance, thus putting the case in the hands of the village court. During her narrative, Rebeka did not elaborate on the reasons the *pastor* did not engage in dealing with the dispute, nor did the *pastor*, when I asked him. There are several possible explications for his advice. One is that the *pastor* was usually not involved in dispute management within the congregation; he had a major position within the church and held church services together with *ngaeng tsaru* and others. But he was not the moral figure to approach for any kind of congregational dispute management. Another explanation might be that, from his point of view as a Lutheran pastor, he probably thought of Tomas and Susan as individually responsible and liable for

---

10   For further examples of the traditional remedy of exclusion from group membership, see Goddard (2009, pp. 243–244). In Christian contexts of dispute management similar practices were also documented for other regions in Papua New Guinea: on the south coast of Papua New Guinea, the London Missionary Society introduced deacons' courts, which used 'refusal of communion and suspension of church membership' as severe penalties. 'This punishment meant exclusion from many of the social activities of the village' (Oram n.d., cited in Goddard, 2009, pp. 40–41).

committing a sin and that this idea would be best reflected at village court. The *pastor* may also have foreseen a structural problem since 'the dispute' involved members of different congregations: Tomas and Rebeka were members of the Lutheran congregation whereas Susan was a member of the Assemblies of God (AOG). The usual remedy of one congregation (Lutheran) would not necessarily have any impact on a member of another congregation. The *pastor* might also have foreseen difficulties in cooperating with his AOG colleague when trying to organise a somewhat ecumenical service to have both Susan and Tomas excluded temporarily from their respective congregations.

A third forum operated by the church for settling disputes—the *bung* or *kibung*, held publicly in the open space of a village square—was run by *ngaeng tsaru*. This public forum was not an option, neither for Rebeka nor for the pastor, for a similar, structural reason: *kibung* was also related to the Lutheran congregation and run by its church elders, and would thus not necessarily have any impact on Susan and her family. Yet, the reluctance to place the dispute at *kibung* may probably be found elsewhere. As pointed out by several interlocutors, disputes related to *pasin pamuk* (adultery or whoring)— also referred to as *man paulim meri* or *meri paulim man* (a man has sexual intercourse with a woman or vice versa)—had increased prior to the dispute discussed here, and the topic had also increasingly been discussed at *kibung*. During *kibung*, children, adolescents, younger and unmarried villagers are present, as well as a majority of adults. The younger part of the audience should not—in the eyes of *ngaeng tsaru*—be in touch with issues such as adultery. To protect them, church elders had decided recently not to discuss *pasin pamuk* in the public realm of *kibung* any longer. With his reluctance to treat the dispute, the *pastor* acted as a gatekeeper and closed church forums to it. Nonetheless, the *pastor* had affirmed Rebeka's grievance against adultery when he indicated where to take it instead: to village court. He emphasised the severity of disputes concerning *pasin pamuk*. The *pastor* referred Rebeka to a forum where the dispute would be handled not in the public of church service or *kibung*, nor without public involvement *long arere*, but in the public forum of the village court.

Approaching village court I

Rebeka turned to Nadzab Village Court the next day. She said she had felt less comfortable approaching village court representatives, since she knew only a little about proceedings and possible outcomes. She had not yet been involved in any case at the village court, neither as a disputant nor as a witness. Rebeka first approached her village's *village court peace officer*. He did not record the dispute, but by directing her to their village's *village court magistrate*, he thus supported her access to this forum. The magistrate listened to Rebeka and advised her how to formulate her grievances for the court records. After having tried kin and her congregation, Rebeka now had found a forum that accepted her grievance and that agreed to treat it. She did not know what kind of framing it would receive in this forum. Following the magistrate's advice, she decided to accuse both Tomas and Susan of adultery. The magistrate wrote two reports in his records, one for each adulterer. The report about Tomas stated that he had contacted Susan and spent time with her, committing adultery. The one about Susan stated the same, adding the information that Tomas was married to Rebeka.

The magistrate decided not to mediate the dispute in his village, as he would usually have done in one of his weekly mediation sessions. Instead, he appointed it directly to *ful kot*. The reason for this was structural and related to a reduction of village court officials' workload: once per month, in weeks when *ful kot* took place, magistrates did not hold their weekly session within their own village. In such weeks, disputes were either postponed for a mediation hearing in the village the following week or, if considered *hevi* (severe) by a local magistrate, they were directly taken to *ful kot*. For Rebeka, the shift from mediation to *ful kot* meant two things: it added uncertainty coupled with awe about proceedings at *ful kot* and it assumed an 'upgrade' of her case to a forum she thought of as more important and probably harder than a mediation within the village. The peace officer handed written summonses to both Tomas and Susan the next day. These summonses held the same wording as the reports and they informed all parties that the dispute would be treated at a full court hearing in a neighbouring village the next week.

Family involvement II

When Tomas received his summons, he became angry with his *spouse*. For several days, Rebeka stayed away from home with their son. *Relatives* and *in-laws* came to see her. One of Tomas's elder sisters remembered how she argued with her brother: 'Tomas, you drink [alcohol] and you hang around, and now [we have] this problem, it is absolutely clear now. You have to stop and behave correctly.'[11] Family members comforted Rebeka, confident that

---

11 '*Tomas, nau, ehm na spak na raunraun ya, nau dispela hevi ya, em kamap ples klia. Na nau yu mas lusim na stap isi.*' (Rebeka, 3 July 2002).

the adultery would be ended by village court. Rebeka remembered another of Tomas's sisters saying to her: 'Listen, you go to sleep at home … Afterwards, we will straight it at court. Next week Tuesday we will go together to court in [the other village].'[12] Rebeka now received the family support she had already expected the previous day.

At village court I

On the day of *ful kot*, some relatives accompanied Rebeka. Tomas had first planned to go to work in Lae as usual that day. But Rebeka had argued with him in the morning and convinced him to come along with her to *ful kot*. When they arrived at the neighbouring village, Susan was present, too. *Ful kot* held its sittings in that village under a large copper roof built close to the Lutheran church, being the area of the village for communal and congregational gatherings. Usually, all official members of the court are present at full court sittings, including, at that time, 15 male adults, acting as village magistrates (7), peace officers (6), and court clerks (2).

When it came to Rebeka's dispute, their village's magistrate read their summons. As both Tomas and Rebeka remember, the accused were directly asked to admit their guilt, which they both fully did. In the proceeding that then developed, a *ful kot* member interrogated Rebeka about her claims against Tomas and Susan. Rebeka explained she wanted to receive money from both. On the one hand, she demanded the sums missing from her husband's salary for about two months (880 kina) and on the other hand, she demanded a sum to be paid by Susan as compensation to her. Rebeka's statement was slightly different from what had been written in the summons. She now, orally, repeated what she had told the magistrate but what had not found its way onto village court forms. She framed her claim in terms of Christian morality as one of adultery and demanded compensation only from Susan, excluding her husband. From him she only demanded the missing fortnightly payments. Rebeka remembered how she explained her point of view at court:

> She too, she must pay me, she has been doing adultery with my husband. She knows that I am truly married. This man, he has truly married me. Now we have a child.[13]

---

12 '*Harim, nau bai yu go bek na slip long hap … Bihain bai mipela stretim long kot … Next week Tuesday, bai mipela go long kot long [the other village].*' (Rebeka, 3 July 2002).
13 '*Em olsem, em mas baim me, em wokim pasin pamuk long man bilong mi. Em save olsem: mi marit pinis. Dispela man ya, em maritim mi pinis. Nau mipela igat pikinini.*' (Rebeka, 3 July 2002).

Rebeka referred to her 'true marriage' (*marit pinis*) and pointed out that Susan knew about it: the marriage had been established through both a parochial ceremony and offspring. At the time, marriages were counted to be 'true' when a couple moved in together, when bride wealth (in kind or in cash) was paid from his family to hers and when offspring was born. Additionally, Christian parochial marriages had become popular. Parochial marriages were celebrated through a large church service, marrying several couples, and participation in the ceremony was made official through marriage certificates. This had also been the case for Rebeka and Tomas. Following Rebeka's statement about her 'true marriage', Rebeka was requested to produce her marriage certificate to prove the correctness of her claim. Village court officials demanded written evidence, thus introducing a framing of state law within its hearing. The demand came without surprise since Rebeka had been informed in advance by the village's peace officer about the probable need to provide it. Rebeka was able to produce the document. From the point of view of the magistrates present, this seemed sufficient to understand the grievance and to formulate related consequences. Both aspects important for the dispute's further management were clear: the accused had admitted guilt concerning sexual relations and a proof for marriage had been given. They had no further questions about Rebeka's claim and no further discussion seemed necessary about 'true marriage', as often is the case in disputes concerning marriage, adultery or child maintenance. At *ful kot*, there was no direct negotiation between the parties about their expectations, and the magistrates did not take long to announce their decision.

The adjudication of *ful kot* was first announced orally, Rebeka remembered. It partly followed Rebeka's claims she had also given orally earlier: both Susan and Tomas were made responsible and 'accused' of adultery and ordered to stop seeing each other. Both accused were fined for identical sums, to be paid in cash to the court. Court fines payable to Nadzab Village Court were fixed at the rate of 50 kina each. Court fines are usually imposed for breaches of criminal law and adultery is not a criminal offence. The court did not elaborate on reasons for fines in this case, and it reflected its adaptation to missing allowances.[14] Neither Rebeka nor Tomas ever

---

14 Elsewhere (Neuhaus, 2020), I engage in an 'anthropology of the bureaucracy', focusing on the administration and management of Nadzab Village Court, by analysing court forms, court records and court archives, as well as the many contradictions produced by village court legislation and the Village Courts' Manual. These contradictions result in village court officials' search for locally acceptable as well as manageable adaptations to the ideal as laid out in the manual, such as collecting fines for non-criminal offences.

questioned these fines. Additionally, compensation sums of 300 kina, due within two months for both accused, were to be paid to 'the complainer', Rebeka. Rebeka explained to me that she understood these payments as compensation to her for the damage of her reputation through adultery.[15] The village court orders issued in writing, addressed to Tomas and Susan individually, omitted the orally stated phrase 'to stop seeing each other'; instead they repeated the amounts and kinds of payment for each accused and the date it was due. As will be seen later, this *ful kot* adjudication did not suffice to settle the dispute enduringly for several reasons.

What Rebeka had initially claimed—roughly 900 kina for four fortnightly pays that Tomas had not transferred to her—was neither discussed nor included in the decision. *Ful kot* did not address this aspect of family life even if it had been an important part of Rebeka's oral claim. At the time of my research, female partners usually kept cash income at home and only very few individuals had bank accounts. Women told me they kept the money because they were less prone to consume important amounts of cash for activities such as drinking, smoking, chewing betel nut and so forth. It was undisputed that Tomas in general had the duty to share his salary with Rebeka to provide cash for the household whereas she provided garden produce for subsistence and the market. Rebeka did not receive any reimbursement for the outstanding sum nor any compensation in kind in this regard. She thus continued lacking an important amount of cash for family life.

Nadzab Village Court had neglected Rebeka's claim for fortnightly payments, but it had ordered compensation payments for both Tomas and Susan to Rebeka. It thus addressed the issue of adultery as it had been stated in reports and summonses. By issuing two orders, it split the dispute and made two individuals liable: one order was addressed to Tomas, the other to Susan. As Tomas explained to me, compensation, traditionally, had not been part of settlements between spouses: 'I think, compensation is not the way our ancestors did. I think, before, they only used to straight such disputes by talking. All elders would talk.'[16] Within the wider family, the dispute was still quite present and several persons repeated Tomas's statement. One woman[17] said that formerly, in times before the installation of Nadzab

---

15   Rebeka wasn't clear about the amount she was to receive; she wavered between 200 and 300 kina in her narration. Court records state the sum of 350 kina per person.

16   '*Mi ting, kompensesin i no, em i no pasin bilong tumbuna. I ting em, bilong bifoa em … ol bai stretim tok tasol. Ol bigmen bai stretim tok.*' (Tomas, 14 July 2002).

17   A female congregational councillor, Matina (17 July 2002).

Village Court, payments would not have been made, but (congregational) *hetmen* would have given *stia talk* to Tomas. Susan's parents would have prevented their daughter from further contacting Tomas (as he was married) and they would have married her even without bride wealth.

Rebeka had adhered to that idea in not asking for compensation from her husband and had instead asked for reimbursement of the missing fortnightly payments. Tomas explained his point of view about the ordered compensation payment: 'I paid for my fault. It's like this: I did wrong like this, and I had to pay Rebeka for the wrong I did.'[18] Tomas understood that he was to compensate his spouse for his wrong behaviour as a husband. His framing can be read as closer to a Christian interpretation: an individual is responsible for one's wrong (adultery in marriage) and is individually liable for its correction. It equally refers to state law in that responsibility and liability are individualised, but it does not reflect state law in substance, since adultery is not a topic of state law in Papua New Guinea. Tomas's perception is slightly different from Rebeka's: she perceived the compensation payment by Tomas as reimbursing her loss in cash through the missing fortnightly payments. The compensation payment by Susan she perceived as restoring her status, which she referred to as 'her reputation'. I will come back to the second order, concerning Susan's compensation and fine, below.

Both Tomas and Susan had to *pay* compensation to Rebeka. I do not know whether compensation *payments* had been introduced solely by Nadzab Village Court or whether they had also been in practice before. For sure, more traditional ways to compensate in kind were turned into compensation in cash with colonisation, as one magistrate explained: 'Compensation *payments* come from white men. They are something new.'[19] Even for a relatively wealthy people like the Wampar, the sum of 300 kina was an important amount of money. And even for Tomas, who earned about 1,000 kina monthly, it was not a small amount. The sum ordered for compensation equalled a year's high school fee for one child. A reason for the fairly high amount fixed by Nadzab Village Court might be found in the increased interest in adultery within the villages. At the time of the dispute, not only village church elders had recently been confronted with an important increase of adultery cases, but also Nadzab Village Court. *Pasin pamuk* had become the second most important issue raised at court.

---

18 '*Mi baim asua bilong mi yet. Olsem, mi wokim rong na, wokim rong olsem na mi baim long Instru, long rong bilong mi.*' (Tomas, 14 July 2002).
19 '*Kompensation bilong mani em bilong wait man. Em niupela samting.*' (Moses, 11 July 2002).

The magistrates of Nadzab Village Court may have used a strict verdict on a dispute about *pasin pamuk* as a deterrent. At village court, Rebeka had received confirmation of her grievance and *ful kot*'s verdict strengthened her claim.

The whole dispute can be reconstructed by reading Nadzab Village Court's records. Written accounts and oral adjudication did not completely match. Written reports, summonses and village court orders stated the amounts to be paid by whom to whom, but no preventive orders existed for the accused 'to stop seeing each other', nor had this phrase entered the orders. What had been missed in the treatment of this dispute in a rather quick and formal *ful kot* hearing was a negotiation between the parties in order to better understand their needs. This resulted in the magistrates not being responsive to all aspects of Rebeka's initial claim, and a shift in the framing of the dispute away from a disruption of family life including missing fortnightly payments. In its verdict, a reciprocal exchange to heal relations between the spouses and between the women was omitted in favour of considering two persons to be responsible and liable for adultery and one aggrieved by it.[20] Instead of placing relationships at the centre of its settlement, Nadzab Village Court had followed a state law approach to find individual fault and guilt. By imposing equal amounts of fines and compensation for both adulterers, the village court did not correspond to Rebeka's perception of liability: Rebeka had seen Susan as liable for adultery, but the magistrates held both adulterers equally liable.

Two months later, as Tomas recounts and as revealed by entries in the court records, Tomas made both his payments at another *ful kot*. He paid the fine to the village court and the compensation to his spouse. He and Rebeka shook hands at that meeting, as he told me. One of the magistrates explained to me that the act of shaking hands to settle a dispute is deeply rooted in custom: 'Yeah, to shake hands really belongs to our traditions.'[21] It is the sign showing that relations between these two parties were healed. Even though the dispute between the married couple now seemed settled, this was not the case for the second dispute, the one concerning Rebeka and Susan. Susan did not pay her fine nor did she come to another *ful kot* to explain her neglect. In her narrative, Rebeka criticised the village court's

---

20   Differentiating responsibility and liability in the context of disputing and justice in Papua New Guinea goes back to Strathern (1972). She proposed that individuals may be seen as individually responsible for an act whereas liability seemed to rest with related persons and groups (Strathern, 1972, pp. 142–143).

21   '*Yeah, sekhan em pasin bilong tumbuna tru.*' (Moses, 11 July 2002).

failure to follow up on Susan. But Rebeka was misinformed, as revealed by entries in the magistrates' written accounts: during a period of four months, the magistrate summonsed Susan monthly to pay her compensation and fine and to come to court. In the meantime, Susan not only missed paying her fine and compensation. She and Tomas also disobeyed the part of the village court's verdict that had been made orally only. The dispute continued through re-adultery between Susan and Tomas.

In its second phase, the process of dispute settlement again entered several forums, in the steps shown in Figure 2.3.

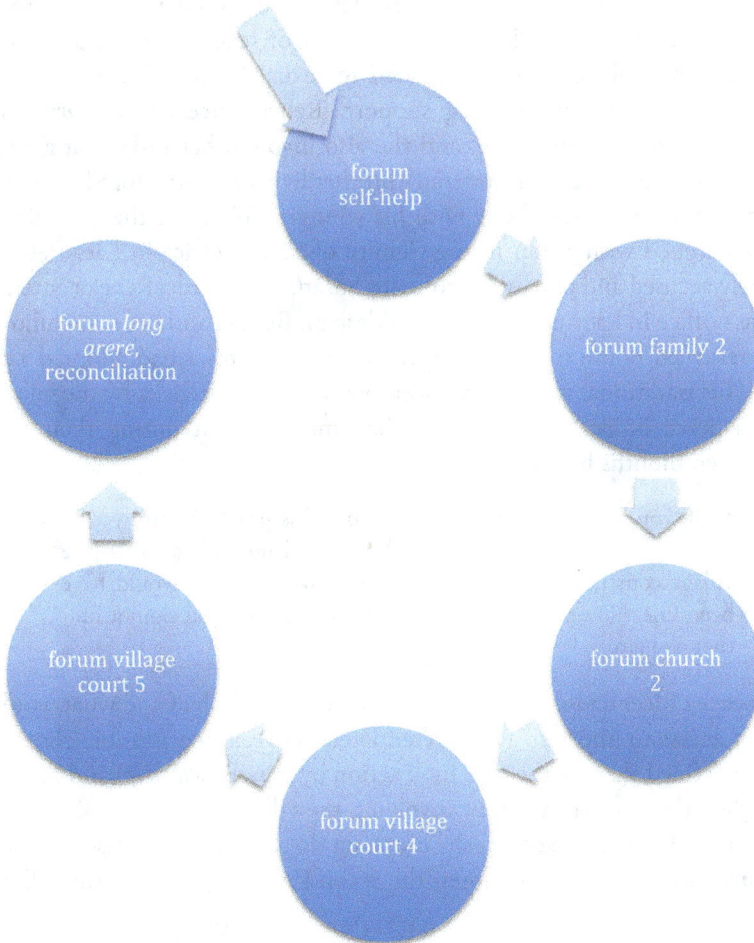

Figure 2.3. Rebeka's dispute, phase 2.
Source: Author's representation.

Getting to know about adultery II, self-help and family

Again, Rebeka was informed about the adultery by a relative— and, again, she broke into tears—this time at the market on the Highlands Highway, where villagers sold their produce. As Rebeka recalled, she rushed to town to immediately see Susan in her office. At this instance, Rebeka was accompanied by two of her sisters. Their refusal to accompany her to Lae would have prevented Rebeka's plan since Wampar women, and women in Papua New Guinea in general, rarely move around on their own, and they do not go to town without company. There are several reasons for this: single women constantly live with the threat of sexual violence and they easily become subject to gossip related to sexual intercourse. So offering accompaniment meant offering support. Rebeka received *support from her kin* immediately this time, and she also involved her in-laws at a later instance: she contacted her husband's brother living in Port Moresby and he had a discussion by telephone with his younger sibling. In the meantime, Rebeka argued with Susan in the vicinity of Susan's office in Lae. Rebeka publicly accused and openly fought with Susan. Afterwards, Rebeka entered Tomas's office in Lae and displayed her despair. Rebeka and her companions then returned home to their village. This time, Rebeka had adopted *self-help*. This traditional remedy had been pointed out to Rebeka by the village court's peace officer earlier on. He had mentioned it during their first encounter, months before:

> Well, you have now informed me about this problem. And you— you cannot beat this woman … If you had not talked to us [the village court], and you had beaten that woman, that would have been fine. Now you have already informed us, and you cannot beat that woman.[22]

The peace officer had shown Rebeka which choices she had and what would restrict access to a forum. He differentiated between two possible choices, and he defined them: either she took action by herself (*self-help*) and fought with the other woman without involving the village court or, if she chose the forum of the village court, she must not do anything else herself. At the first instance, Rebeka had chosen the second way, approached the village

---

22 '*Sapos … nau, yu tokim mi long dispela hevi pinis. Na yu no – i no inap go paitim dispela meri … Sapos yu no tokim mipela, na yu go paitim dispela meri, em inap. Na nau yu tokim mipela pinis, nau yu no ken go paitim dispela meri.*' (Rebeka, 3 July 2002).

court and followed its proceedings. As Rebeka perceived this later adultery as a new case, at this instance she chose a combination of several options she had come to know: she first applied self-help when travelling to Lae, and she involved family. Afterwards she put the dispute to court. In between, she tried again to involve the church.

Addressing the church II

Back in the village from town, and still quite desperate, Rebeka contacted the *pastor* for a second time, again expecting support from his side. Again, she was left without a positive response. The pastor explained his denial to her, saying that the case had already been to village court and would have to be resolved there. He perceived this second instance of adultery as a continuation of the dispute already treated at court. He separated the legal realms of church and village court and refused to mix them.

At village court II

Rebeka then informed the local *village magistrate*. She expected a big fine or even imprisonment for her husband, as she was outraged: 'I have taken him to court. He has paid his court fine. Now I have to put him into a cell, and he will sleep in a cell.'[23] Rebeka expected the local *peace officer* to arrest Tomas at his office in town and send him to prison. Her expectations were not met. In contrast to what Rebeka had expected, and in accordance with the pastor, the *magistrate* classified the adultery at this instance as a continuation of the first dispute, and not a new one. The magistrate put it on the agenda of the next *ful kot* and, again, the dispute was not mediated at the village level. The reason for this was that *ful kot* had been its last instance. Susan was informed by a summons to come to the next *ful kot* hearing, as can be read in the magistrates' records. This time, the summons did not mention adultery; instead, it stated a disobedience of the older village court order and the missing payments, and it indicated the date and place of *ful kot*. At the hearing, Tomas and Rebeka were present, and Susan was not. Since all officials of Nadzab Village Court knew Tomas and Susan had been orally ordered 'to stop seeing each other', even if this had not been spelled out in order forms or in preventive orders, the magistrates at this instance just reinforced their former orders. By doing so, the magistrates framed

---

23   'Mi bin karim em long kot, karim em i go long kot na em i baim kot fain pinis. Na nau mi mas putim em long ser. Na i slip long ser.' (Rebeka, 3 July 2000).

the dispute not as a civil case (adultery) but as a criminal case: a breach of former village court orders. No further action was taken by *ful kot*, in stark contrast to what Rebeka had expected. As both Rebeka and Tomas confided to me, Tomas and Susan have not dated again since. But Susan still did not pay her fine or compensation.

Waiting for compensation

Rebeka remembered that for nearly a year the dispute remained unsettled since she was still waiting for compensation from Susan. Rebeka developed anger not only towards Susan but also towards Nadzab Village Court. From Rebeka's point of view, neither the local magistrate nor his colleagues from *ful kot*, where the dispute was filed, took any further steps to force Susan to realise compensation and fine payments. Rebeka had the impression that nothing was undertaken to settle this part of her dispute. She felt neglected by the village court. Court records show that Nadzab Village Court tried Susan in September 2000, without informing Rebeka. *Ful kot* even ordered two months of imprisonment for Susan for her continued disobedience of the very first court order. Thus, bad communication from the village court to the complainant had produced anger and mistrust in the context of a dispute that had been at least half resolved. Rebeka was mainly disappointed by her village magistrate's seeming inaction, as for her he was the main contact person of Nadzab Village Court. She had the impression that he had done nothing.

At this point, Rebeka and her son Matias fell ill without any clear medical diagnosis. Illness in general is a threat to life in rural Papua New Guinea for two reasons. It often is understood as related to anger and sorcery (Strathern & Stewart, 2007). 'Most physical illnesses are understood to be caused by anger—either the sick person's anger or that directed at them by others with whom they are in dispute' (Robbins, 2004, p. 267). For this reason, people generally are hesitant to seek treatment either at the local aid post or at hospital. They not only fear the expenses, but they also doubt the effectiveness of medical services as they understand that the root of their illness lies elsewhere. After having been in hospital in Lae without a medical diagnosis, Rebeka decided to reach for non-medical treatment for the illnesses. As she remembered, a *ngaeng tsaru* treated her with prayers and consecrated water—a treatment used when sorcery or anger is thought to be the reason for an illness. And she remembered how he had formulated his advice:

> You are still sticking to this disagreement. This dispute has been going on for a long time. The problem will come back to you. Do you know well how God ends disputes? Well, you have to forgive the sin of your sister.[24]

The *ngaeng tsaru* explained that Rebeka's illness was caused by the lingering dispute and that this had also become manifest in her son's illness. In his advice, he related the Christian virtue of forgiving someone's sin with the traditional value of healing relationships between the two women. This was seen to be ever more important, as Susan and Rebeka belonged to the same *sagaseg* (lineage), as the *ngaeng tsaru* stressed when using the term 'sister'. Rebeka was thus advised to forgive her sister Susan for her sin, to end Rebeka's and her son's illnesses. Rebeka said she herself had not seen a relation between her illness and the lingering dispute, but she became afraid of an expected endlessness of her suffering.

Rebeka now manoeuvred the dispute to its final stage: she officially withdrew it from village court and informed the local peace officer how she planned to end the dispute. Rebeka had decided not to forgive Susan 'just' by herself, which would have been an outcome of self-help led by Christian morality. Rebeka had chosen the forum *long arere* (elsewhere), including Susan and others, for the settlement of her dispute. By treating the dispute in a reconciliation ceremony, she planned to forgive Susan and expected to reconcile through *kaikai na sikhan* (to eat and shake hands).

Reconciliation *long arere* (church III, and family involvement III)

Rebeka organised the meeting *long arere*. Usually, mediators organised this kind of meeting, which is traditionally the domain of church and village dispute processes, but Rebeka took it into her own hands. She informed church elders (*ol hetmen*, as she formulated it), the pastor and members of her *sagaseg* within her village that she planned to perform reconciliation to

---

24 '*Yu wok long holim dispela kros. Dispela kros stap go longpela taim. Em bai hevi bai kam bek long yu. Na yu save long pasim long God pinis? Ok, yu mas lusim sin bilong narapela sista bilong yu.*' (Rebeka, 3 July 2002).

end the dispute: 'I will make tea and we two women will shake hands and this will have to end.'[25] She also informed Susan by sending a message to her via Susan's parents. Tomas was also informed. However, his closest kin, his step-parents, were not invited, neither by Rebeka, nor by Tomas, nor by anybody else. Until several years later, his step-parents were still outraged for not having been invited: they did not understand the reasons for this and they felt excluded from an important family issue. In my understanding, this omission had been made consciously and points to a new framing of the dispute. In earlier stages of the dispute, Rebeka had always involved her kin (her family of origin and her *sagaseg*) as well as Tomas's kin. This time, it seems that she perceived the settlement no longer involved Tomas and his kin: his part in the dispute had already been finished. Rebecca followed the framing of the *ngaeng tsaru*: the dispute belonged to Rebeka in that she was to forgive Susan and it concerned affected relations between women belonging to the same *sagaseg*. Thus, relatives of these two women and their *sagaseg* members were involved, Tomas only played a minor role, and Tomas's relatives did not have a role to play in the reconciliation ceremony at all.

The reconciliation ceremony was held at the premises of Susan's parents, where she lived as an unmarried daughter. Participants were Susan and her parents, Rebeka and her parents, Tomas, the political councillor of the village (belonging to the same lineage as Rebeka and Susan), several *ngaeng tsaru* (church elders or *hetmen*) and the pastor. Rebeka arrived together with the village councillor. She recalled that they first prayed together. Then *stia tok* (steering talk) was given to Tomas and Susan. *Stia tok* was a usual part of dispute settlement; it meant that elders pointed out misconduct in a way that put shame on the accused, and they advised about ideal behaviour. In church services, sermons had a similar function, as they were often used in a more general way to explain ideal behaviour to the congregation.[26] *Stia tok* included reprimand and exhortation, and Tomas still felt ashamed, when we talked about it. *Stia tok* emphasised that adultery had to be finished altogether and forever, and Susan was advised to get married soon and to stop dating men. *Stia tok* indirectly also included Susan's parents—by their participation in the ceremony—they were also made knowledgeable about their daughter's misconduct and made responsible for getting her married.

---

25 '*Bai mi boilim ti, na bai mitupela meri ya sikhan na dispela samting mas pinis.*' (Rebeka, 3 July 2002).
26 Robbins (2004, pp. 226–231) gives a detailed account of an Urapmin sermon that is very interesting with regards to how, in an indigenous religious form, the Bible is read and interpreted.

As Matina, the leader of the congregational women's group in the village, explained to me, it was seen as the responsibility of parents to find a man for their daughter.[27]

As a third step of the ceremony, Rebeka forgave Susan for her sin. The two women then shook hands, demonstrating that there was no anger left between them and the dispute was ended. Collectively, all participants to the ceremony shared a meal. Both Susan and Rebeka provided food and beverages. Susan had prepared tea and stew with rice, Rebeka had prepared tea and bread. All participants to the ceremony—*sagaseg* members of both parties to the dispute and village elders—exchanged substances in that they shared food and beverages prepared by others. All participants renewed their relationships in this way. The reconciliation ceremony included Christian values in that Rebeka had forgiven Susan for her sin and it included traditional values in that relationships were healed and reaffirmed.

An enduring settlement

Regularly, reconciliation ceremonies were the outcome of church and village dispute management processes, and Nadzab Village Court records also regularly mention the remedy of *kaikai na sikhan* for disputes treated in mediations as well as in *ful kot* hearings. In the verdict of Nadzab Village Court on the dispute discussed here, it had been left out. Nadzab Village Court's initial verdict of one-sided compensations paid in cash had not been sufficient to settle the dispute enduringly. Failures to reach an enduring settlement also may be interpreted in the light of several unfavourable coincidences and their unintended consequences: inaccessibility of several forums led to transformations of the dispute's framing and to a non-treatment of affected relations. In the end, Rebeka was fine. She was contented with the outcome of reconciliation and she has received support from the forums she had addressed in the very beginning: family and church. Rebeka finished her narrative about the dispute with the expression: '*Mi bel kol nau*' ('My belly is cold')—she no longer felt any anger.[28]

---

27 '*Em wok bilong mama na papa, long painim man. Em i stap yet.*' (Matina, 17 July 2002).
28 This expression is widely used to express inner peace reached after an argument or dispute. *Bel* literally refers to the stomach, the insides, and idiomatically refers to a person's emotional centre. Podolefsky (1978, 1986) locates the feeling he refers to (*belkol*) in the belly, whereas Robbins (2004) locates it (*belisi*) in the heart. The reason for this may be the old problem of translation: one may translate *belisi* as 'light-<u>hearted</u>'.

Her final phrase relates to people following an individualistic (Christian) paramount value: they reach for the ideal of an individual state of inner peace. This can be understood as a result of Rebeka adhering to the advice given to her by a *ngaeng tsaru*. She followed the example of God and forgave Susan for her sin. She has calmed her will and dismissed her former claim to compensation from Susan.

Her expression '*Mi bel kol nau*' could also be interpreted as relating to people following a relationist paramount value: several authors discuss expressions that describe the re-establishment of social relationships through an individual state of wellbeing. Podolefsky used the term *belkol* (1978, pp. 219–220; 1986, pp. 42–46); Robbins (2004) uses *belisi*. Slightly differently, Troolin discusses the meaning of *wanbel*, referring to harmony between two or more individuals or groups or within a group (2018, pp. 27–28). As *wanbel* includes acting in ways keeping the welfare of another person or group in mind (Troolin, 2018, pp. 194–195), one could conclude that all three terms follow a paramount value of so-called *gutpela sindaun* (literally: 'sitting well'; referring to communal wellbeing, 'in a peaceful state', 'having a good life'). The disturbance of *gutpela sindaun* is called *brukim sindaun* (literally: 'to break the sitting', meaning 'to disturb the peace'). Ideally, disputing parties arrive at healing affected relationships, which leads to an agreement (*wanbel*) inner calm (*bel kol*), both of which are essential for individual as well as communal wellbeing (*gutpela sindaun*).

Accordingly, Demian (2003, p. 102) also describes dispute management as a 'social technique', as 'the means of finding a route through the complexity of a dispute and its desired outcome', which is, in the end, 'straightening relationships', not disputes. In the same vein, Robbins proposed to call the kind of justice prevalent in Melanesia 'relational justice' (Robbins, 2009; see Demian, 2016), with the aim of healing relations, and contrasting it to Western conceptions of justice based on the individual and individual gain.[29]

In my interpretation, Rebeka has achieved an inner state of peace because affected relationships have finally been healed by forgiving Susan for her sin, and by embracing Susan. In the end, Rebeka, as a relational being, was

---

29   The question of 'traditional conceptions of justice' in Papua New Guinea has been discussed ever since the invention of village courts (see Lawrence, 1969, p. 35; Chalmers, 1982, p. 179; to name just two). The relation between a 'harmony ideology' and Christianity (Nader, 1990) has only been discussed more recently for this region (Barker, 2007; Goddard, 2009, pp. 6–7; Robbins, 2004).

oriented to an ideal of relational Christianity, meaning a combination of *bel kol* (inner peace) for herself and *wanbel* (agreement) between the families and the women, in order to have *gutpela sindaun* (communal harmony).

When I last met them in person in 2009, Rebeka and Tomas still lived together. They considered their marriage to be harmonious and good (*gutpela sindaun*). In general, they agreed (*wanbel*), even if minor quarrels about Tomas's alcohol consumption occurred from time to time. To the best of my knowledge they have lived happily ever after. The third person to the dispute—Susan—was then married to a man from Siassi, had two children and lived patri-uxorilocally,[30] close to her father's premises.

Susan and her family appear somehow shallow in my discussion. This is a result of some ethical considerations of mine: I have not spoken with Susan and her family about the dispute. Listening to them, understanding their perceptions, frustrations and motivations and giving them a voice would have, of course, completed my story. The reasons for my omission are these: on the one hand, I was not a neutral party to the dispute. By living with Tomas's step-parents, I was considered kin of Tomas. I also had a close relationship with his spouse, Rebeka. In 2002, I had felt reluctant to approach Susan because of the little time that had passed since reconciliation. I did not want to stir the issue up. In 2009, I reconsidered meeting her but decided against doing so, since I did not want to disrupt Susan and her husband by getting back to an issue pre-dating their marriage.

Conclusions

My chapter aimed to show the importance of rural village courts as part of a multifaceted local legal scenery in Morobe Province, Papua New Guinea. Using an extended case history as my example allowed me to better understand the local legal amalgamation and its interconnectedness. The paths this dispute followed are quite usual in the Markham River Valley. Following one family's marital dispute displays how a difficult situation was handled in a complex social field through forum shopping by the plaintiff as well as forums shopping the dispute.

---

30   When men from elsewhere in the country marry Wampar women, the couple often lives with the wife's father's family, thus being able to access gardens to which female partners have use rights.

The example helps to better understand individual choices in moments of conflict and dilemma, how they relate to the changing and conflicting moral orientations and related framings the dispute received, and what these imply for the outcome of a dispute. It also helps to better understand how to find a solution conceived of as just in order to settle a dispute enduringly.[31] In summary, I point out important aspects that may, as in this dispute, lead to an enduring settlement:

- Legally conscious disputants better understand procedures and probable outcomes in different forums, and they become legal actors better capable of taking efficacious action.

- Supporting a claim at every node of the dispute settlement process enhances a disputant's affective legal consciousness.

- Negotiations between all parties to a dispute involved facilitates finding out what disputants need, and what kinds of outcomes are expected by the parties to a dispute.

- Goals for outcomes may change in the process of dispute management, depending on grievances, parties and forums: to exchange for some loss or damage, to restore one's position or prestige, or to heal affected social relations.

- In face-to-face communities with multiplex and highly valued relationships, it seems to be appropriate to steer towards reconciliation instead of adjudication as an outcome of the dispute management process.

- In keeping dispute management local, it is conceived of as less daunting, and both mediators and parties to a dispute are knowledgeable about histories of disputes and histories of relations.

- Involvement of family and lineage adds to social control within the village.

- Every existing forum and its dispute management process is enforced through forums' interconnectedness and cooperation between mediators.

---

31 Surprisingly, the enduring settlement of disputes has not been at the centre of attention paid to village courts, an exception being Podolefsky (1978, 1986). Unfortunately, his careful insights did not receive the attention they merit, probably because they are not easily accessible: his PhD thesis (1978) remains unpublished and is only available as a microcopy. His other work concerned with the relation of dispute settlement and local conceptions of justice (1986) was published in an edited volume also only accessible with difficulties. Elsewhere, I take a more detailed look at aspects causing the initial failure to reach an enduring settlement as well as at aspects that led to a 'successful' settlement (Neuhaus, 2020).

Many of these ideal aspects were (at least sometimes) part of everyday dispute management in the villages along the Markham River. And many of these aspects were—in various combinations—taken into account in processes of forum shopping and shopping forums within a multifaceted local legal scenery. Nadzab Village Court was one among several 'participants' in a vivid semi-autonomous social field with various forums at hand which, together, but yet discrete, created and shaped their own law, influenced by the state, by traditions and customs, and closely interwoven with Christianity.

Nadzab Village Court is probably deemed to heal affected relationships in the forums of counselling and *mediesin* (mediation), but less so in the forum of *ful kot*. I would thus alter Wormsley's earlier interpretation that 'Village Courts are successful at resolving certain types of cases involving persons related closely' (Wormsley, 1986, p. 74) by focusing on certain forums within the realm of a village court instead of disputant relations.

By tracing how legal consciousness develops through the interaction between and within these forums, my analysis answers the questions about how contemporary Papua New Guineans conceive of law and what they expect of law when using local legal institutions. We have seen their complex and competing perspectives on their rights, obligations and relationships. Individuals are willing to become legal actors—be they complainants, defendants, mediators or magistrates. Their legal consciousness is shaped in the realm of a village court. Knowledge about legal institutions becomes more detailed once involved in the settlement of a dispute. Rebeka learned to make use of the laws. She was able to use her growing understanding of the law as a type of efficacious action at several instances: when using self-help, then putting the conflict back to court, and also when she finally withdrew it from the court and organised the reconciliation ceremony. The course of her search shaped Rebeka's legal consciousness in various ways. Not all her expectations were met, not all her perceptions proved correct and not all her claims were fulfilled. Rebeka suffered from a loss during the treatment of her case at Nadzab Village Court. She had become alienated from her initial position about how to treat the dispute. In the beginning, she had sought entities closer to her; she wanted to frame the dispute as a problem to be resolved within the family. She then accepted and adopted the standpoint of Nadzab Village Court but always felt a dear need for reconciliation in a more customary sense. She actively manoeuvred the dispute between forums and, in the course of this, she was advised and supported as well as—sometimes—rejected. In my understanding, Rebeka never felt her claims were treated as unimportant or unreasonable. Even the pastor, who indeed had disappointed her several times, had stressed the importance of her claim through forwarding it to court. On the contrary, from the beginning, she experienced her claiming as positive, in that institutional actors supported and validated it. This is what Merry calls the affects of legal consciousness (Merry, 2006a, p. 215). Positive affects helped Rebeka manoeuvre her dispute with such endurance and, at the same time, strengthened her claim. Even if forums were inaccessible, denied access or shopped the dispute between them, every forum supported her and affirmed her claims. Merry stresses the importance for individuals of positive affects to 'see themselves as right-bearing subjects and to claim rights in the next crisis' (p. 215).

Analysing this case also provides an example against the tattered reputation of village courts with regards to gender. Taking a close look at a kind of case very common in Papua New Guinea ('adultery' or *pasin pamuk* in Tok Pisin), reveals a counter image of village courts and shows that they may give power to women, even by just hearing their cases. My case analysis underlines the importance of Nadzab Village Court for the protection of women's rights within the local legal scenery, even if its settlements are not always effective. If Nadzab Village Court had taken into account lineage relations and endowed relatives with responsibility through a reconciliation ceremony, the dispute would probably have ended months earlier. Nevertheless, Nadzab Village Court's handling of the adultery case, acknowledging compensation to Rebeka, was a way of strengthening women and their rights. It added to Rebeka's legal consciousness. From the beginning, it was important for Rebeka to feel the correctness of her claims, to have them acknowledged. In the course of her struggle, she was able to express her feelings and her views in most of the forums she approached. She was able to put her dispute to court publicly. Nadzab Village Court's handling of the adultery case—acknowledging compensation to Rebeka, hearing it several times, following up on Susan for months, even without result—is a way of strengthening a woman and her rights. Rebeka's position in the village was improved through the recognition of her claims by the court. As an unintended consequence, she was finally also heard in a forum closer to herself. She had addressed family and church in the first place and only in the end was she able to make herself heard in the more private realm of a reconciliation ceremony. Thus, the interplay of court and non-court dispute settlement in this case leads to the realisation of a woman's rights in the broad sense used by Merry.

Coming back to Merry's concept of vernacularisation briefly mentioned at the beginning of this chapter, I'm able to add another set of actors to Merry's vernacularisers.

The 'targets' of processes of vernacularisation—rural Papua New Guineans in my case—do very well act as translators, contrary to what Merry expects (2006a, p. 134). People engaging in dispute settlement are actually vernacularisers at the local level. These local vernacularisers are separated in two groups, broadly speaking: dispute managers and disputants. Members of both groups have influence and the means to spread their opinion. Yet, they are different from what Levitt and Merry (2009) call 'local vernacularisers' in that they are not part of a social movement promoting a package of international law or good governance. They do not necessarily engage intentionally in the translation of such a package of international law concerning women's rights as Levitt and Merry's vernacularisers, even though village court officials do receive training about these issues, at least occasionally. And, more generally, rural Papua New Guineans are informed people, continuously broadening their legal consciousness: they have school education, some have studied abroad, some have trained on a job; they engage in congregational and other vocations; they read the news and listen to radio broadcasting (usually in Tok Pisin); they read information on posters (i.e. about women's rights) placed near Nadzab airport, the Highlands Highway and in the town of Lae; and they exchange what they hear and read. Men and women build up networks, both private and work-related, that connect them with at least the rest of Morobe Province. Knowledge, ideas and information all travel up and down these lines and have done so for many decades. Those at the 'grassroots' thus described do themselves translate (legal) information and (legal) knowledge into local legal consciousness. People engaging in dispute resolution are vernacularisers at the local level. And they have influence and the means to spread their opinion. An example of knowledge and information reaching the village level concerns the increase of adultery as well as *pasin pamuk* cases at Nadzab Village Court since the year 2000, occupying all legal institutions in the area. I see a correlation between the stated increase of such disputes and an increase in knowledge about women's rights in the whole country and in Morobe Province. The increase may be related to public debates around women's rights in village courts and elsewhere in Papua New Guinea. And this may be a welcome outcome of the work of social movements and of women's rights actors in Papua New Guinea.

References

Alayza Mujica, R., & Crisóstomo Meza, M. (2009). Women's rights in Peru: Insights from two organizations. *Global Networks, 9*(4), 485–506. doi.org/10.1111/j.1471-0374.2009.00265.x.

Barker, J. (2007). Introduction: The anthropological study of morality in Melanesia. In J. Barker (ed.), *The anthropology of morality in Melanesia and beyond* (pp. 1–21). Routledge. doi.org/10.4324/9781315612454-1.

Beer, B. (2006). Interethnic marriages: Changing rules and shifting boundaries among the Wampar of Papua New Guinea. In B. Waldis and R. Byron (eds), *Migration and marriage: Heterogamy and homogamy in a changing world* (pp. 20–39). Lit.

Beer, B., & Schroedter, J. (2014). Social reproduction and ethnic boundaries: Marriage patterns through time and space among the Wampar, Papua New Guinea. *Sociologus, 64*(1), 1–28. doi.org/10.3790/soc.64.1.1.

Biersack, A., Jolly, M., & Macintyre, M. (eds). (2016). *Gender violence & human rights: Seeking justice in Fiji, Papua New Guinea & Vanuatu.* ANU Press. doi.org/10.22459/GVHR.12.2016.

Chalmers, D.R.C. (1982). A history of the role of traditional dispute settlement procedures in the courts of Papua New Guinea. In D. Weisbrot, A. Paliwala, and A. Sawyerr (eds), *Law and social change in Papua New Guinea* (pp. 169–189). Butterworths.

Comaroff, J., & Comaroff, J.L. (1997). Postcolonial politics and discourses of democracy in southern Africa: An anthropological reflection on African political modernities. *Journal of Anthropological Research, 53*(2), 123–146. doi.org/10.1086/jar.53.2.3631274.

Demian, M. (2003). Custom in the courtroom, law in the village: Legal transformations in Papua New Guinea. *Journal of the Royal Anthropological Institute,* (n.s.), *9*, 97–115. doi.org/10.1111/1467-9655.t01-2-00006.

Demian, M. (2016). Court in between: The spaces of relational justice in Papua New Guinea. *Australian Feminist Law Journal 42*(1), 13–30. doi.org/10.1080/13200968.2016.1191118.

Felstiner, W.L.F., Abel, R.L., & Sarat, A. (1980/1981). The emergence and transformation of disputes: Naming, blaming, claiming … *Law and Society Review, 15*(3/4), 631–654. doi.org/10.2307/3053505.

Garap, S. (2000). Struggles of women and girls – Simbu Province, Papua New Guinea. In S. Dinnen & A. Ley (eds), *Reflections on violence in Melanesia* (pp. 159–171). Hawkins and Asia Pacific Press.

Goddard, M. (2004). *Women in Papua New Guinea's village courts* (State, Society and Governance in Melanesia: Discussion Paper 2004/3). Research School of Pacific and Asian Studies, The Australian National University.

Goddard, M. (2009). *Substantial justice. An anthropology of village courts in Papua New Guinea*. Berghahn Books.

Lawrence, P. (1969). The state versus stateless societies in Papua and New Guinea. In B.J. Brown (ed.), *Fashion of law in New Guinea* (pp. 15–37). Butterworths.

Levitt, P., & Merry, S.E. (2009). Vernacularization on the ground: Local uses of global women's rights in Peru, China, India and the United States. *Global Networks, 9*(4), 441–461. doi.org/10.1111/j.1471-0374.2009.00263.x.

Liu, M., Hu, Y., & Liao, M. (2009). Travelling theory in China: Contextualization, compromise and combination. *Global Networks, 9*(4), 529–554. doi.org/10.1111/j.1471-0374.2009.00267.x.

Merry, S.E. (1996). Legal vernacularization and Ka Ho'okolokolonui Kanaka Maoli, the People's International Tribunal, Hawai'i 1993. *PoLAR, 19*(1), 67–82. doi.org/10.1525/plar.1996.19.1.67.

Merry, S.E. (2006a). *Human rights and gender violence. Translating international law into local justice*. University of Chicago Press. doi.org/10.7208/chicago/9780226520759.001.0001.

Merry, S.E. (2006b). Transnational human rights and local activism: Mapping the middle. *American Anthropologist, 108*(1), 38–51. doi.org/10.1525/aa.2006.108.1.38.

Merry, S.E., Levitt, P., Rosen, M.H., & Yoon, D.H. (2010). Law from below: Women's human rights and social movements in New York City. *Law & Society Review, 44*(1), 101–128. doi.org/10.1111/j.1540-5893.2010.00397.x.

Michelutti, L. (2007). The vernacularization of democracy: Political participation and popular politics in North India. *Journal of the Royal Anthropological Institute, 13*(3), 639–656. doi.org/10.1111/j.1467-9655.2007.00448.x.

Michelutti, L. (2008). *The vernacularisation of democracy: Politics, caste and religion in India*. Routledge.

Moore, S.F. (1973). Law and social change: The semi-autonomous social field as an appropriate subject of study. *Law and Society Review, 7*, 719–746. doi.org/10.2307/3052967.

Nader, L. (1990). *Harmony ideology. Justice and control in a Zapotec mountain village.* Stanford University Press.

Neuhaus, J. (2020). *It takes more than a village court: Plural dispute management and Christian morality in rural Papua New Guinea* [Unpublished PhD thesis]. University of Zürich.

Podolefsky, A. (1978). *Pattern, process, and decision-making in New Guinea Highlands dispute handling* [PhD thesis]. State University of New York at Stony Brook.

Podolefsky, A. (1986). To make the belly cold: Conceptions of justice in the New Guinea Highlands. *Journal of Anthropology* (Special Issue on Customary Law and Legal Development in Papua New Guinea, ed. by R. Scaglion), *6*(2), 35–54.

Rajaram, N., & Zararia, V. (2009). Translating women's human rights in a globalizing world: The spiral process in reducing gender injustice in Baroda, India. *Global Networks, 9*(4), 462–484. doi.org/10.1111/j.1471-0374.2009.00264.x.

Robbins, J. (2004). *Becoming sinners: Christianity and moral torment in a Papua New Guinea society.* University of California Press.

Robbins, J. (2009). Recognition, reciprocity, and justice: Melanesian reflections on the rights of relationships. In K.M. Clarke and M. Goodale (eds), *Mirrors of justice: Law and power in the post–Cold War era* (pp. 171–190). Cambridge University Press. doi.org/10.1017/CBO9780511657511.

Scaglion, R. (1981). Samukundi Abelam conflict management: Implications for legal planning in Papua New Guinea. *Oceania, 52*(1), 28–38. doi.org/10.1002/j.1834-4461.1981.tb01483.x.

Scaglion, R. (1983). The effects of mediation styles on successful dispute resolution: The Abelam case. *Windsor Yearbook of Access to Justice, 3*, 256–269.

Serban Rosen, M., & Yoon, D.H. (2009). 'Bringing coals to Newcastle?' Human rights, civil rights and social movements in New York City. *Global Networks, 9*(4), 507–528. doi.org/10.1111/j.1471-0374.2009.00266.x.

Silbey, S.S. (2005). After legal consciousness. *Annual Review of Law and Social Science, 1*, 323–368. doi.org/10.1146/annurev.lawsocsci.1.041604.115938.

Strathern, A., & Stewart, P.J. (2007). Morality and cosmology: What do exemplars exemplify? In J. Barker (ed.), *The anthropology of morality in Melanesia and beyond* (pp. xiii–xxi). Routledge.

Strathern, M. (1972). *Official and unofficial courts: Legal assumptions and expectations in a Highlands community* (New Guinea Research Bulletin No. 47). The Australian National University.

Troolin, D.E. (2018). *'Wanbel': Conflict, reconciliation and personhood among the Sam people, Madang Province* [Unpublished PhD thesis]. University of Adelaide.

von Benda-Beckmann, K. (1981). Forum shopping and shopping forums: Dispute processing in a Minangkabau village. *Journal of Legal Pluralism and Unofficial Law, 13*(19), 117–159. doi.org/10.1080/07329113.1981.10756260.

von Benda-Beckmann, K. (2001). Legal pluralism. *Tai Culture, VI*(1/2), 18–40.

von Benda-Beckmann, K. (2003). The environment of disputes. In W. Van Binsberg in collaboration with R. Pelgrim (eds), *The dynamics of power and the rule of law: Essays in honour of Emile Adriaan B. van Rouveroy van Nieuwaal* (pp. 235–245). Lit Verlag.

Wormsley, W.E. (1986). Courts, custom, and tribal warfare in Enga. *Journal of Anthropology* (Special Issue on Customary Law and Legal Development in Papua New Guinea, ed. by R. Scaglion)*, 6*(2), 55–107.

Zorn, J. (2016). Translating and internalising international human rights law: The courts of Melanesia confront gendered violence. In A. Biersack, M. Jolly, & M. Macintyre (eds), *Gender violence & human rights: Seeking justice in Fiji, Papua New Guinea and Vanuatu* (pp. 229–269). ANU Press. doi.org/10.22459/GVHR.12.2016.06.

3

'Making *kastam* full' in the Sepik: The Awim Village Court as a spectral gift of shells

Tomi Bartole

Introduction

Village courts were introduced in Papua New Guinea in 1975 as a result of recommendations by the outgoing Australian colonial power in 1971 and the Committee Investigating Tribal Fighting in the Highlands in 1973. The considerations, motivations and reasons for the institution of the village court were many, comprising, but not limited to, the impracticality of local courts and the desire for an efficient and cost-effective justice system that would reach rural people (Goddard, 2009, pp. 47–50). Village courts became a reality, however, only once mainly juridical arguments acquired political and nationalistic grounds. This chapter explores the village court as a political idea, because, as some commentators have pointed out, this has the form of a gift or exchange of power; Goddard thus says, for example, that the village court aims at developing self-governance by way of 'giving a modicum of power to indigenous people' (Goddard, 2009, p. 49), while Strathern and Stewart (2000) claim that the village court has as its goal the restitution of the power to the people that had been removed during colonisation. The interest in the village court as a form of exchange or gift of power stems from the fact that exchanges constitute the prominent analytical situation in Melanesian ethnography, but also from a rather fascinating statement recounted to me by my brother Tony from the Sepik village of Awim, where

I conducted fieldwork. Tony told me that *lo*, a Tok Pisin word that in this case includes juridical institutions such as the village court, had not come yet into their distant area, called Arafundi. He told me that the *waitmen* had not brought it yet. Tony's statement propels us to question today's relationship between the people, their indigenous government and the *waitmen*, especially because the village court as a form of exchange or gift of power was part of the idea of an independent state of Papua New Guinea that sought to turn away from its colonial past and to partly reaffirm precontact customs and tradition (Goddard, 2009; Zorn, 1990). The project turned out to be, however, a difficult one (see Goddard, 1992, 2009). While the state reaffirms customs and tradition, and in the same process affirms itself, Ottley and Zorn point out that the state is hesitant to fully adapt to custom. The state might affirm itself through custom and tradition, but the state is at the same time authorised and legitimised through law, which custom might undermine (Ottley & Zorn, 1983). The full adoption of custom and tradition by the state, which was imagined to be achieved through, among other things, the village courts, was an attempt to integrate customary law into the formal legal system (Zorn, 1990, p. 279), to constitute a law based on custom (Aleck, 1991) or to adapt law to custom (Ottley & Zorn, 1983). This attempt, however, remained an unfulfilled idea that gave rise to a series of complexities (see Goddard, 1992).

To comprehend these complexities, legal anthropology has rendered the village court a critical and prominent analytical situation. Thus, the village court, for example, works as a scaling device to register the transformations (Zorn, 1990) of the problematic relationship between custom and law (Demian, 2015b). This relationship contains other relations, such as the complex integration of introduced law and neo-customary regulatory procedure (Goddard, 1998), custom and court (Zorn, 1990), local customary law and official customary law, and also what happens in the legal system of a given jurisdiction and what people might be doing in their everyday lives (Ubink, in Demian, 2015a, p. 3). The relations between the categories of indigenous and introduced, on the one hand, and English and Tok Pisin words, on the other hand, proved to be extraordinarily complex. For instance, the concept of *kastam*, distinct from that of custom (Keesing & Tonkinson, 1982; Otto, 1992; Schwartz, 2010; Thomas, 1992), brings considerable tumult for anthropologists, jurists and ordinary Papua New Guineans when dealing with custom and law (Demian, 2015b). The village court reveals relations between custom and *kastam*, but also between law and the Tok Pisin *lo* (Filer, 2006), and shows how *kastam* itself can be indigenous, introduced or both (Demian, 2003).

Demian shows, for example, that people background some of these elements and thus foreground others as strategic acts for constituting the sources of authority (Demian, 2003, 2015b). I take Demian's formulation as a cue to contemplate Strathern and Stewart's observation that with the introduction of the village court, people were given back not the power to fight each other but the power to sanction each other—to send offenders to jail and call the local police for people to be taken away (Strathern & Stewart, 2000). After making this observation, Strathern and Stewart ask implicitly whether this exchange was a fair one or not, and whether the things exchanged were equivalents. While this is, without doubt, a significant question, I suggest that in its current form it obviates an equally pertinent one: whether this exchange was a successful one—that is, whether the village court has been given by the *waitmen* as a gift and whether this gift has been received or accepted by the Awim people. Moreover, I suggest posing the question about whether the village court in Awim works (produces effects) precisely because this has not yet arrived.

Demian says that while jurists regard the village courts instrumentally (in combining custom and law), anthropologists use them descriptively and analytically (Demian, 2008, p. 440). To use village courts descriptively and analytically, however, they need to be enacted and practised by the people. Assuming this is not the case, the anthropologist is left with nothing to describe and nothing to analyse.

Village courts have been observed by many to not fully work as imagined (Aleck, 1992; Evans et al., 2011; Goddard, 1992, 2000; Scaglion, 1979, 1990; Westermark, 1986, 1991; Zorn, 1990). For scholars to be able to make assessments of this kind, however, village courts need to work in a more elementary way—that is, they need to appear to be enacted and practised by the people or, in a word, they need to be visible; only then can village courts be made into analytical situations that allow observations and analyses. In short, the village court works as it is enacted and practised, even though it might not work as imagined, for example, by those who introduced it.

The village of Awim where I conducted fieldwork in 2013–14 is situated in the south of the East Sepik Province of Papua New Guinea, in the Arafundi area. The Awim people speak the lingua franca Tok Pisin and Tape, one of the four languages spoken in the area (Hoenigman, 2015, p. 46). Currently, the village has around 200 people and is the result of the merging, under the influence of patrol officers (Amboin [ABN], 1963, pp. 10–11, 1964, p. 2; Roscoe & Telban, 2004, p. 99), of two moieties or major clans—the Mukumbae and the Wandukumbae (Telban, 2001, p. 5; Roscoe & Telban, 2004, p. 103). The people of Awim know of and have the institution of the village court—the court's representatives are regularly elected alongside the election for the village councillor—but the village court is very rarely enacted. When the village court is 'enacted', this has the form of a messenger delivering to the people the decision of the court, which usually relates to extremely minor offences, such as the destruction of garden plants as collateral damage in quarrels. Awim people do not enact the court—the court is regularly invoked, but not convened, and the people say that it does not work. It could be said that in Awim the village court is consistently present in people's speeches and talks, but it does not manifest in a form that would make it visible to all. The invisibility of the village court is a significant point to make, due to the prominent relationship that vision, sight and display have with acting and efficacy in Melanesia (Strong, 2017, p. 86). This fact does not, however, necessarily imply that the village court does not produce certain effects. Antithetical to the formula proposed above (village courts are enacted—they work, but do not work as imagined), I show that the village court in Awim works (produces effects) precisely because it does not work (it is not enacted). When the court does work as an effect, this is not registered within the legal context of the village court itself, but rather within the traditional problem-solving technique that has the form of a ritualised handshake (*kores-spendo* in Tape, lit. their two hands are copulating; *sekhan* in Tok Pisin).[1] During the 'handshake' ritual, two persons stand facing each other, shaking hands and expressing their regrets for any past thoughts, words and deeds that might have brought adversities into their lives. I write this ritualised form as 'handshake' to distinguish it from a handshake, the action in which two persons hold each other's hands and move them vertically, because although handshakes do occur in a 'handshake', the handshakes are not what the 'handshake' is about.

I approach the Awim Village Court as a form of observable exchange— a critical analytical situation in Melanesian ethnography. My contribution about village courts to the anthropology of law is, however, negative, because I focus on the equally significant reality of failed exchanges (Kirsch, 2006, pp. 1–2)—an instance in which the village court fails to be enacted, because, as I argue, it has not been fully gifted, that is, received by the Awim people. The methodological goal set in this chapter is to sever the phenomenal—

---

1   The meaning of *spendo* could be rendered with the word 'fucking', but due to the vulgarity of both the English and the Tape words I choose to translate it as 'copulating'.

that is, what manifests itself in a form that can be seen—from the analytical. By way of turning a failed manifestation (the non-enacted village court in Awim) into an analytical situation, I envision claiming for the former the same ethnographic and theoretical dignity of an analytical situation that is grounded in visible phenomena.

This methodological goal has several theoretical implications. Unlike the state of Papua New Guinea, which resiliently attempts to integrate customs fully into its legal system (Aleck, 1991; Ottley & Zorn, 1983; Zorn, 1990, p. 279), thus resulting in a partial integration, the Awim people desire to 'make *kastam* full', but not by subscribing to the abovementioned logic of amalgamation and unification, which is nothing more than an idealistic conception of the synthesis of dualism, where law would be assimilated with customs. For the Awim people *lo*, embodied in the village court, is not substantial in the sense that custom is for the state. While in the state's eyes custom can be said to be something (it can be seen and even touched), for the Awim people the village court is not. Neither can it be said, however, that the Awim Village Court does not exist. The Awim Village Court is not an entity, but it does nevertheless produce certain effects. This is why I suggest conceiving of this court as neither an entity nor a nonentity, neither an institution nor a non-institution, it is, in a word, a spectral court: a descriptive term for which I present support throughout the chapter.

When Awim people say that they want to make *kastam* full, it might appear at first as though *kastam* is lacking, while *lo* appears as the supplement to this lack that potentially enables the rehabilitation of *kastam* by making it whole again. The lack, however, is on the side not of *kastam*, but of *lo*, or the village court itself, insofar as the village court is never enacted. While in the case of the state, there is a symmetry between custom and law that sustains the relation, in the Awim case, there is no such symmetry and thus neither is there a relation.

In this chapter, I show that Awim people do indeed render *kastam* full, but without integrating within it a substantiated *lo*. *Kastam* here appears as never being complete or finished, because each intervention of the effects of *lo* make *kastam* full only partially, to the extent that *lo* enables people to exercise certain efficacies through *kastam* only temporarily. In this process of strengthening *kastam*, *lo* appears as a gift of the colonial era that has not yet fully been delivered to the people, but is nevertheless awaited and still on its way.

By presenting a problem-solving case between my brother Tony and the village of Yimas, I draw out the choices the Awim people had at their disposal to solve their problem: either the 'handshake', which they say belongs to their ancestors, or the village court, which they say belongs to the *waitmen*. I analyse this problem-solving situation, first, through the choices people made between the 'handshake' and the village court, and second, when one of them was chosen instead of the other, to show the ways these two problem-solving modes continued to be implicated in each other. At first, the two choices appeared to the ethnographer and perhaps to the people as well as symmetrically opposed equivalents: either village court or 'handshake', which suggests a relationship between them. Later events reveal, however, that either the two choices were never equivalent from the start or the two choices became non-equivalent after the choice was made. The latter is a question I do not intend to answer as I lack the necessary data, but I continue to dwell upon it as it suggests a non-relationality between the 'handshake' and the village court. Before proceeding to the presentation of the problem-solving case, I propose to acquaint the reader with Tony's thoughts about the relation between *kastam* and *lo*. He shared his thoughts with me about a month after his problem with Yimas was resolved. I use his account to establish the coordinates of an indigenous analysis.

The village of Awim and Tony

Awim is a relatively poor village, sometimes designated as a 'one-kina'[2] community. The amounts of money and goods circulating are meagre, and only two men possess a canoe. During my stay, the people sought to achieve a form of efficacy that would once and for all fulfil their hopes for a better life. These hopes were reiterated in their own life-project motto: 'change and development'. The people hoped for change and development, but not, as Sahlins (1992, p. 13) says, to become just like us, but rather, to become more like themselves. At the base of the motto, I argue, was the idea of changing and developing their *kastam* by way of making it powerful once again, and consequently to change the world in which they lived. The efficacy of the 'handshake' was a constant concern for the people because this played a central role in the strengthening of *kastam* insofar as problems and problematic relations were conceived to be halting processes of change and development.

---

2   The kina is the Papua New Guinean currency. In 2018, 1 kina was worth €0.26, £0.24 and AU$0.41.

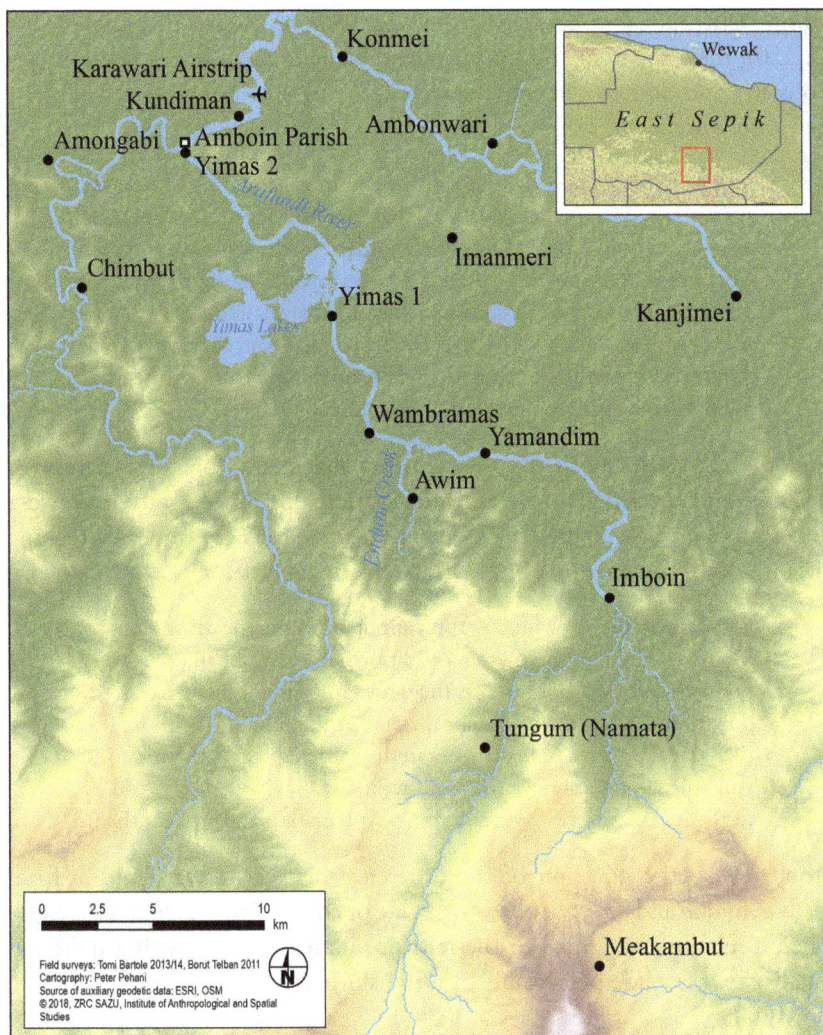

Map 3.1. Awim and neighbouring villages.

Source: Map by Peter Pehani, based on field surveys by the author (2013–14) and Borut Telban (2001), supplemented with data from Esri, OSM (OpenStreetMap) and ZRC SAZU (Research Centre of the Slovenian Academy of Sciences and Arts), Institute of Anthropological and Spatial Studies.

About a month after Tony's problem with Yimas was solved, I asked him about the difference between *kastam* and *lo*, and he replied:

> Some *kastam* and *lo* are the same. There is a little change, from one to the other. But the full *kastam*, you know, it is *kastam-lo*. This *lo* has not come into [our area]. The *waitmen* has not brought it yet.

Tony institutes a pseudo-identity between *kastam* and *lo* (cf. Lipset, 1997, p. 220), their apparent combination, and he talks about *lo* as something yet to come and be received. He then proceeds by strengthening the identity between *kastam* and *lo*:

> There is this *kastam*, *lo* that says you cannot break [cross] another man's boundary mark. If you do that you will meet with enemies. You have to stay inside your own boundary mark. You have to touch [interact with] something that belongs to you. The same goes for government's *lo*. It is the same with health, quarrels and fights. Before they also had some *kastam* to solve problems. I can say that today's *kastam* and *lo* on the one hand, and *lo* and *kastam* from before, they are the same, of the same kind, one kind.

Kastam and *lo* are posited as equivalents that allow for combination or relation and, in order to evince the historical difference, Tony makes use of a simple inversion between the two terms. He then continues by making a synthesis of the previously established historical difference:

> You cannot play too much. You cannot run underneath the house; if you are a young man, you will lose your strength, then you will not be able to work. Now it is the same. You cannot just sleep in the house. You have to work. Remove the [penile] blood.[3] With *lo*, it is the same. You have to make work in the garden, plant something and you will see the money. You hunt animals; then you marry, you go to the bush. You cut the trees, you grow bananas, and you eat them.

Tony reveals the question of the difference between *kastam* and *lo* from before, and *lo* and *kastam* today, to be one of continuity. He does not simply elicit a relation, but through the relation, he tells a story with a temporal quality that is made perceivable by a transformation:

> *Lo* has come in and is supporting *kastam*. *Kastam-lo*, *kastam*, relationship, *kastam*, brother system. *Lo* has come in. The *waitman* system has come in, and we have these thoughts. It is not that *lo* came in and my thoughts developed. We already had *kastam*, so when *lo* came in, it makes the *kastam* possible. *Lo* fulfils *kastam*, and this is why it is still related. This is why we have to follow it [*lo*].

---

3   This is an allusion to past initiation rituals in Awim of penile bloodletting and blood sprinkling (Roscoe & Telban, 2004, p. 110; Telban, 2001, pp. 6, 18), which is still practised individually by some of the younger men secretly in their gardens and the bush.

At this point in the story, *lo* has come. *Lo* has come as related to *kastam*; *lo* is what fulfils *kastam* (makes it possible) and, because *lo* is grounded in *kastam*, people have to follow it. At the beginning of the story, Tony suggested a combination between *kastam* and *lo* (*kastam-lo*), as was the case with the state and, at the end of the story, this relation is elaborated as one in which *kastam* is depleted and abated, while *lo* becomes *kastam*'s supplement and complement. In the next section, I present Tony's case and show how *kastam*'s depletion and *lo*'s supplementarity are turned into *lo*'s depletion, which breaks the relation between them.

Tony's problem and the choice

When I arrived in the village of Awim in September 2013, discussions about a certain 'problem' were an everyday occurrence. Awim people made more frequent use of the Tok Pisin word *problem* than *hevi*, because these follow more closely the Tape distinction between problems categorised as *mem* and *piya*, respectively, in which the first is a serious matter concerning all and the second refers to the personal experience related to the former. Tony was said to have been accused by the village of Yimas of bribery while working for a candidate in the electoral campaign for the 2012 Karawari Local-Level Government elections. I have never fully learned about the details of this alleged bribery. What was widely known, however, was that Yimas supported another candidate in the electoral race and thus the accusations made might have been politically motivated.

Notwithstanding the reasons behind the accusations, Tony steadfastly claimed his innocence but was deeply affected by the accusations that had been made. He was worried, *piya*, a state deemed extremely dangerous, because, in a manner similar to touching or interacting with prohibited things, it might lead him and sometimes others to be 'held by sickness' or even to death. At the same time, Tony's efficacy in business and other everyday activities was disrupted. He even fled to his father's bush camp in fear of a Yimas ambush, which actually occurred one night once he was back. He stayed in the bush camp for a number of weeks. Although far from Yimas, Tony was in great danger because 'walking with worries in the bush' is not advisable—one might cross a spirit's grounds, which is considered dangerous in such states.[4] Tony's problematic relation with Yimas and his worries became a 'problem', *mem*, for the whole community once the people recognised that everyone was prone to fall sick or even die. Tony's singular problem became a problem for many people, because the dangers this presented had become not only a remote possibility, but also an actual one. Also, in making one person's problem into a problem of many, people in Awim were efficaciously instantiating their relations. This is why it was the whole community that chose the most adequate problem-solving ritualised form and took care to organise it.

While people were discussing Tony's problem with Yimas, many said at first that they should take Yimas to court, but in the end, they opted for the 'handshake' instead. This decision and the argument in support of it were given in a single statement: 'We must solve this [problem] the ancestral way.' After they chose to solve the problem via the 'handshake', the village court started to become problematic in people's talk. The village court was problematic in the same way Tony's problem was problematic for the whole community—that is, the village court could have potentially ruined and killed the whole community.

The problem with the village court resides at the end of an imagined, but no less efficacious, course of events that the invocation of the court would trigger. People in Awim say that the village court will not be able to solve problems and problematic relations and, because of this, once it is invoked it will inevitably transfer the matter to higher courts, first to the Angoram District Court and finally to the 'provincial court'[5] in Wewak (see Goddard, 1992, p. 90, 1996, p. 60). As neither the village nor the district court will solve the problem, the people will find themselves in the Wewak court almost automatically. The Wewak court is unique in being associated with the police, who are said either to kill (see Hirsch, 1999, p. 814) or to ruin people's lives in the same way that problems do. The police would witness the process in court, and people perceive them to be too strong and dangerous a witness for them.

---

4   This is especially true of the two hills on which the spirits of the people reside—one of them is very close to Tony's father's bush camp, where it is dangerous to even circle the hills. Similarly to Kanjimei, a village that belongs to the same language group, but is situated outside the Arafundi area, people stay in the village if they are worried (Hoenigman, 2015, p. 104). See also Telban (2001, p. 6) for a similar account of spiritual dangers encountered in the bush.

5   There is no Papua New Guinean court system designated as provincial. There are, however, district courts in the provincial capitals. It will become apparent below why for the Awim the district court in Wewak is not identical to other district courts—for example, the one found in Angoram—and thus why the Wewak court cannot simply be a district court. I thus continue to either refer to this court as the Wewak court or present it in quotation marks as 'provincial court'.

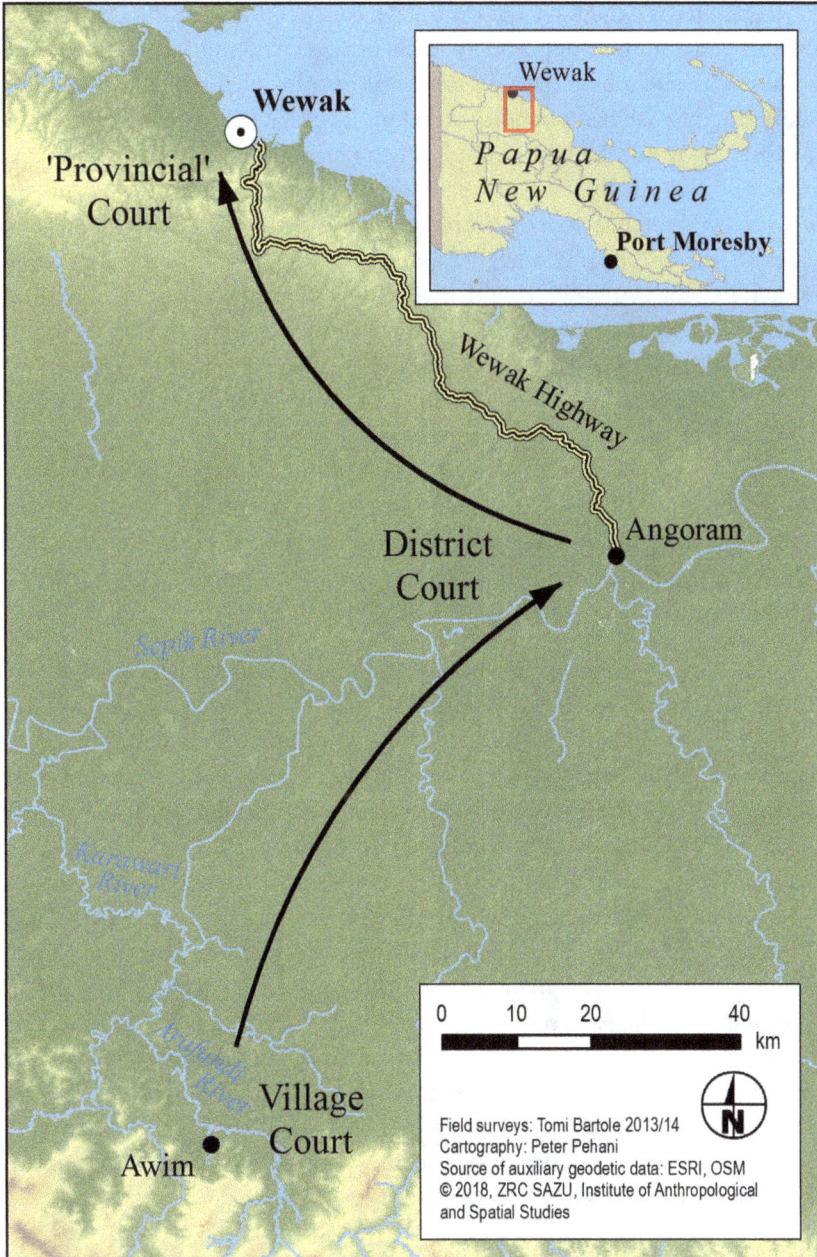

Map 3.2. Imagined path leading from lower to higher juridical instances.

Source: Map by Peter Pehani, based on field surveys by the author (2013–14), supplemented with data from Esri, OSM (OpenStreetMap) and ZRC SAZU (Research Centre of the Slovenian Academy of Sciences and Arts), Institute of Anthropological and Spatial Studies.

Furthermore, the dynamics of the village court and that of the 'handshake' are different, almost opposite to each other. First, the village court was considered to belong to the *waitman* or, as people called it, the 'new system', while the 'handshake' was said to belong to their ancestors, although the 'handshake' would be best glossed as neo-customary (see Goddard, 1998). I was told that, in the past, the people's ancestors would 'shake hands with arrows'—a reference to the problem-solving rituals in which both sides would break spears and other weapons in front of each other. I was told numerous stories in Awim and in the neighbouring village of Chimbut about a 'handshake' they performed three generations ago to stop the fights between them. Each and every storyteller claimed that the participants in the 'handshake' both shook hands and broke arrows. In 1966, a patrol officer witnessed and documented one such 'handshake' between the neighbouring villages of Imboin and Meakambut, who did not shake hands in the ceremony, but at its conclusion the patrol officer Classen 'moved among the men shaking hands [with them] and giving [a] small handful of salt to each man' (ABN, 1966, p. 8), by which he might have contributed to the transformation of the ritual as well as its name.

Second, the enactment of the 'handshake' and its efficacy depended on the mutuality of both parties involved. Both parties had to agree and commit themselves to take part in the ritual. In the case of the village court, however, anyone could be brought to court at any time by anyone for almost any reason, even for the refusal to release one's sister into marriage. In these instances, the village court is mainly used by people as a threat to substantiate their claims and requests.[6] During my entire stay in Awim, these threats never actually led the village court to assemble, and the village court simply remained a threat. On the day of the 'handshake' between Tony and Yimas, people gathered in the main meeting house, *haus win*. A church leader from another village started a brief service in which he asked God to give power to the people gathered there. He welcomed and thanked everyone for gathering. These were acts that elicited, as the church leader emphasised, people's goodwill and determination to solve the problem between Tony and Yimas, although the names of the people involved and the actual problem were never pronounced.

---

6   I single this example out because this is what happened to my brother Mark. After being threatened with the village court, he left the village with his sister and stayed in Yimas for two or three months. He was, however, afraid not of the court itself, but rather of what he might do due to the threats.

Everyone was asked to pray to God, and people did so, each on their own and so loudly that their voices were overlapping, while their words were hardly discernible. After a while, they stopped praying all at once, without an obvious sign to do so, and the church leader asked everyone to shake each other's hand, which is otherwise a constant feature of Sunday services in many Papua New Guinean denominations (Robbins, 2004, p. 267).

Once the decision to solve the problem the *kastam* way with a 'handshake' was taken and this process was underway, a transformation occurred, in which the village court, which was not chosen as a means to solve the problem, appeared in the 'handshake' through people's speeches. In fact, the speeches during the 'handshake' between Tony and Yimas were opened by one of the village magistrates saying: 'If anyone breaks this "handshake" I will call the police and send everyone to [the Wewak] court.'

The village court had become no longer opposed to the 'handshake', but the anticipated effects of the series of courts (village → district → 'provincial') became integral to its proceedings and its efficacy. The magistrate did not invoke the village court so much as the problematic aspect of the Wewak court that figures in the police and jail. The series proceeding from a lower juridical instance to a higher one—that is, from village to district and finally to 'provincial' court—is missing or cut short. The last juridical instance is made to appear directly. The reason for this lies in the first two juridical instances being deemed 'useless'—that is, without power or as lifeless— while the last, because it is associated with the police, is deemed powerful, although dangerous. The village court, which eventually triggers the series of courts leading finally to the Wewak court, is symmetrically opposed to the traditional way of solving problems only before the 'handshake' commences, but once this has started, the court together with the police become, in absentia, conditions of the 'handshake's' efficacy.

After the prayers, men started delivering their speeches, which consisted mostly of introductions emphasising gratitude for people coming and the goodwill demonstrated by this very act. Besides Tony, only *big men* from Awim, Yimas and other invited villages (Yamandim, Wambramas and Imboin) spoke, while young men and women listened. Tony was not a defendant—a term that would be more suited for a court. By accepting to take part in the 'handshake', which was in this case organised by the Awim Local-Level Government Councillor and Tony's brother Augustin, a person accepts equal responsibility in the matter at hand, and this held true for Tony as well as for the people of Yimas. Faults and mistakes were never brought up in the speeches during the 'handshake', even when the speeches became focused on the purpose of the ritual—that is, to solve the problem. Of Tony's alleged bribery or Yimas's accusations, one did not hear a single word. The intention to solve the problem was placed in the foreground. The problem itself, although never articulated, was very much present in the background and remained there through appropriate or 'good' talk. This good talk, although avoiding a direct enunciation of the problem at hand, served to organise the 'handshake' by setting the coordinates of the problem. This then determined the organisation of the 'handshake', in particular, through discussion of who besides Tony would become a participant in the shaking of hands and expressions of regrets. At first, the talks identified the problem as one of parenting, and thus these talks foregrounded the adults. Later, however, adult speakers distanced themselves from the problem and rearticulated it as one concerning the youth of Awim and Yimas.

The last speeches also shaped the proceeding of the 'handshake' and were thus transformational. In order for the 'handshake' to proceed and the expression of regret to occur, two groups of people or lines (the Tok Pisin *lain* is an idiom in this case for family or clan) had to take their respective places along the sides of the meeting house so that the two sides were then facing each other. The two lines were divided by two persons standing at the centre and holding hands throughout this stage of the 'handshake'. These two persons are referred to as witnesses and, besides the spectators, God and God's predecessor the Sun, they constitute the set of witnesses who are considered key for the efficacy of the 'handshake'. In the Tape language, the figure of the witness is referred to as *panga*—that is, someone who makes one strong, who supports, reassures or makes one's talk become true. While God and the Sun observe the 'handshake' from above and the spectators from the periphery, the two witnesses holding hands and separating as well as uniting the two lines are situated at the very centre of the 'handshake', the closest to the persons shaking hands. In the past, these witnesses were important *big men* from uninvolved clans, while today these positions are taken mainly by village court magistrates.

After the handshakes and expressions of regret between Tony's and Yimas's lines were concluded, the participants were reminded of the court invoked at the beginning of the proceedings. The same magistrate said:

> Suppose you will make another problem after you have solved this one. I will take note. I will take you and carry you out, to the *bik lo*, where all the police will witness, to the district court.

In this speech, the police have been moved from Wewak to the district court in Angoram, which suggests that the path leading to them is shortened by one court. The magistrate emphasised not the solution to the problem, but the repetition of the problem. The 'handshake' has as its goal the solution to the problem at hand, but also the prevention of the re-emergence of problems related to the first and, at the same time, preventing problems from re-occurring. This is also the reason people prefer not to avail themselves of the village court as this might bring new problems.

The magistrate's speech had an impact on Tony, who told me:

> It would not be good to cause another problem, or I will go to jail. I am really afraid, so I will start with a talk, but if we touch the wrong side, we will just hide.

Tony is afraid of jail, but also of making a mistake with words while shaking hands. If Tony were to 'touch the wrong side' of the discussions he could create another problem and his ultimate choice would be to hide again in the bush camp.

'Handshakes' and shells

In the introduction to this chapter, I put forward the trope of exchange for the village court found in Strathern and Stewart's comment about the suggested unfair and non-equivalent exchange between the village court and its power to sanction, on the one hand, and the power to fight, on the other hand (Strathern & Stewart, 2000). I have foregrounded this trope because, in the abovementioned 'handshake' dating from three generations ago between the villages of Awim and Chimbut, the people of Chimbut gave a shell to the people of Awim. The shell is still today held by the Patam clan of Awim, and people say that it is the shell that made the 'handshake' efficacious. The shell was and still is very powerful, people say. The shell is not powerful in itself, but it required Chimbut people to empower it—a process that is understood by the people as efficacy rendition. Chimbut people achieved this by dressing up and, more importantly, by giving a three-month-old boy named Kapyak to Awim. Chimbut and Awim people said that this is what empowered the shell, which in turn made the 'handshake' between them efficacious, in contrast to other 'handshakes' performed at the time with other villages. The shell has power because now it contains within itself the story of the problem between both villages, kinship relations instantiated by the child given, the proceedings of the 'handshake' and the final resolution to the problem.

When my great-grandmother Kakuai took the child from Chimbut people into her own hands at the end of the above presented 'handshake', she proclaimed to everyone present:

> I came with Kapyak, and you should all look. Suppose you Chimbut hurt or ruin Awim, suppose you stand up and strike Awim, I will kill you all. If Awim strikes Chimbut, this shell will kill all Awim.

Keropin, the Chimbut man who told me this story, said that the shell holds a great promise and that their (Awim and Chimbut) ancestors have created true power.

The shell has the power to destroy whichever village strikes the other village first and thus breaches the agreement made in the 'handshake'. Although it was a gift from Chimbut given to Awim, this could potentially affect both. While both villages, and especially Chimbut, agreed to 'shake hands' because they recognised the potential danger of being destroyed due to the mutual exchange of attacks, they found in the shell, which could equally destroy one of the villages, the guarantee that enabled them to cease fighting. I suggest that this is an instance in which one problem was exchanged for another problem: the problem of fighting was exchanged for the shell, while the shell itself has all the makings of a problem, because this could potentially destroy one of the villages. In this exchange of one form of problem for another resides a significant achievement. The shell, precisely by being a problem and functioning as one, instead of ruining lives now saves them. A comparison between the 'handshake' performed between the villages of Awim and Chimbut and the 'handshake' between Tony and the people of Yimas suggests that the shell, in the first case, and the village court, in the second case, operate and are operated upon in a similar manner. The shell and the village court both take the place of the initial problem to be solved through the 'handshake'—fighting in the first case and problematic relations in the second—precisely through their qualities as problems themselves. There is a further reason that I have been proposing the trope of exchange as an analytical category in the case of the Awim Village Court, and this resides in Marilyn Strathern's analysis of a first contact in the Highlands that had the form of a certain, and importantly, successful exchange (Strathern, 1992). Strathern tells us that Australians were interested in souvenirs and that they wanted to trade with steel axes, knives and spears. The Hageners remained impassive to Australians' requests until the gold prospector Michael Leahy opened a bag of shells. At that moment, as Strathern says: 'The strangers had found their medium' (Strathern, 1992, p. 248). Strathern suggests that at the heart of the matter was the revelation that the Australians had things that would elicit from the Hageners things they valued: pigs. For the Hageners, Strathern points out, forms (shells) are made of other forms (humans), unlike forms that appear by themselves, as the spirits in the Highlands do. The shell 'was the one item that already belonged to Hagen; everything else was a mere curio' (Strathern, 1992, p. 250). Strathern concludes with the supposition and suggestion that what made the strangers human was that they could be perceived as procreative conduits through which Hagen men could continue to reproduce themselves (Strathern, 1992, pp. 249–252), which implies that the Australians were made of and were able to procure the very same stuff of which the Hageners were made. I suggest, via Strathern's analysis of the pearl shells as 'the medium', that there is an anti-analogy between the shell Awim people received from the Chimbut people three generations ago and the village court the Awim people 'received' after 1975. I term this comparison an anti-analogy because although the shell and the village court elicit the same thing—the actual possibility of ruin and death of one of the parties taking part in the 'handshake'—the analogy is nevertheless a negative one due to the spectral status of the Awim Village Court. For while the Chimbut shell was a form made efficacious and made as such of a Chimbut human form, the village court is a form that appeared by itself, unmediated, as spirits in the Highlands do in Strathern's account. The term anti-analogy employed here aims to highlight the fact that there is no relation between the 'handshake' and the village court once the former commences. I approach the claim that there is no relation between the two through Strathern's definition of relations, according to which relations have two properties—a relation is both holographic and complex. The first property could be said to establish the conditions of comparison for a relation can be applied to any order of connection irrespective of scale, thus potentially establishing connections everywhere. The second property is a continuation of the first, and it could be said to have to do with the two ways relations reproduce as a self-organising figure. The first occurs by way of modelling phenomena to produce instances of itself. The second occurs by way of elicitation and complementarity. As Strathern says, relations summon entities other than themselves in order for the latter to complete the former (Strathern, 1995, pp. 17–19). This second property rests on the idea that a relation's minimal number is two (things/relations) and that two only makes a relation whole. One begins with a 'faulty' relation and, in the process of its elicitation, one ends with a complemented and fulfilled one.

The Awim Village Court, however, does not function as a complementary element in regard to an incomplete relation: the Awim Village Court does not complete the 'handshake'. This is because the two are not made of the same stuff; as Strathern would have put it, the village court is not to be found on the 'same earthly plane' as the 'handshake' (Strathern, 1995, p. 18).

The village court exists in between the being given and being received. On the one hand, Awims recognise in the village court the same elicitory powers previously known in the shell that was given to them by Chimbut. On the other hand, Awims prefer not to enact the village court, as they know what course of events such an enactment would trigger: the inevitable transference of the problem at hand to the Wewak court, where the police will act as a witness, and which figures as the ruin and death previously contained in the Chimbut shell. If it is true, as Strathern and Stewart (2000) argue, that peoples in Papua New Guinea had the power to fight taken away and were given in exchange the power to sanction, it could be suggested that the Awim people accepted the above transaction only partially, or they accepted only the spectral aspect and form of the village court.

Herein lies the difference between the exchange of shells analysed by Strathern and the exchange of the village court as a shell in Awim. In Strathern's case, the shells were actually and successfully transacted, not only because they elicited pigs but because the shells changed hands. Awim people, however, accepted the village court only partially, as it is never fully enacted, and thus it has spectral status. The village court as shell elicits the problem it contains only partially, through its effects from the distant town of Wewak, and never fully as the village court's presence in Awim and consequently as Awim people's presence in Wewak.

Conclusion

The colonial-era gift of the village court to the people of Awim is a gift that has not been fully realised as a gift, because both its delivery and its reception remain uncertain. The spectrality of the village court as a gift can be appreciated in Tony's discordant story about the ways in which *lo* has not come yet or has not been brought yet by the *waitmen*—that is, the colonial system, and the ways in which *lo* has come.

This chapter's goal was to turn the attention from successful exchanges, which constitute the critical and prominent analytical situation in Melanesian ethnography, to the equally significant reality of failed exchanges (Kirsch, 2006, pp. 1–2). I showed that, via Strathern and Stewart's suggestion about the exchange of the power to fight for the power to sanction, implied in the introduction of village courts to Papua New Guinea, the Awim Village Court is an item of transaction or a gift, while in this regard I posed the question about whether this gift was transacted successfully or not. In other words, I posed the question about whether the village court as a gift has been actually gifted by the colonial era and received by the Awim people, and thus constituted as a proper gift—after all, what is a gift that has not been gifted? The question form either/or reveals, however, an inability to capture the spectral phenomenality of the Awim Village Court as this has an existence that could be rendered through the neither/nor form instead: neither entity nor nonentity. This form highlights the fact that the limits of ontology do not always coincide with the limits of epistemology: the enactment and thus existence of the village court are not necessarily a condition of it serving analytical purposes. On the contrary, it was precisely the spectral status of the Awim Village Court that allowed the development of the analytics for the 'handshake' and village court that touch directly upon the central issue of this chapter—what 'making *kastam* full' might mean and imply in Awim?

Tony, for example, posited a relation between *kastam* ('handshake') and *lo* (village court). He postulated, according to Strathern (1995, pp. 17–19), a symmetry and complementarity between them when saying that 'when *lo* came in, it makes the *kastam* possible … *Lo* fulfils *kastam,* and this is why it is still related'. The enactment of the 'handshake' between Tony and the people of Yimas revealed that the relation between the two is of a particular kind. I call this kind of relation an anti-relation, and I bring it about through a focus on Tony's mention about *kastam*'s condition of possibility. An anti-relation is essentially asymmetrical and, on account of this asymmetry, it could be claimed that there is no relation proper. I put all the stakes on the meaning of the phrase 'making *kastam* full' for making sense is exactly what relations are about. As Strathern says, a relation can be thought of in the same way as a linguistic sign: as a relation between signifier and signified (Strathern, 1999, p. 6). What is *kastam* then, made full? My argument in this chapter points to sense-relation—a relation that makes sense and a sense that makes relations. The making full of *kastam* appears as a propensity to close a gap or lack internal to *kastam*. I believe the true question lies here, in this gap or lack found within *kastam* itself, which could be, however, conceived in two different ways. I argue that there is a relational and an anti-relational reading of this gap. According to a relational reading, *kastam* elicits *lo*, specifically, and 'handshake' elicits the village court, in order for the latter to complete the former. In this case, the lack is itself conceived of relationally, and directionally, insofar as this directs and is directed at something other than itself. 'Making *kastam* full' would then imply counting the 'handshake' and the village court together as two halves of a completed whole. If this lack is conceived of as a depletion of *kastam*, as I have initially suggested in following Tony's words, the village court can appear as a supplement and complement that makes *kastam* whole or complete. This is how one arrives at a relation as far as the village court is the other half of the 'handshake' that the latter has elicited. Relational analytics is grounded in the idea that a relation is a complemented being; *kastam* signifies and expresses *lo* and the 'handshake' refers to or is the village court. What about non-complemented beings and signs, then? Anti-relational analytics, in contrast, acknowledges the limits of relational complementarity, for it posits the lack at the core of the relation, which brings a significant implication. The division no longer runs between different relations/entities, but between a relation/entity and the lack—a lack that surrounds the relation/thing as its own limit and thus makes them count as an indivisible one. While the complexity of a relation assumes this is made of two—a relation and its other element or entity (Strathern, 1995, p. 18)—the complexity of an anti-relation assumes a split relation/entity, split into itself and the lack. More concretely, once the lack in *kastam* of the 'handshake' is transposed onto *lo* or the village court as lack itself, the village court starts functioning as the internal limit and possibility of the 'handshake'. As its internal limit, the village court is, as it were, the definition of the 'handshake'. Alternatively, as Tony also put it, 'when *lo* came in, it makes the *kastam* possible', except that *lo*, rather than entering the Arafundi area *lo* (village court), has entered first into *kastam* ('handshake'). Making *kastam* full is thus only practicable on the ground if one assumes a relational analytics, as this allows for a totalisation, which is provided by complementarity and symmetry. In contrast, an anti-relational analytics does not allow for such totalisation and completion to occur because it does not obviate the split within *kastam* ('handshake'), which is *lo* (village court) itself, and follows instead the repetition of claims of 'making *kastam* full' into an open future that is prone to other forms of entries, besides those of the Chimbut shell and the village court.

References

Primary sources

Amboin [ABN]. (1963). *Amboin Patrol Report, No. 4, 1962/63*. National Archives of Papua New Guinea.

Amboin [ABN]. (1964). *Amboin Patrol Report No. 8, 1963/64*. National Archives of Papua New Guinea.

Amboin [ABN]. (1966). *Amboin Patrol Report No. 1, 1966–67*. National Archives of Papua New Guinea.

Secondary sources

Aleck, J. (1991). Beyond recognition: Contemporary jurisprudence in the Pacific Islands and the common law tradition. *QUT Law Review, 7*, 137–143. doi.org/10.5204/qutlr.v7i0.347.

Aleck, J. (1992). The village court system of Papua New Guinea. *Research in Melanesia, 16*, 101–128.

Demian, M. (2003). Custom in the courtroom, law in the village: Legal transformations in Papua New Guinea. *Journal of the Royal Anthropological Institute, 9*(1), 97–115. doi.org/10.1111/1467-9655.t01-2-00006.

Demian, M. (2008). Fictions of intention in the 'cultural defense'. *American Anthropologist, 110*(4), 432–442. doi.org/10.1111/j.1548-1433.2008.00076.x.

Demian, M. (2015a). Introduction: Internationalizing custom and localizing law. *Political and Legal Anthropology Review, 38*(1), 3–8. doi.org/10.1111/plar.12083.

Demian, M. (2015b). Dislocating custom. *Political and Legal Anthropology Review, 38*(1), 91–107. doi.org/10.1111/plar.12088.

Evans, D., Goddard, M., & Paterson, D. (2011). *The hybrid courts of Melanesia: A comparative analysis of village courts of Papua New Guinea, island courts of Vanuatu and local courts of Solomon Islands* (World Bank Justice and Development Working Paper Series 13). The Legal Vice Presidency of the International Bank for Reconstruction and Development.

Filer, C. (2006). Custom, law and ideology in Papua New Guinea. *The Asia Pacific Journal of Anthropology, 7*(1), 65–84. doi.org/10.1080/14442210600554499.

Goddard, M. (1992). Of handcuffs and foodbaskets: Theory and practice in Papua New Guinea's village courts. *Research in Melanesia, 16*, 79–94.

Goddard, M. (1996). The snake bone case: Law, custom and justice in a Papua New Guinea village court. *Oceania, 67*(1), 50–63. doi.org/10.1002/j.1834-4461. 1996.tb02571.x.

Goddard, M. (1998). Off the record: Village court praxis and the politics of settlement life in Port Moresby, Papua New Guinea. *Canberra Anthropology, 21*(1), 41–62. doi.org/10.1080/03149099809508373.

Goddard, M. (2000). Three urban village courts in Papua New Guinea: Some comparative observations. In S. Dinnen & A. Ley (eds), *Reflections on violence in Melanesia* (pp. 241–253). Hawkins Press and Asia Pacific Press.

Goddard, M. (2009). *Substantial justice: An anthropology of village courts in Papua New Guinea.* Berghahn Books.

Hirsch, E. (1999). Colonial units and ritual units: Historical transformations of persons and horizons in Highland Papua. *Comparative Studies in Society and History, 41*(4), 805–828. doi.org/10.1017/S001041759900314X.

Hoenigman, D. (2015). *'The talk goes many ways': Registers of language and modes of performance in Kanjimeni, East Sepik Province, Papua New Guinea* [PhD thesis]. The Australian National University.

Keesing, R., & Tonkinson, R. (eds). (1982). *Reinventing traditional culture: The politics of kastom in island Melanesia.* Anthropological Society of New South Wales.

Kirsch, S. (2006). *Reverse anthropology: Indigenous analysis of social and environmental relations in New Guinea.* Stanford University Press. doi.org/10.1515/97815 03625747.

Lipset, D. (1997). *Mangrove man: Dialogics of culture in the Sepik Estuary.* Cambridge University Press. doi.org/10.1017/CBO9781139166867.

Ottley, B.L., & Zorn, J.G. (1983). Criminal law in Papua New Guinea: Code, custom and the courts in conflict. *American Journal of Comparative Law, 31*(2), 251–300. doi.org/10.2307/839827.

Otto, T. (1992). The ways of *kastam*: Tradition as category and practice in a Manus village. *Oceania, 62*(4), 264–283. doi.org/10.1002/j.1834-4461.1992. tb00357.x.

Robbins, J. (2004). *Becoming sinners: Christianity and moral torment in a Papua New Guinea society.* University of California Press.

Roscoe, P., & Telban, B. (2004). The people of the Lower Arafundi: Tropical foragers of the New Guinea rainforest. *Ethnology, 43*(2), 93–115. doi.org/10.2307/ 3773948.

Sahlins, M. (1992). The economics of develop-man in the Pacific. *RES: Anthropology and Aesthetics, 21*, 12–25. doi.org/10.1086/RESv21n1ms20166839.

Scaglion, R. (1979). Formal and informal operations of a village court in Maprik. *Melanesian Law Journal, 7*(1), 116–129.

Scaglion, R. (1990). Legal adaptation in a Papua New Guinea village court. *Ethnology, 29*(1), 17–33. doi.org/10.2307/3773479.

Schwartz, T. (2010). *Kastom*, 'custom', and culture: Conspicuous culture and culture-constructs. *Anthropological Forum, 6*(4), 515–540. doi.org/10.1080/00664677.1993.9967430.

Strathern, A., & Stewart, P.J. (2000). *Stories, strength and self-narration: Western Highlands, Papua New Guinea.* Crawford House Publishing.

Strathern, M. (1992). The decomposition of an event. *Cultural Anthropology, 7*, 244–254. doi.org/10.1525/can.1992.7.2.02a00060.

Strathern, M. (1995). *The relation: Issues in complexity and scale.* Prickly Pear Press.

Strathern, M. (1999). *Property, substance and effect: Anthropological essays on persons and things.* The Athlone Press.

Strong, T. (2017). Becoming witches: Sight, sin, and social change in the Eastern Highlands of Papua New Guinea. In K. Rio, M. MacCarthy, & R. Blanes (eds), *Pentecostalism and witchcraft: Contemporary anthropology of religion* (pp. 67–92). Palgrave Macmillan. doi.org/10.1007/978-3-319-56068-7_3.

Telban, B. (2001). *Arafundi River 2001* [Unpublished report]. ZRC SAZU (Research Centre of the Slovenian Academy of Sciences and Arts).

Thomas, N. (1992). The inversion of tradition. *American Ethnologist, 19*(2), 213–232. doi.org/10.1525/ae.1992.19.2.02a00020.

Westermark, G.D. (1986). Court is an arrow: Legal pluralism in Papua New Guinea. *Ethnology, 25*(2), 131–149. doi.org/10.2307/3773665.

Westermark, G.D. (1991). Village courts in Papua New Guinea: A comparative perspective. *Law and Anthropology: Internationales Jahrbuch für Rechtsanthropologie, 6*, 67–79.

Zorn, J.G. (1990). Customary law in the Papua New Guinea village courts. *The Contemporary Pacific, 2*(2), 279–311.

4

Unmaking a village court: The invisible workings of an alternative dispute forum

Eve Houghton

[Law] is hesitantly coming round to the realisation that it can no longer be considered a grand bastion of certainty but merely one process running along other processes on a space of fleeting, fragile, almost imaginary consistency.

– Andreas Philippopoulos-Mihalopoulos (2010, p. 208)

Introduction

This chapter explores the ramifications that theories of spatial justice and the co-creation of law and space have when examining dispute forums in Papua New Guinea. Building on work in which I explored conceptions of justice and their intersections with the everyday in a village court (Houghton, 2019) and based on 12 months of fieldwork in Bialla, a town in the Papua New Guinean province of West New Britain, this chapter challenges the official/ unofficial distinction upheld between the village courts and 'alternative' dispute forums. In my previous work, I described the making of a village court by tracing the paths of court summonses and exploring their ability to carry relational ties. I identified the village court as a flexible space that gains temporary fixity through physical attributes such as chairs and flags, allowing it to take shape around and in direct response to the disputes it oversees.

Here, I build on this work by discussing the significance of the mediation forum that materialises when a village court is unmade, and how this connection between the emerging and withdrawing dispute forums extends the influence of the village court, making it possible for a wider range of local requirements to be addressed in different ways, irrespective of any legal prescriptions that limit the village court itself. Crucially, I will use this connection to reveal why the absence of data relating to these 'alternative' forums when assessing the role and use of village courts limits the viability of the conclusions usually drawn about how well they are functioning and the services they provide.

Established in the *Village Courts Act 1973* (later replaced with the *Village Courts Act 1989*) as part of the country's shift towards independence, the village courts of Papua New Guinea (PNG) are often considered in relation to their performance as part of the country's official legal system. This origin in legislation means they are commonly seen to stand apart from other dispute venues that exist outside state-sanctioned parameters. Currently, the village courts are made visible to state authorities through physical documentation in the form of court registration and periodic reports. Meanwhile, any unregistered and undocumented forums remain invisible to centralised government bodies. Even if residents refer to a dispute forum as a village court and local authorities run it as such, these venues are still regarded as alternative forms of law arising in response to the absent state (Schwoerer, 2018). As a result, questions about the effectiveness and success of the village courts are usually measured against official court documentation in the form of the records that are kept by court officials at a local level and the village court handbook that outlines the remit and purpose of the courts. This approach renders village courts as static spaces providing local backgrounds against which state laws are interpreted and applied. This conceptualisation conceals the existence and capacity of other dispute venues and the connection they have to the workings of the village court as a flexible legal space. To borrow from Andreas Philippopoulos-Mihalopoulos, this chapter is driven by the conceit that:

> Space and its conceptualisations have greatly changed, and law, both as a discipline and as a social function, must keep up with it. Space is no longer the local background but the radically disorienting factor of law's self-description. (2010, p. 214)

Dispute forums in Bialla

Alternative dispute forums in Bialla are both diverse and numerous. I could not hazard a guess as to the actual number, but as an example, within the village of Ewasse where I was resident there were at least five—four linked to the head figures from each Christian denomination in the village (Catholic, Seventh-day Adventist, Reformed Protestant and Evangelical Pentecostal Protestant) and one village-wide *komiti*. In Ewasse, the *komiti* is a public gathering that includes representatives from each of Ewasse's 15 clans. It is used to discuss issues relevant to everyone in the village. Anyone can present an issue at *komiti* meetings, and for that reason it covers a huge range of topics, from bake sales to riots. Included in this were a wide range of disputes.

Having five dispute forums in a single village illustrates the variety required to address the needs of the population and the kinds of disputes they have. The authority embodied by leaders from different denominations reveals some of the existing broader hierarchies that are well established beyond a dispute forum context and are intertwined with the space, laws and relationships through which these disputes are handled.

Ewasse has one of the more homogeneous populations in Bialla. The village consists of 15 clans, all established as being from the area and all with rights to land.[1] Identifying shared authorities who were able to act as dispute overseers was relatively straightforward for residents who used their family, faith and clan as initial guidelines for this. Residents of villages like Ewasse would often provide examples to illustrate a stark contrast between their lives and the lives of residents on nearby settlements owned by oil palm companies (Koczberski & Curry, 2004). These examples covered many topics, such as health, wealth and marriage. Dispute forums were no exception to this. These settlements are sites of high in-migration, with workers coming from all over PNG to move into houses that are provided by one of the two large oil palm companies working in West New Britain, New Britain Palm Oil Limited and Hargy Oil Palm Limited. These sites consist of large numbers of breeze-block residences and disputes arise on these shared plots of land like any of the other villages in the region. As a

---

1   Much has been written on the significance of customary land and ownership in Melanesia. McDonnell et al. (2017) provide a good overview. Tammisto (2019) explores the significance of work and landscape as the materialisation of personal and group histories, providing useful context for New Britain specifically.

result, there are also dispute forums in the settlements, but dealing with residents who have moved into the area from all over the country makes dealing with disputes and identifying a shared respected authority to oversee a dispute more complex. Not only that, but without shared clans or religious leaders on the settlements who might otherwise represent authority, I was told almost anyone could become an overseer of disputes, and if disputants didn't like a ruling they were easy to ignore as a result. 'In the settlements [dispute overseers] can be anyone and do not represent everyone', a pastor in Ewasse told me in a succinct condemnation of settlement dispute forums.

Thus, it is in this environment of varied villages, settlements and alternative dispute forums that the state-sanctioned village court materialises each week. Despite the wide range of cases that Bialla's village court manages to address, there are also disputes that cannot be resolved there. One reason for this is that many disputes in Bialla involve payments of more money than the village court is able to award to disputing parties.[2] These larger settlement sums were common in Bialla, as debt cases linked to the harvesting of oil palm often easily exceeded the village court's legal K1,000 compensation cap. In these instances, the village court is unable to make any official ruling that could possibly resolve the dispute with any finality. Therefore, disputants need to seek a more appropriate forum.[3] Some alternative forums in Bialla can be seen to emerge almost solely in an effort to cater to this need, and it is this kind of forum that I will be discussing in this chapter. I will describe how the village court, with its legal prescriptions and physical realisation, helps to inform the materialisation and uses of an alternative forum that occupies that same physical space. This is most easily identifiable when the magistrates explicitly decide to oversee certain disputes not as cases, but instead as what they referred to as 'mediations'. This chapter begins by revisiting the unmaking of Bialla's village court, as described in my previous article exploring the court's materialisation (Houghton, 2019), and goes on to explore a specific dispute that was overseen in the alternative forum that emerged in its stead.

---

2   Limits on payments are broken down in the Village Courts Act based on the type of case magistrates deem a dispute to be. The highest of these relate to compensation, damages and debt, which are limited to K1,000 (*Village Courts Act 1989*, section 4(45)). An exception to this is in the case of bride price, custody of children or death where 'a Village Court may award such amount in compensation or damages as to the Village Court seems just' (1989, section 4(46)).

3   The seriousness that is given to the compensation cap in Bialla is not true of every village court in PNG where larger amounts have been demanded as part of official village court rulings (Demian, 2015b). Notably, the village court in Bialla also chose not to make rulings in debt cases where compensation was paid in any form other than money (e.g., pigs or store goods, which are highly valued and have no legal cap attached).

A note on terminology

The term 'mediation' will be used repeatedly throughout this chapter to describe a type of dispute forum that exists outside the remit of the village court. This term will be extended to describe the process used to address disputes ('mediated') and the role that certain actors take during this process ('mediators'). The reason for my use of this term is that it was the word used in Bialla to describe many of the dispute resolution processes that existed outside the village court. Although many of the forums had their own names that differed from this (*wanbel kot, stretim kot, komiti*), the process used to oversee disputes was often considered to be 'mediating'. This term is therefore the most appropriate to use throughout my discussion of the following disputes.

I acknowledge that the word mediation also has a place in PNG legislation. Mediations are a legally sanctioned part of the PNG Government's effort to allow for alternative dispute resolution processes.[4] Enough disparity exists between the legislative definition and the events that took place in Bialla that there is a need to distinguish between the two. As a result, the term mediation will appear throughout this chapter, but its use is in no way linked to the legislative definition of this term unless explicitly stated. To maintain this distinction and allow for a clear division between the two processes, I will refer to Mediations as they exist in legislation in capitalised form. This rule extends to any additional descriptors stemming from the same term (Mediators, Mediating).

In the absence of a court: Unmaking as a means of creation

The physical elements that constitute each of PNG's village courts differ. Usually marked by the presence of a flag, village courts can range from a table in a busy urban market (Hukula, 2019, p. 176) to boxes drawn into the sand on a beach (Demian, 2016, p. 14). In Bialla, the village court occupies a large wooden bandstand and is identifiable from the careful positioning of chairs, a table and a provincial flag (Figure 4.1). Despite

---

4 Full details of the government guidelines for a Mediation and the proper processes attached to registering as a Mediator can be found in the *Rules Relating to the Accreditation, Regulation and Conduct of Mediators* (2010).

their differences, how and where they are physically realised shapes the work they all do—from making relationships observable to defining in/justice. Considering this, what happens when the physicality of a village court is intentionally altered or disrupted? To help navigate this question I draw on two existing theories relating to spatial justice. The first is the idea that in/justices are embedded 'in the spaces and places in which they are produced, enacted, contested and neglected' (Brunnegger, 2019, p. 16). The second is my adoption of an idea that has gained popularity in the field of legal geography: that law and space are not independent of one another but instead 'mutually constitutive' (Blomley & Labove, 2015, p. 474) or 'intertwined' (Delaney, 2010, p. 4). These theories provide the groundwork for my argument that the unmaking of the village court in Bialla does not just remove a legal space, or a space's capacity to 'do' law, but instead has the ability to conjure another legal forum entirely. Throughout this chapter, legal forums demonstrate how conceptions of in/justice inform the articulation of disputes in place, and how the intertwining of law and space shapes the forum that materially emerges in response to this dispute. To better understand this, I will describe the steps through which the village court is unmade and the proceedings in the alternative dispute forum that follow as they relate to a single dispute.

Figure 4.1. The village court in Bialla.
Source: Eve Houghton (2014).

My discussion is divided into three sections. The first focuses on the case study itself, detailing both the dispute's content and the mediation forum's material existence. The second section consists of the analysis of this case study. It considers the material attributes that define the mediation forum as a legal space in order to discuss why unmaking the village court is so important to its existence. The third and final section looks at how the mediation forum oversees the dispute. Seen together, the shifting legal spaces that contribute to dispute resolution in Bialla demonstrate the capabilities and restrictions of these interrelated forums, and encourage us to revise how we approach the subject of village courts and their capacity as legal institutions in PNG.

Case study: Anna, Noah and the promise

We were four cases into a village court session when the peace officer called a new pair of disputing parties up to the bandstand for their case to be heard.[5] Both parties arrived before the magistrates, diligently handed over their summonses and stood awaiting instruction. The magistrates read through the case as it had been described on both summonses. At this point, the magistrates would usually ask the complainant to describe the case to them. The case would then progress in a routine way. However, on this occasion neither party was given the opportunity to speak. Instead, one of the magistrates told the disputants that the village court would not hear this case. As this announcement was made, another magistrate took hold of both summonses and ripped them dramatically right down the centre. He stood holding the torn pages aloft for a moment before returning them to the table and himself to his seat. The sense of drama that had been created through the public destruction of the summonses was unlike the dismissal of any other case I had seen. It was also quite unexpected, as both parties were present and both had presented their summonses—these being the most common requirements disputants fail to meet that lead to a case's suspension or dismissal.

Following the summonses' destruction, the magistrates stood and announced that the court was closed, much like it had been at the end of every court session I had witnessed since my arrival. As per usual, everyone standing briefly bowed their heads to mark the occasion. The provincial flag was removed from its place on the table and carefully folded. The magistrates relinquished their chairs and the peace officer carried them back into the nearby office buildings along with the flag, table and green court notebook in which cases are officially documented. The bandstand stood vacant of all village court paraphernalia save for the magistrates themselves, yet no-one showed signs of drifting back to town like they usually would at the end of

5   Peace officers play supporting roles in the village court. They help maintain order by telling people where to stand, correcting any poor behaviour and collecting evidence or summonses that are passed to the magistrates. They also call disputants to the bandstand to begin a case.

a hearing. Instead, the parties from the case that had just been dismissed returned to the stage. They sat where they would have been standing if the case had taken place—defendant on the right, complainant on the left. The magistrates and peace officer remained on the bandstand, but rather than sitting in the centre at a table they instead took up residence in spots across the floor and on the bannisters around the edge of the stage. One of the magistrates announced that they were ready to take care of this mediation, and he invited one party to begin by describing the dispute.

The bandstand had changed quite a lot in the short time since the village court closed. Not only were the flag and chairs removed, but also an evident change in atmosphere had occurred. The parties sat on the floor, with friends clustered on either side of the bandstand—their positions signifying their loyalties. As a marked change from the village court, rather than one of the magistrates leading proceedings, it was now the peace officer who was orchestrating events. The magistrates had donned caps and sat drinking canned drinks. Some were even chewing *buai* (betel nut)—a habit that called for them to regularly spit red saliva from the edge of the bandstand and into the grass below. The disputing parties also showed none of the signs of formality usually required during village court sessions. They sat with their bags, and every so often a child would wander up onto the bandstand to get the attention of one of the contributing parties. In the village court, this behaviour would have been strictly forbidden and in some cases even punishable. In the mediation, these actions were not even mentioned.[6]

One of the magistrates explained that because this dispute would be overseen as a mediation, it meant no ruling would be made. Instead, the conclusion of the dispute was reliant on the two parties agreeing on a resolution together. The magistrates and peace officer saw themselves merely as facilitators for this agreement. They were there to point the disputants along a certain track rather than to make any judgements of their own. The magistrate emphasised that nothing in the mediation would have any legal ramifications and that the aim was only to create peace—not to punish. In this way, the magistrates define the mediation forum as one in which injustice is countered by peace, rather than justice in more judicial terms. This is a sentiment that the village court magistrates use

---

6   In one of Kimbe's village courts, which as a rule were even stricter than Bialla's, I saw a man held in 'contempt of court' when he was seen to be chewing *buai* and then his nephew ran into the courtroom to see him as the case was taking place. He was charged K50 as punishment following this second offence. The combination of these events was too much for one magistrate, who threatened that the next time the case was interrupted he would be charged again and asked to return next week instead.

to explicitly distinguish the role of the mediation forum from the village court. Notably, this interpretation differs to how the role of village courts has been described by senior court officials in Port Moresby. In the capital, the purpose of village courts is seen to be 'peace not justice' (Demian, 2016, p. 13)—evidence of the profound divide that can exist between national vision and local implementations of dispute management.

The complainant in this instance was a man called Noah, who looked to be in his twenties.[7] He sat cross-legged on the bandstand across from the defendant—a woman of similar age called Anna. She had come with her mother, who sat beside her chewing *buai* and leaning back on her hands, her bare feet jutting out towards the magistrates. Noah began by describing why he wanted to have a mediation. The fact that the case was originally presented in the village court was never mentioned again. Noah spoke as though the mediation was what he had sought for his dispute from the very beginning. He claimed that Anna had '*promisim marit*' or promised to marry him, and he had given her money to pay for her school fees based on this belief. Later, Anna had told Noah that she never wanted to marry him and had also refused to pay him back the school fees. When it came her time to speak, Anna claimed that she was only ever Noah's friend. She asserted that she had made him a promise of friendship and nothing else. Debate continued between the parties for some time until eventually the dispute was reduced to one core concern: did Anna break her promise?

Having so far done little more than prevent the parties from talking over one another, it was at this point that the peace officer and magistrates, in their new positions as mediators rather than representatives of the village court, began to guide the discussion forward.[8] They made it clear that if Anna was found to have broken her promise of marriage to Noah, she would need to repay him for her school fees as she would have gained that money by lying. If she never promised him anything more than friendship and he chose to give her the money anyway, she would not be required to pay.

Anna's mother, who had until this point only spoken in confirmation of points Anna had made, began to speak passionately about her dislike of Noah. She described how Noah had tried to buy Anna's love and that, as soon as he realised his love had been rejected, he had decided to try to get

---

7   All names have been changed to protect the identities of the people involved.
8   To mark this shift in their roles overseeing the dispute, I refer to the village court magistrates and peace officer as 'mediators' while describing their actions during the mediation.

the money back. She also said that she would never have let Anna marry him, so he should never have assumed she could. Anna, she claimed, could never have promised to do so. It was not Anna's promise to make.

This debate continued to bounce between disputants for some time, until one of the mediators voiced his opinion. He summarised his understanding of events and announced that as soon as Anna discovered her parents did not like Noah, she should never have taken any money from him in case it could have been confused as a payment towards marriage in the future. This conclusion demonstrates that this mediator and Anna's mother share the understanding that Anna and Noah are not free to make promises of marriage without family consent. This is because in West New Britain, and many parts of PNG, marriage revolves around families exchanging bride price. Bride price is most commonly an exchange of goods made between families in recognition of a marriage between two individuals. Depending on the region the items exchanged can differ greatly. In West New Britain, a bride price is usually paid by a groom's family to the parents or family of his bride. A bride price is agreed before a couple marry, but the exchange itself does not always take place before a marriage and may take years to pay in full. An understanding of the value of this exchange and the period over which it is to be paid is therefore a fundamental part of a marriage. Families are intimately tied together for years through the ongoing acts of exchange and of calling upon outstanding bride-price debts as a reminder of familial obligations to one another. As part of this, the bride and groom are both expected to fulfil certain obligations to one another within their new roles as husband and wife. This often impacts brides to a greater extent, as in West New Britain this would involve moving to their husband's village and working on his land to provide for their family. This makes matters of marriage very much a family affair—a point to which the mediator and Anna's mother refer, knowing that everyone will have this shared understanding of what a promise of marriage really involves.[9]

This also indicates why the promise becomes such an important part of this discussion, as it could entirely change what the financial exchange meant and did to Noah's and Anna's (and their families') relationships as a

---

9   There were marriages that were recognised in Bialla that did not involve bride-price payments. However, couples in these marriages were often described with explicit reference to the lack of bride price, clearly demonstrating these marriages are still outliers in the region.

result.[10] Thus, the mediator's view that the promise was not Anna's to make and that the exchange of money could be misconstrued had an immediate effect. As soon as the mediator finished talking, Anna admitted that it was she who had originally phoned Noah to ask for the money—he had not offered it unprompted. At this point the mediators all agreed that Anna had effectively stolen the money. They stopped there and said any repayment should be agreed by the disputing parties. It should not require a ruling from them. This was all that the mediators said, but it was enough to shape the rest of the mediation as it was now clear to everyone present that Anna should be expected to pay Noah back.

Upon hearing this, both Anna and her mother ceased all arguments against having to pay anything at all and instead turned their attention to discussing how much money was owed. Noah claimed that Anna owed him K5,000, and he provided a crumpled handful of receipts from the school Anna attended as proof of payment. These receipts were passed around the bandstand between the mediators, ending with one who took the time to add up the costs. He reported that the receipts did not add up to K5,000, and Noah explained that these were only the receipts he remembered to keep. Anna was noticeably quiet for the rest of the mediation. Instead, her mother spoke, stating that she and Anna would only pay for an amount that could be proven. She asked Noah to write down all the dates he claimed to have paid school fees. Once he had finished, she sat and compared what he had written with her own knowledge of Anna's schooling. This was a lengthy process, during which both sides continued to voice their dissatisfaction with one another.

Eventually, the mediators brought an end to proceedings as the two parties could not agree. I asked whether that meant that this dispute would be overseen in the village court in future, and one of the mediators informed me that unless the disputants came to an agreement, the conflict would require a district court hearing, bypassing the village court altogether because of the K1,000 compensation cap. The consensus was that it would be much better to reach an agreement and come back for further mediation than to take the dispute to the district court. I asked whether the mediators thought they had helped the parties with their problem and their response was overwhelmingly positive:

---

10   See Strathern (1984) for just one example of the numerous publications that explore the importance of exchanges and bride price as they relate to personhood and relationships in different parts of Melanesia.

> Before it was not clear. Now this is about debt. Anna broke her promise and this mediation helped her say this. Noah doesn't have his receipts, but when he does have these receipts, he will be able to get his money. Anna will have to pay this.[11]

To close the mediation, there was no visual cue as clear as the bowing that closes proceedings in the village court. The mediators merely suggested that both parties go away and come up with an amount to be paid. They should then meet again and try to reach a mutual agreement. They would be allowed to return for another mediation if they needed to, especially if they wanted people to witness the final payment. Anna, her mother and Noah all nodded at this suggestion and gathered their things before exiting the shade of the bandstand. At this point some of the mediators began to drift back towards the nearby offices, while others remained. They were joined on the bandstand by other people who had previously been sitting on the surrounding field or were simply passing by on their way home from town. This was a dispute forum no longer, just a bandstand full of people.

What unmaking does

In previous work, I have established how certain actors are vital to the making of the village court in Bialla—for example, a summons, a chair, a flag and a magistrate (Houghton, 2019). Looking at the treatment of these same actors as the court transitions into a space for mediation, we can see how their contributions to the village court's existence are intentionally interrupted for the village court to be unmade. This section explores exactly how this interruption not only unmakes the village court but also establishes a new alternative dispute forum.

Benefiting from the progress made in the past decades in the field of legal geography, it has become increasingly straightforward to understand the ways that law and space are 'mutually constitutive, political and socially consequential' (Blomley & Labove, 2015, p. 474). So, how can this intertwining of law and space extend into our understanding of the significance of unmaking Bialla's village court and the emergence of an alternative dispute forum? In this endeavour, I am informed by the groundwork laid by Melissa Demian (2016), who, while also examining

---

11 This explanation took place in a mixture of English and Tok Pisin. For this reason, I have not included a separate Tok Pisin quotation.

the village courts of PNG, brings together theories of spatial justice—in which space is inherently ethical (see also Philippopoulos-Mihalopoulos, 2010)—with relational justice that identifies relationships as the bearers of rights over individuals or groups (see also Robbins, 2009). Demian's amalgamation of these two threads allows her to conclude that 'the only way to achieve relational justice is through its instantiation in spatial justice' (2016, p. 30). In the context of PNG's dispute forums this approach means relationships are the bearers of rights and in disputes must find footing in/as space to become observable or public, and hence give overseers and onlookers the ability to acknowledge, define and provide justice in response to them. In the case of Anna and Noah, they were each able to voice their understanding of their relationship, with Anna claiming they were friends and Noah claiming that there was a promise of marriage. Subsequently, the mediators used descriptions of events that took place in this relationship as indicators to define the specifics of the relationship, ultimately siding with Noah in viewing Anna's request for financial support as indicative of a more than platonic arrangement. Anna's mother was also integral to this as she was able to physically (and vocally) represent the extended relationships actively involved in any promises of marriage that may or may not have been made—a relationship that was not captured on the village court's summons that only called Anna and Noah onto the bandstand. This theoretical groundwork enables us to examine how the unmaking of the village court creates a dispute forum that is entirely suited to both making the disputants' relationship(s) observable in space and providing a form of justice that prioritises said relationship(s), seeking to mediate a peaceful outcome that satisfies the requirements of the relationships involved, rather than make a court ruling setting a debt. This relational dimension is part of the 'embeddedness' of in/justice in PNG that is then made observable in dispute forums (Brunnegger, 2019).

The mediation forum used to oversee Noah and Anna's dispute emerges in response to a relationship and is shaped by a shared understanding that it stands apart from, but in reference to, the legal parameters of the village court it has replaced. I will be referring to this lingering influence of the village court and associated actors as active absence. It is through this active absence that this emerging forum gains the mediating abilities required to oversee this dispute. To examine this proposition in greater detail, it is worth returning to the most easily identifiable influence demonstrated by any one actor in the making and unmaking process: a village court summons. When a case is successfully concluded in the village court, the summonses that worked towards its creation cease to exist. Their material form is artfully disappeared by magistrates, usually concealed in stacks of paper or the backs of notebooks to be disposed of later. As the summonses vanish, so too does the dispute—at least in its legal form.

The importance that summonses play in the making of a case, and of the court itself (see Houghton, 2019), makes the act of tearing them in front of an audience particularly striking. This is the first physical event that works to distinguish the mediation from the village court that preceded it. Prior to the ripping of the summonses, every step that was required for Anna and Noah's dispute to be overseen in the village court took place. Unlike other instances when the magistrates sent disputants away claiming they have 'no case', in Noah and Anna's dispute the magistrates initially acknowledge the case's existence. Through their receipt of both summonses the case comes into being and it is no longer in the magistrates' power alone to undo this.[12] Instead, the magistrates must rely on a new process if they wish to avoid overseeing the case that has been created. The only way to do this is to somehow undo the effects of those actors that define both the case and the village court as a space that cannot oversee the dispute. It is for this reason that, rather than simply putting the summonses aside, the magistrates publicly destroy them.

Within the village court context that the summonses help to create, as soon as they are handled in a way that strays from convention, there are ramifications for both law and space as they continue to co-create with new parameters, with relational justice remaining paramount. In this case, the summonses' destruction highlights a limitation of the village court—namely, this dispute and the relationship it refers to cannot receive satisfactory justice here—which in turn provides a guide for what the mediation forum that follows can do. The unmaking then continues through the removal of other physical attributes that worked to stabilise the village court. The peace officer and magistrates remove the remaining furnishings of court from the bandstand and return them to the nearby office buildings. It is not a quick process and has an air of ceremony about it, as everything is handled carefully and quietly. This public procedure helps to maintain threads of connection and establish active absences from which the alternative mediation forum gains shape and legitimacy. The peace

---

12 I never saw the magistrates dismiss another case where summonses had been provided by both disputants, as Anna and Noah did. Cases were often reframed or required other witnesses to attend before magistrates would address it, but this is radically different from the immediate dismissal of cases I observed when summonses were not provided.

officer and magistrates are the only feature of the village court that is not removed or destroyed during this unmaking process, but they do undergo a physical and public transformation that helps simultaneously to illustrate connection and distinction between the village court and the mediation forum that follows. The magistrates change their positions, language and behaviour: sitting on the same level as everyone else, moving to the edges of the bandstand and openly consuming *buai*. These visible changes are significant because it is precisely their being witnessed that creates such a powerful juxtaposition between the venues. How this juxtaposition works can be explained with reference to Franz and Keebet von Benda-Beckmann's 'Places that come and go' (2014), in which they explore what happens to theories of legal geography when combined with theories of legal pluralism. They describe how fading places can 'linger' or cast 'shadows' on what comes next. People take risks by anticipating legal spaces and parameters that may not have materialised yet. In the context of the village court, people share such a clear image of what the village court looks like and is capable of that unmaking it casts a shadow informing any forum that emerges in its stead. Held in direct and immediate comparison with one another, the new roles of people and objects that had been court-making actors divide the two dispute forums extremely effectively. In the case of the magistrates, their authority remains, but their roles and even how they are addressed shift into that of mediators who are seen as facilitators who do not make rulings. Concurrently, the peace officer's authority is elevated as he takes on a more prominent role in proceedings—physically indicated as he takes a central position on the bandstand. For both the magistrates and the peace officer, their physical transformation helps redefine the space as, simultaneously, the emerging legal space redefines their roles within it.

Why unmaking matters

Having established how a mediation forum is created as the result of unmaking a village court, it is now possible to identify what this new forum gains from the process and what that means for Anna and Noah's dispute. Despite ostensible commonalities such as a shared goal to create peace between Anna and Noah, as well as the bandstand itself as a location, clear distinctions can be made between the roles of the village court and the mediation forum. Many of these differences stem from the change that court-making actors undergo in the village court's unmaking. The expectations of those witnessing disputing events and interacting with the forum shift accordingly as a result of these changes. For example, when Noah presented his argument, he automatically altered his discussion to acknowledge the new venue in which it was being overseen. It was as though he had planned to have his dispute mediated all along. The process by which the dispute would be concluded also differed to village court practices. The clear division between the two forums frees the mediation from certain legislative restrictions, while the connection maintained between the two forums sustains authority and shapes the forum's purpose—that is, to create peace and not punish as the village court is seen to do. Having described how unmaking takes place, I want to focus on how legislative limitations applicable in the village court shape the use of the mediation. I consider how these limitations are regarded and acknowledged as the connection between the absent village court and the mediation forum that takes its place, revealing how alternative mediation forums expand the local capacity to settle disputes.

In Anna and Noah's case, the most obvious reason for the forum change is that the village court is legally unable to deal with disputes that may require more than K1,000 compensation or debt repayment (*Village Courts Act 1989*). However, this summary does not account for why the case was not referred 'up' to the district court or why it was not simply catalogued as a formal Mediation that is allowed for in village court legislation. Instead, the chosen forum places the dispute outside the gaze of any state legislation, rulings or court setting entirely. The magistrates call upon a forum where they intentionally take on the role of mediators—a distinction that removes them from positions of legal authority, while still allowing them to facilitate proceedings. This returns us to the influence of relational justice. The need for this kind of mediation stems from the fact that when the dispute was originally brought forward, it was not a case about a debt of more than K1,000, it was about how to reconcile two people's differing accounts of a relationship and the obligations within that relationship. Therefore, the duty of whichever forum oversaw the dispute would be to discern whether Anna had made a promise and, as part of that, make a moral judgement with regard to her behaviour within the context of the relationship at stake.

At first glance, this kind of action does not seem to lie outside the village court's remit, especially when one considers Fiona Hukula's (2019) observations that village courts are often moral forums as much as anything else. In addition, when the Village Courts Act states that 'in all matters before it a Village Court shall apply any relevant custom' and that it should do so 'whether or not it is inconsistent with any Act' (1989, section 8(57)), it provides legislative parameters that allow customary laws to supersede all other legislative Acts within the village court context. This Act indicates that custom is really supposed to be a village court's forte. However, in Anna and Noah's case, two difficult matters must be considered, both of which make the village court a less than ideal venue for this ruling to take place. First, if Anna were deemed to have broken a promise of marriage, the magistrates foresaw that the settlement could include a debt involving an exchange of sums exceeding village court allowances. Therefore, the village court would not be able oversee the dispute, at least not with any kind of court record or legal sanctions to support it. In isolation perhaps this issue would not have been enough to lead to the court's unmaking. Magistrates do sometimes oversee cases to the point of discerning what the next step should be, and simply refrain from ruling on the compensation amount itself.

However, in this instance there is a second factor to take into account that was enough to encourage the forum shift. If Noah and Anna's case had been overseen as a matter of custom, the magistrates would be dealing with (and making a ruling based upon) their moral assessment of a promise of marriage and what that means in Bialla. The problem for the magistrates arises when they are required to document their rulings. Although free to describe cases as they choose on court documents, magistrates must use a certain language to describe cases. Most are catalogued under certain titles and even defined as the case takes place by magistrates as 'adultery', 'debt' or 'assault'. These terms have legal connotations that usually have some impact upon the compensation ruling that follows. In theory, in the case of a broken promise the magistrates are free to make a customary ruling, although this can come with its own nightmarish complexity (see Demian, 2015b). However, this kind of customary ruling was not something I ever saw in the village court at Bialla. Cases that lacked a definition deemed sufficiently 'legal' in the magistrates' eyes would often move into a mediation forum to be seen there—forums where no paperwork was ever required. One of Bialla's magistrates attempted to describe this distinction to me, saying, 'We can't write that we punished a person for breaking a promise! They are not married yet. It would not work.' It is striking that interpretations such as this one, rendering some disputes as more legal in the eyes of the state than others, result in official records lacking any evidence of precisely the sorts of cases that village courts were originally established to handle.

The magistrates read the summonses describing Anna and Noah's case and immediately realised they would be stuck if they oversaw it in the village court. If they deemed the case to be a matter of stealing, and were therefore able to document the case, they would be outside their remit because of the amount involved. If, however, they attempted to address it as a matter of custom by categorising it as a dispute over a broken promise, in their position as legal actors they felt they would be undermining the position of the village court. Without mediation forums such as that which emerges through the village court's unmaking, the only alternative would be for this case to register for the lengthy and serious process of a district court hearing, or not be addressed at all.

Between the potential amount of compensation required to resolve the case and the lingering question of how to rule on a broken promise with many relationships attached to that, the village court seemed too restrictive to those attempting to run it. As a result, the clear distinctions established between the court and the mediation forum by the court's unmaking process allowed for those present to work through these issues in a space that emerged with the aim specifically of overcoming these issues. In this forum we can see how the unmaking of the magistrates' positions, and their emergence in the role of mediators, allowed them to reveal the relationship and discuss large sums of money while simultaneously removing their responsibility to make a legal ruling subject to government guidelines.

Not only does unmaking the village court distance the mediators from external state authority, it also protects them from any repercussions instigated by unhappy disputants following a ruling. This fear of taking responsibility for rulings was often given by magistrates as a reason for a move into a mediation, especially when disputes involved extended clans and *lain* (families, groups). Some dispute forums are considered to provide this freedom from personal responsibility in a way that the village court is not.

The village court magistrates, on the other hand, often felt more vulnerable through their perceived connection to many disputes they oversaw. Rather than stepping in to merely symbolise or represent the village court or a disputing party, magistrates contribute to the temporary materialisation of the court. They simultaneously shape and are shaped by the justice that disputants can access there. In this way, they become part of the embodiment of the forum and its authority. As a result, magistrates are held as responsible for the rulings made there as the court is itself. Concerns about repercussions stemming from dispute rulings have also been identified by other academics observing village courts, most commonly those relating to sorcery (Demian, 2015a; Goddard, 2009), because of the responsibility and risk involved in the job. The risk people spoke of in Bialla always concerned unresolved disputes or unhappy disputants seeking 'payback' for magistrates' rulings deemed to be unfair. This concern applied mostly to the village court, but precautionary measures were also sometimes taken in larger mediations. For example, when a dispute involved families from outside Bialla, risk was mitigated through the presence of mediators from other regions to create a shared authority that all disputants would recognise. Another cautionary measure available was to invite the *lain* (extended families) of disputants to attend. This enabled mediators to attempt to create widespread agreement between more people connected to a dispute and to limit the likelihood that someone would reject the outcome in the future.

Although I saw no actions taken against the magistrates explicitly due to their involvement in cases, a negative event in a magistrate's life, such as sickness, was likely to be associated with a past dispute and considered a repercussion, although notably this was not always an association made by the magistrates themselves. This risk of repercussions was enough to influence how disputes were dealt with in Bialla. For example, there was sometimes a significant increase in the number of mediators called upon to help facilitate proceedings in order to further distribute responsibility, despite the impossibility of actual rulings being made in that forum.

When the village court is unmade, the effort of court-making actors to facilitate peaceful relations between Bialla's residents continues. By removing any formal ruling body in the form of the magistrates, mediations limit the chances of any escalation of conflict. The same effect is achieved when the number of mediators overseeing a dispute is increased. These changes indicate that the end of conflict and the maintenance of peace are always paramount to the process, regardless of the forum.

What does this shift in responsibility actually mean for the mediation, other than allowing the mediators to enjoy *buai* while they work? In Anna and Noah's dispute, the changes that the magistrates underwent in order to become mediators and their combined contribution to the unmaking of the village court allowed them to explore what the financial exchange did to the relationships it engaged with (namely, that it was not just between Noah and Anna) and to treat Anna's promise as a serious matter relating to this without worrying about how it could be catalogued. Anna and Noah's dispute provides just one example of the perceived limitations of the village court, the significance of the village court's unmaking and the necessity of the mediation forum and others like it that are used in its stead.

Conclusion

The commonalities between the village court and alternative forums can be significant in terms of the authority they hold in local communities and some of the physical attributes that contribute to the creation of legal spaces. However, the legal distinctions made between these venues and how these differences are evoked through physical space can be used to reveal just how important these other forums are. Ultimately, the interrelation between these legal venues demonstrates not a divide between the 'official' and 'unofficial', but instead that no single venue or type of case (adultery, debt, bride price) should be considered entirely in isolation if we wish to discover what it is they truly do. The treatment of Anna and Noah's dispute in Bialla illustrates how legal spaces can temporarily hold a relationship up for public examination and define aspects of it to shape what may happen to it in the future. When restrictions or broader social concerns limit the capacity of the village court, space and law find a new form created in reference both to the relationship it needs to serve and the village court that it complements. Despite the differences in the ways they materialise and the processes that take place within them, dispute forums are interrelated. The unmaking of the village court is what allows the mediation forum to take shape—it relies on the active absence of the village court to exist. As a result, Bialla's mediation forum can oversee disputes outside any strict legal remit and still make use of similar processes that are used in the village court setting with many of the same court officials.

By acknowledging the workings of this venue, we can see not only where the village court magistrates feel unable to oversee disputes, but also how they go about overcoming limitations in order to try to provide disputants with useful insights. This process also demonstrates the type of disputes that go unreported by the village court magistrates. This reveals some of the limitations of village courts' collection of data on which both the provincial and the national governments rely for gauging the workings of the courts across PNG. This lack of data becomes even more pronounced if we take into account the numerous alternative forums that emerge in every village or settlement in the country.

The village court also provides a procedural connection with which (and in some instances against which) the mediation forum can define its own identity and remit as a dispute forum (see Galanter, 1981). By physically unmaking the village court to establish differences between it and other dispute forums, magistrates are recast in a new role and contribute to the realisation of a new law in a new space that is able to tend to the dispute at hand. All this is done while simultaneously upholding several similarities between the venues that define the mediation's legitimacy, authority and capacity. In combination, these attributes create a unifying effect between forums. They function not as independent venues divided by imagined counterpoints such as law/custom, official/unofficial or local/national oversight, but as two different parts of one dispute mediation system that are dependent on one another to tend to people's relationships. This connection does not give the village court a position of authority in a hierarchy of dispute forums. Rather, it establishes each forum on an equal footing in an expansive constellation of forums that are all working towards the same goal, each with the ability to keep different local requirements and relationships in mind.

References

Blomley, N., & Labove, J. (2015). Law and geography. In J.D. Wright (ed.), *International encyclopedia of the social & behavioral sciences* (pp. 474–478). Elsevier. doi.org/10.1016/B978-0-08-097086-8.86123-1.

Brunnegger, S. (2019). Theorizing everyday justice. In S. Brunnegger (ed.), *Everyday justice: Law, ethnography and injustice* (pp. 1–34). Cambridge University Press. doi.org/10.1017/9781108763530.

Delaney, D. (2010). *The spatial, the legal and the pragmatics of world-making: Nomospheric investigations.* Routledge. doi.org/10.4324/9780203849101.

Demian, M. (2015a). Dislocating custom. *Political and Legal Anthropology Review, 38*(1), 91–107. doi.org/10.1111/plar.12088.

Demian, M. (2015b). *Sorcery cases in Papua New Guinea's village courts: Legal innovation Part IV* (In Brief 2015/27). The Australian National University.

Demian, M. (2016). Court in between: The spaces of relational justice in Papua New Guinea. *Australian Feminist Law Journal, 42*(1), 13–30. doi.org/10.1080/13200968.2016.1191118.

Galanter, M. (1981). Justice in many rooms: Courts, private ordering and indigenous law. *The Journal of Legal Pluralism and Unofficial Law, 13*(19), 1–47. doi.org/10.1080/07329113.1981.10756257.

Goddard, M. (2009). *Substantial justice: An anthropology of village courts in Papua New Guinea.* Berghahn Books.

Houghton, E. (2019). Ever in the making: Actors and injustice in a Papua New Guinea village court. In S. Brunnegger (ed.), *Everyday justice: Law, ethnography, injustice* (pp. 182–205). Cambridge University Press. doi.org/10.1017/9781108763530.011.

Hukula, F. (2019). Morality and a Mosbi market. *Oceania, 89*(2), 169–181. doi.org/10.1002/ocea.5216.

Koczberski, G., & Curry, G.N. (2004). Divided communities and contested landscapes: Mobility, development and shifting identities in migrant destination sites in Papua New Guinea. *Asia Pacific Viewpoint, 45*, 357–371. doi.org/10.1111/j.1467-8373.2004.00252.x.

McDonnell, S., Allen, M.G., & Filer, C. (eds). (2017). *Kastom, property and ideology: Land transformations in Melanesia.* ANU Press. doi.org/10.22459/KPI.03.2017.

Philippopoulos-Mihalopoulos, A. (2010). Spatial justice: Law and the geography of withdrawal. *International Journal of Law in Context, 6*(3), 201–216. doi.org/10.1017/S174455231000011X.

Robbins, J. (2009). Recognition, reciprocity, and justice: Melanesian reflections on the rights of relationships. In K.M. Clarke & M. Goodale (eds), *Mirrors of justice: Law and power in the post–Cold War era* (pp. 171–190). Cambridge University Press. doi.org/10.1017/CBO9780511657511.010.

Schwoerer, T. (2018). *Mipela makim gavman*: Unofficial village courts and local perceptions of order in the Eastern Highlands of Papua New Guinea. *Anthropological Forum, 28*(4), 342–358. doi.org/10.1080/00664677.2018.1541786.

Strathern, M. (1984). Marriage exchanges: A Melanesian comment. *Annual Review of Anthropology, 13*, 41–73. doi.org/10.1146/annurev.an.13.100184.000353.

Tammisto, T. (2019). Making temporal environments: Work, places and history in the Mengen landscape. In A. Lounela, E.K. Berglund, & T. Kallinen (eds), *Dwelling in political landscapes: Contemporary anthropological perspectives* (pp. 247–263). SKS (Finnish Literature Society).

Village Courts Act 1989, No. 37 of 1989, Papua New Guinea. (1989). www.paclii.org/pg/legis/consol_act/vca1989172/.

von Benda-Beckmann, F., & von Benda-Beckmann, K. (2014). Places that come and go: A legal anthropological perspective on the temporalities of space in plural legal orders. In I. Braverman, N. Blomley, & D. Delaney (eds), *The expanding spaces of law: A timely legal geography* (pp. 30–52). Stanford University Press. doi.org/10.2307/j.ctvqsdzbj.6.

Part II: The courts, the law and the Papua New Guinean state

5

Keeping the sky up: Papua New Guinea's village courts in the age of capacity building

Michael Goddard

Introduction

The anthropologist Peter Lawrence once wrote that, contra the legal maxim *fiat justitia, ruat coelum* (loosely, 'let justice be done, though the sky may fall'), Melanesians were more concerned to keep the sky up (Lawrence, 1970, p. 46). His comparison was topical during late colonial attempts to bridge the gap between law and 'custom' with the introduction of state-sanctioned village-level courts. It remains apt in contemporary times when development aid organisations have increased their attention to community-level institutions in Papua New Guinea (PNG). Their interventions, holding the promise of functional improvement conducive to globalised imperatives such as human rights and the rule of law, have been glossed with terms such as 'capacity building' and 'institutional strengthening' (see, for example, Eade, 2005; Pacific Women Support Unit [PWSU], 2018; Talao, 2009). PNG's 'village court' system has been an intermittent recipient of development aid interest since its inauguration in 1974. The village courts are currently regarded as an important community-based component of the pursuit of 'law and order' and human rights, at a time when major resource extraction projects are contributing to unprecedented transformations and social problems in far-flung communities that, not so long ago, were popularly portrayed as autonomous, 'traditional' and sustained by 'custom'.

In this chapter I revisit some themes in traditional Melanesian dispute management and review the fortunes of the village courts, which were intended to incorporate 'custom' (including 'customary law') into their practice and are increasingly influenced by recent capacity-building and strengthening endeavours. I suggest that development aid assumptions and strategies risk undermining the very aspect of the village court system that has made it such a successful institution: the intimate relationship the courts have had with the communities they serve. More specifically, I question an axiom chain that informs the strategies of aid intervention in institutions like the village courts. The first axiom is that the courts' practice can be dichotomised as referencing law on the one hand and 'custom' or 'customary law' (terms implying rule-like 'tradition' in popular discourse) on the other. The second axiom is that custom and tradition are liable to impede justice and the pursuit of human rights and that Western law is more reliable. The third axiom is that while local culture should be respected, it is wise to incorporate principles derived from Western legal culture in the training of village courts officials in the interests of their just practice.

I argue instead that village courts' practice has not followed 'custom', 'customary law' or tradition in the popular sense. The courts have, though, been sensitive to local understandings of what is right and just. These understandings are generated by a sociality governed by a disposition towards sociocentric obligations and responsibilities that is liable to subordinate the interests of individuals to the interests of groups. The successful local practice of village courts has been substantially due to their nuanced understanding of this sociality, and may be undermined by a gradual conditioning into juridical practice based on more individualistic principles of justice.

Traditional dispute management

The diversity of the hundreds of societies we call Melanesia is well known, and it was matched in former times by a great diversity among disputing procedures. However, from the extensive available ethnographic literature, as well as studies specifically of disputing and responses to perceived wrongdoing,[1] three general and integrated themes are discernible: the social contextualisation of disputes, the extended historical processes that frame disputes and the sociocentrism that largely determines matters of liability.

The social contextualisation of disputes has become commonplace in the legal anthropology of Melanesia, as indicated by Epstein's generalisation that 'what is crucial in New Guinean thought is that the nature of an offence is defined not so much by the act itself as by the social context within which the act occurs' (1972, p. 632). Indeed, while Malinowski oriented his seminal book-length discussion of 'crime and custom' explicitly to a principle of reciprocity (1959, pp. 15–21, 58), it included a case study in which he contextualised a suicide in *ambiguous* attitudes towards incest and exogamy (1959, pp. 77–84), nicely exemplifying Epstein's later point. The comparative importance of this is that no matter how ritualised traditional disputing processes might have been—for instance, a moot or public inquisition—the discursive content was not particularly exclusive. This contrasts with modern Western legal proceedings, which have highly developed and strictly kept rules about admissible evidence, relevance of argument and testimony, and so on. In this respect, the anthropological contextualisation of traditional disputes in wider issues of politics, kinship and religion in society indicates the transparency of dynamic influences beyond what an outsider might assume to be simply a dispute between two parties. As Sally Falk Moore put it, disputes could be 'events on which various durable organisational interests impinged, and in which they competed for effectiveness' (Moore, 1977, p. 186).

Consider the following incident from my mid-1980s fieldwork in the upper Kaugel Valley, in the Western Highlands of PNG. One day I attended a gathering that the community called a *kot* (Tok Pisin for court). The kin of a young woman were in dispute with the kin of a young man, who they said had neglected his husbandly duties. The couple had originally entered into a quasi-marital relationship immediately after a ritual communal courting session for young people, but after many months a *braidprais* (marriage payment) had not yet been paid and the young woman, dissatisfied with her husband, had gone back to her parents. The *kot* was held to determine whether the couple should stay together, in which case the *braidprais* should be paid, or whether they were irreconcilable, in which case the young man

---

1   The first fieldwork-derived discussion of traditional Melanesian treatment of social breaches is generally acknowledged to be Malinowski's 1926 *Crime and Custom in Savage Society* (Malinowski, 1959). Others of significance include Hogbin (1938), Todd (1936), Kaberry (1942), Burridge (1957) and Pospisil (1958).

(or more correctly his kin group) should pay compensation. The putative *kot* continued for two days, most of which time was occupied by long harangues and declamations by elderly people lamenting a perceived decline in morals in the community and recalling the more measured and responsible attitudes towards courtship and marriage that had prevailed in former times. Eventually discussion turned back to the 'case' at hand and a presiding elder shortly decided that the young couple was irreconcilable and that compensation should be paid. Everyone present expressed agreement and the elder nominated an initial *bel kol* (anger-cooling) payment of 100 kina, which the father of the young man immediately took from his waistband—where it had been in readiness from the outset of the hearing—and handed over.

For the community, then, the 'decision' of the *kot* had been completely predictable, including the appropriate compensation amount and the *bel kol* payment. The public arbitration was a necessary ritual but, importantly, while it had the superficial trappings of a dispute settlement procedure, its more important social function was to provide a forum for the community's moral self-appraisal and critique. The local appropriation of the English term 'court' to describe the process exemplifies an adaptation of an introduced concept to a local context in which much more than a dispute is actually taking place. It would be a misrepresentation to abstract the specific dispute as though it were a circumscribed ritual like a Western court hearing.

Integrated with the social contextualisation of disputes is the second theme that I identified above: the extended historical processes that generate and shape disputes. Here I invoke what Comaroff and Roberts (1986) have called the 'processual' paradigm, in contrast to the 'rule-centred' paradigm that typified earlier legal anthropology (see, for example, Llewellyn & Hoebel, 1941; Pospisil, 1958). According to the processual paradigm, conflict is treated as endemic in social life, so the analysis of order should ultimately be grounded in social processes, not institutions. Analytically this demands a historical dimension, the necessity to understand the genesis of a dispute, successive efforts to manage it and the subsequent history of the relationship between the parties (Comaroff & Roberts, 1986, pp. 12–13).

In researching disputes in Melanesia, I have encountered many cases where a dispute seemingly 'of the moment' is actually a manifestation of a very long-running and socially extensive problem—perhaps stretching back to antiquity—which cannot in itself be resolved, as the community mostly recognises. For example, small contemporary disputes among the traditional inhabitants of the territory that is now the National Capital District of PNG can frequently be related to the beginnings of colonialism, or even before. The colonial town of Port Moresby was established at the end of the nineteenth century and its subsequent spread created a growing land shortage and therewith land disputes among the indigenes, the Motu and Koita peoples (Goddard, 2010, 2011). The two groups, long intermarried, are nowadays avowedly Christian and 'peaceful' from missionisation more than a century ago (Goddard, 2005a, pp. 179–205; 2013). They have attempted for decades to maintain a diplomatic amnesia about their irresolvable land problems. Nevertheless, my research on small village-level disputes (drunken brawls, insults, garden thefts and the like; see Goddard, 2009) that at first sight are relatively spontaneous has found many of them to be periodic manifestations of transgenerational tensions generated by long-suppressed land disputes. Certainly, as Zorn wrote (1992, p. 29), 'dispute settlement' in Melanesia might be better called 'dispute management'.

The third theme that emerges from a broad range of ethnography is the sociocentrism of Melanesian societies. Anthropological literature has for a long time conventionally portrayed Melanesians as traditionally lacking the individualism of Westerners and subjugating individual 'rights' to those of the group (see, for example, Leenhardt, 1998, pp. 248–251; Malinowski, 1959). This does not mean there were no individual aspirations, but that any such aspirations were constricted by the relationships in which a person was inextricably enmeshed (Hogbin, 1947; Malinowski, 1959, pp. 28–59; Read, 1955). Dichotomous terms such as 'individual' and 'communal' were frequently applied to this sociality. More recently the dichotomy has been problematised by the introduction of the concept of the 'dividual' (Strathern, 1988) and of 'relationality'. Strathern adopted the term 'dividual' from Marriott's representation of Hindu ideas about persons:

> To exist, dividual persons absorb heterogenous material influences. They must also give out from themselves particles of their own coded substances—essences, residues, or other active influences—that may then reproduce in others something of the nature of the persons in whom they have originated. (Marriott, 1976, p. 111, cited in Strathern, 1988, p. 348n7)

Relationality is exemplified in Robbins' observation that:

> Melanesian cultures value the creation of relationships over that of
> other cultural forms (e.g., individuals, wholes) and … reckon the
> value of relationships rather than of the individuals who make them
> up or the larger structures of which they may empirically be a part.
> (Robbins, 2004, p. 292)

One way and another, these various characterisations have been used in attempts to represent important aspects of Melanesian sociality contrasting with a Western emphasis on individualism including, most relevantly for my discussion here, the legal individual.

In respect of disputes and perceived wrongdoing the distinction has important implications for matters of 'rights', obligations and liabilities, for traditionally Melanesian societies were less preoccupied with *individual* rights and liability than with the restoration of some kind of stability among *groups* affected by a dispute, often through a logic of reciprocation. Anthropologists have long observed that dispute settlement in Melanesia can be a matter of reconciling the interests of the groups rather than of the individuals directly affected (see, for example, Reay, 1974, pp. 199–200). Lindstrom (2010) has discussed a variety of ways with which social breaches were traditionally dealt among the Tannese of Vanuatu, including a response between groups whereby a person who had been killed was physically replaced with a person from the group of the killer (Lindstrom gives an example in which the killer was the replacement (2010, pp. 10–11)). The response follows a principle found elsewhere in Melanesia placing an emphasis on the restoration of social balance: in the Tannese instance, for example, a person lost required a person gained.

These processes contrast with Western legal individualism, in which an individual responsible for a crime or offence is held to be individually liable. Marilyn Strathern wrote in 1972 that Hageners (of the Western Highlands of PNG) had a concept of individual responsibility without necessarily an individual liability to make amends for it (1972, p. 142). Further, she noted that '"settlement" may seem to be more important than the rights of individuals' (1972, p. 143). This brings us back to Lawrence's comment, on the *'fiat justitia'* maxim, that Melanesians were more concerned to keep the sky up. Melanesian tendencies to place the concerns of the group ahead of the rights of individuals have been an ongoing problem for legal conservatives and human rights advocates.

In combination, these three themes—the social contextualisation of disputes, the processual paradigm and Melanesian sociocentrism—demonstrate the folly of representing Melanesian disputing processes as static and structurally stable systems of 'customary law'. Not only does this risk the reification of elements of a complex social whole at the expense of recognising their role in more substantial social processes, but it also denies their flexibility and adaptability. Indeed, most contemporary anthropologists of law have discarded the conception of 'customary law' as a set of applicable rules. In Melanesia, Pospisil's account of the Kapauku (in what was then Netherlands New Guinea) in the 1950s was already problematising the distinction between 'customary law' and 'authoritarian law' (Pospisil, 1958, pp. 248–289). Historical studies in Africa and the Pacific have indicated that the conventional notion of customary law was a colonial product generated by the effects of missionaries, colonial courts and the responses of indigenous peoples (see, for example, Chanock, 1998; Merry, 1999). In these and other colonised societies customary law did not exist 'until the introduction of a sphere of political activity from which it had to be differentiated' (Demian, 2003, p. 100; see also Fitzpatrick, 1980, p. 68). The polemical attacks on Western law by Melanesian politicians at the end of the colonial era that invoked a notion of customary law as representative of 'ancient laws, values and institutions' (Narakobi cited in Gordon & Meggitt, 1985) were a legacy of this colonial creation.

An important aspect of the flexibility and adaptability of traditional dispute processes has been their ability to assimilate aspects of legal or quasi-legal procedure from other societies with which they interact. This of course includes the procedures introduced by Christian missions and European colonisers, although in postcolonial rhetoric opposing custom to 'white men's ways', these kinds of assimilations are largely forgotten. For example, Edward Hviding has shown how contemporary 'custom' in the Marovo area of New Georgia (Solomon Islands) is presented by local people as oppositional to Western ways when in fact it shows the complex influence of interaction with foreign traders, Christianity and colonial bureaucracy over a long period (Hviding, 1993). Lindstrom has written about 'legal pluralism' on Tanna, Vanuatu, that has since the early 1900s been affected by experience of Christianity and colonial court styles. Similar influences have been noted among long-Christianised south coast PNG societies (Belshaw, 1957, pp. 182–191, 211–226; Goddard, 2009, pp. 118–123; Oram, n.d., p. 6). Also, after long exposure to Western legal culture, Melanesian mimesis of spatial and procedural aspects of 'courts' was common by the mid-twentieth century (Berndt, 1962, pp. 314–327; Strathern, 1972). By the late colonial period these mimetic processes were being seen as a problem by administrators, who referred to them as 'unofficial courts'.

Introduced village-level courts

Systems of 'official' village-level courts were introduced into Melanesia at the end of the colonial period (Evans et al., 2011). They were initially intended to address local and so-called customary issues, with little distinction between civil and criminal jurisdictions, and it was hoped that they would obviate unofficial courts. As state-sanctioned courts dealing with putatively parochial disputes or offences, they were expected to integrate simple principles of introduced law with the imagined set of local dispositions called 'custom' or, by the end of colonialism, 'customary law' (see, for example, Law Reform Commission of Papua New Guinea, 1977). The liberal attempt at recognition of 'custom' (connoting also 'tradition' and 'cultural' variety) was hedged with directives to the effect that custom should not be applied if it was in conflict with law, or if it traduced Western ideas of justice. This problematic discursive binary of law and custom has particularly dogged the 'village court' system that was introduced in PNG in 1974 (Goddard, 2009, pp. 95–111).

PNG's village court magistrates were intended to be 'persons whom the people respect and feel confident about, that is, who know the customs of the area well, and can be relied upon to make fair decisions' (Village Court Secretariat, 1975, p. 1). They required no formal educational qualifications. A stipulation in the *Village Courts Act 1973* that the courts should 'adjourn from time to time and place to place' reinforced the intention that they should be informal. The types of cases the courts could hear, according to the Act, were limited and excluded, for example, divorce applications, offences involving motor vehicles and land claims as well as indictable offences such as manslaughter and murder. Village court magistrates could write prison orders against disputants who failed to abide by court decisions, but these had to be countersigned by a district court magistrate. Village court activities could be overseen by members of the formal judiciary who could also hear appeals by disputants against village court decisions. A 'village court handbook' was issued for magistrates (Village Court Secretariat, 1976), listing the types of offences village courts could, and could not, hear and the maximum penalties they could impose.

The village courts soon came to suffer state neglect, in both provision of resources and regular and systematic oversight (Goddard, 2009, pp. 57–71). Left largely to their own devices, they adapted themselves to local sociality, and their handling of cases involved a deft blending of introduced law and local practice. Legislation allowed them to find individuals guilty or innocent and to impose fines, compensation and maybe community work. They were also encouraged to attempt mediations where appropriate. The courts were supposed to have reinforcements for their decisions, such as referrals to the next level of courts, police assistance and so on. Much of the time these reinforcements were not practically available to them. The magistrates were deliberately untrained in law and assumed to be knowledgeable about local 'custom'. The courts were remarkably successful despite the lack of state support. They grew from a handful in 1975 to more than 1,000 by the year 2000,[2] and have been very popular in village society, hearing thousands of cases across the country yearly and playing an important role in preventing parochial disputes from escalating into major conflicts requiring the intervention of higher state agencies. Importantly in the context of traditional gender politics and women's general lack of access to legal institutions, anthropological research throughout PNG since the 1980s has found that village courts have provided a previously absent forum for women, who have used them extensively and successfully in parochial disputing (Goddard, 2005b, 2009, pp. 255–262; Neuhaus, 2009; Scaglion, 1990; Scaglion & Whittingham, 1985; Tuzin, 1997, pp. 50–55; Westermark, 1985).

Village courts have managed to creatively satisfy the demands of the introduced law as well as their communities' understandings of what is fair and just. This has largely been due to their officers' immersion in local society, knowledge of the background of cases and their ability to interact informally with interested parties and reach comfortable compromises. Importantly, the courts have not been driven in practice by a definable set of 'customs', even though village court magistrates have become conditioned into invoking both 'custom' and 'customary law' in discussing cases (see, for example, Goddard, 2009, 100–109; Pupu & Wiessner, 2018). Rather, they reflect the sociality of the particular community served by each of them and apply a complex integration of introduced law and a variety of local conventions in dispute management procedures (see, for example, Brison,

---

2   Exact figures are hard to achieve. There are possibly 1,500 courts active at time of writing, but lack of regular state support and resources has caused many gazetted courts to close over the past four decades.

1999; Demian, 2003; Errington & Gewertz, 2007; Goddard, 2009; Scaglion, 1990; Westermark, 1986; Young, 1992; Zorn, 1990). Negotiating sociocentrism, and historical and socio-political factors, they have been 'keeping the sky up'. Given the local social context in which any village court operates, the fate of individuals in court is sometimes determined more by the need for harmony and good order in the community at large than by principles of either Western or 'customary' law, and the subjugation of individual 'rights' to wider community concerns is intrinsic to local understandings of what should be done about a conflict. Under the circumstances, decisions that appear to a Western observer to be unfair to an individual disputant may be regarded as perfectly just by the local community. Legal individualism, embedded in Western jurisprudence, needs careful negotiation when magistrates are attempting to manage underlying conflicts in their community. This is a burden that judges and magistrates are spared in conventional courts in Western societies.

While the village courts have operated for several decades, surviving through the dedication of their officers and their amenability to villagers, they have not (as they were intended to do)[3] displaced so-called unofficial courts, which can be found everywhere. These have evolved into various forms of dispute-managing forums commonly referred to locally by the Tok Pisin term *kot*. There have been Christian church courts in many places since the beginning of the twentieth century, and latterly there have been, for example, ethnically based courts in migrant compounds in towns, 'settlement committees' in informal urban housing areas, as well as 'chiefs' courts, and so on (Goddard, 2009, pp. 93–94). A more recent phenomenon are community-generated non-official 'village courts', modelled on the official courts, where the latter have been discontinued through lack of state support or in areas where the official system was never introduced. Schwoerer gives an apt example of such a court in PNG's Eastern Highlands whose magistrates 'base their decisions on local perceptions of order and justice, all the while emulating elements of state justice and constantly referring to the state as the source of their legitimacy' (2018, p. 342).

---

3   See Curtis and Greenwell (1971); Desailly and Iramu (1972).

Development aid, human rights and the rule of law

Two conventional themes have stimulated the interest of development aid organisations in PNG's village court system in recent years. One is 'law and justice', which incorporates not only matters of judicial reform but also concern about PNG's 'law and order' problem. The other is women's rights, which for some years has been a major focus of human rights discourse in relation to PNG (see, for example, Brouwer et al., 1998; PWSU, 2018; Talao, 2009). Further, as the village court system is a state-governed institution by virtue of an Act of Parliament—the Village Courts Act—it has the potential to serve attempts to combine the enterprise of strengthening national governance processes with that of building the 'capacity' of those community-level institutions judged to be contributing constructively to development (see, for example, AusAID, 2007; Department of Foreign Affairs and Trade [DFaT], 2015).

Given the large number and variety of societies in PNG, and the resulting 'stylistic' differences among village courts in accordance with their integration into communities, the generalisations we can make about their practice are limited. Accordingly, it is unwise to assume that training village court magistrates towards a single universalised model of justice would satisfy local understandings of injustice and its remedies throughout PNG. Indeed, the colonial-era planners of the village court system were careful to avoid training the magistrates beyond ensuring they understood the limits of their jurisdiction and the penalties they could impose, and that they kept basic records of cases heard and their decisions (Desailly & Iramu, 1972; Village Court Secretariat, 1976). However, a different politico-juridical sensibility is now being brought to bear on village courts in interventions by development aid organisations in the village court system attempting to make their practice compatible with development policy and to draw them into the body of community-based institutions supported by development aid. The new interventions are largely aimed at educating them about (Western) jurisprudence and human rights.

The Australian Agency for International Development (AusAID)[4] began its interest in the village courts in the 1990s, with early initiatives to regularise the previously haphazard training programs for magistrates and to 'strengthen'

---

4   AusAID was absorbed into the Australian Government's Department of Foreign Affairs and Trade (DFaT) in 2013 and is no longer an executive agency.

the Village Court Secretariat, which was annexed to the PNG Department of Justice and Attorney General. As Sachs observed, 'development' connotes the best of intentions and also 'allows any intervention to be sanctified in the name of a higher goal' (1992, p. 4). Village court magistrates had for years been complaining of government neglect, poor remuneration and a lack of support from other agencies (Goddard, 2009, pp. 60–71). AusAID's interventions partly addressed their grievances in the (very) short term, achieving some payments of long-overdue remuneration and the production of an updated handbook for magistrates.[5] Later the Australian Government's Department of Foreign Affairs and Trade provided assistance to improve pay and conditions and to reinvigorate training programs (DFaT, 2015).[6] However, development aid agencies' responses in general are 'no longer decided by the cry, but by some external standard of normality' (Gronemeyer, 1992, p. 54; cf. Kyed, 2011, pp. 8–9), and a common contingency of development aid is a need to make recipient organisations' practice compatible with international principles to which the aid donors subscribe (Kyed, 2011, pp. 6–10). In the case of village courts, the linked principles are the rule of law and human rights.

The rule-of-law enterprise has been described as 'big business', connecting national legal systems, transnational powerbrokers, Western ideas of democracy, human rights and other issues related to global economics (Nader, 2006, 104; see also Carothers, 2006a). Indeed, the 'rule of law' is a repetitive phrase in UN statements on human rights, and the connection between the two is taken for granted in development-related literature:

> The rule of law can be defined as a system in which the laws are public knowledge, are clear in meaning, and apply equally to everyone. They enshrine and uphold the political and civil liberties that have gained status as universal human rights over the last half-century. (Carothers, 2006b, p. 4)

Some doubts have been expressed about the effectiveness of the rule-of-law enterprise particularly in relation to improving the conditions of the poor. Golub (2006), for example, delineates a 'rule-of-law orthodoxy' as

5   Back payments were successfully distributed in some areas, but not all. The updated handbooks had limited distribution.
6   Due to the logistical impossibility of contacting all village courts and transporting magistrates to a training venue, only a limited number of magistrates actually receive this 'training'.

a top-down, state-centred approach focused on formal judiciaries, and he moots in preference a 'legal empowerment' alternative grounded in grassroots needs and activities, but still incorporating human rights.

A conventional human rights discourse, reflecting UN definitions and disseminated especially by the United Nations Educational, Scientific and Cultural Organization (UNESCO), has been brought to bear on village courts particularly in relation to women's rights. Historically this has continuity with the reconceptualisation among international agencies of gender inequality issues during the 1990s as 'women's human rights', and the advent of a 'rights-based' approach to development (Wilson, 2007, p. 237). The interest of development aid organisations in women's rights in PNG has been informed by a view that women are disadvantaged in that country economically and politically (see, for example, Garap, 2004; Topo, 2004; Vatnabar, 2003) and also as victims of misogyny and male violence (Bradley, 1998; Macintyre, 1998; Dinnen & Ley, 2000). Commentaries on women's rights in relation to 'development' in PNG have situated men as women's competitors, maintaining traditional male dominance using political strategies that are rationalised by appeals to 'custom' or tradition (Bradley, 1998; Macintyre, 1998, 2005; DFaT, 2015, p. 62).

Until very recently the anthropological research evidence that women are successful users of village courts relative to men (see above) barely appeared in policy-related discussions even among academics, who instead cited unreliable reports referring to the earliest days of the village court system and the influence of 'custom' and 'tradition' (see, for example, Macintyre, 1998, p. 218; O'Collins, 2000, p. 6; Oram, 1979, p. 73; cf. Goddard, 2009, pp. 85–86) or anecdotal accounts of women's travails in seeking justice that appear to not understand the jurisdictional limits of village courts.[7] Resultant generalisations that village courts 'demonstrate "excess traditionalism" when dealing with cases of violence against women' (McLeod, 2005, p. 115) reflect the powerful influence of internationalised discourses of law and rights, which displace cautious anthropological discussion of concepts such as 'rights', 'tradition', 'custom' and 'culture' in favour of more familiar Western imagery of countries such as PNG. More recently aid organisations

---

7   For example, a paper frequently cited in development and human rights literature on PNG about women and village courts gave nine examples of complaints of injustice by women in the Highlands Simbu Province (Garap, 2000), of which only two mentioned village courts. In the form briefly presented by the author, at least, the determinations unsuccessfully sought by the women in those two cases were actually beyond a village court's jurisdiction, which suggests there was some local misunderstanding of the village courts' powers.

have begun to recognise that village courts are a useful resource for women (see, for example, Independent State of Papua New Guinea [ISPNG], 2010, p. 19). Resultant strategies have included an attempt to stipulate that every village court should have at least one female magistrate and to include human rights awareness in magistrates' training programs (see, for example, ISPNG, 2010, pp. 22–23; DFaT, 2015, pp. 62, 79). However, a concern for human rights awareness brought aid organisations to the dilemma of 'culture'.

The problem of culture

In addition to deconstructing the colonial origins of 'customary law' and critiquing the postcolonial politics of 'customs' in Melanesia (see, for example, Keesing & Tonkinson, 1982) in recent decades, anthropologists have problematised the concept of culture, displacing earlier representations that implied that non-Western cultures were homogeneous, bounded and historically static, and correctively emphasising their hybridity and mutability. Inasmuch as the difficulty of satisfactorily defining 'culture' has consequently increased, the practical value of the concept has even become a matter of debate (see, for example, Abu-Lughod, 1991; Kuper, 1999; Sahlins, 1999). In contrast, development aid organisations tend to adopt the earlier image of 'culture', thereby rendering it interchangeable with 'custom' and 'tradition', and are inclined towards equivocal assumptions about the effect of indigenous culture on their endeavours. Critical literature since at least the 1990s has drawn attention to the way development aid agencies view traditional culture as a hindrance, in need of transformation because 'many "old ways" of living turned out to be "obstacles to development"' (Sachs, 1993, pp. 4–5). Development-related discussion of the cultural dimensions of history shows a 'tendency to treat cultural characteristics as trans-historical constants' (Amin, 1990, p. 2). A disposition to see culture/custom/tradition as an obstacle to the progress of, particularly, women's rights is a manifestation of a wider concern among human rights organisations, in whose view anachronistic sets of beliefs and values are liable to be used to justify discriminatory social behaviour (Harper, 2011, pp. 34–38). Recourse to this outdated notion of culture has been seen by some anthropologists as having hampered progress in developing universally workable models of human rights (Eriksen, 2001; Merry, 2003).

Paradoxically, though, human rights discourse acknowledges the need for sensitivity to culture. It attempts to recognise culturally different views of personhood and humanity and the political consequences of the way individual and collective rights can be understood (see, for example, Messer, 2002, pp. 322–330). In policy about human rights and village courts in PNG, UNESCO and Australia's government-sanctioned development aid organisations have attempted to incorporate human rights awareness into village court officials' training, particularly in relation to the rights of women. A concern for sensitivity to 'culture' while promoting human rights has accompanied an ideal that aid organisations should facilitate changes that come from 'within society' (Garap, 2005). However, a dilemma arises from the acknowledgement of what one advocate has called a 'traditional' system of dispute resolution in PNG societies 'based on collective rights' (Garap, 2005, p. 9). The 'collective rights' are seen as 'difficult to reconcile with the individual's rights based on contemporary western systems' and may pose 'a threat to the rule of law' (2005, p. 9). Accordingly, 'traditional responses' to crime are likely to breach human rights, and the 'values' underlying such responses are seen to require attention (2005, p. 9). An example is a concern expressed in a 'law and justice' initiative about family and sexual violence in rural areas, where 'cultural norms are the only "rules"' (DFaT, 2015, p. 62), reinforced by the hasty generalisation that 'rape and sexual assault are typically treated as offences against a woman's male relatives with compensation paid to them to restore community harmony' (DFaT, 2015, p. 62). Training in human rights, especially of women and children, is recommended, 'recognising that these are sometimes sacrificed in the use of local cultural approaches to justice' (2015, p. 79).

Implicit in this discourse is the Western concept of the individualised person that persistently underlies UN policy (see United Nations, 1993, p. 1). Eriksen (2001, p. 141) argues that UNESCO has a basic commitment to individual human rights and therefore a contradiction occurs when it attempts to accommodate notions of group rights and 'culture'. While human rights training for village court magistrates has been intended to contribute to the development of 'models for conflict resolution that manage the dilemma between collective and individual rights' (Garap, 2005, p. 4), a distrust of 'custom' and 'tradition' and a concern for the 'rule of law' indicate a desire to make village court practice adhere more closely to formal legal practice. Where custom and tradition are taken to be characteristics of local 'culture' (imagined as a bounded and historically constant set of values), the concern about village courts resonates with what Merry (2003, pp. 60–64) has depicted as an attitude towards culture that accompanies human rights assessments globally. Conformity to universal standards is inevitably demanded as human rights lawyers and activists are committed to implementing these rather than subscribing to a complex variety of ideas about the nature of rights and obligations (Merry, 2003, p. 68).

Conclusion

The management of disputes and social breaches in Melanesian societies did not traditionally adhere to structurally stable 'customs' or 'customary laws'. It was flexible and adaptable, dependent on social context and historical processes, and largely determined by sociocentric, rather than individualistic, considerations particularly in respect of matters of liability. When the village court system was introduced at the end of the colonial period, it was supposed to blend a simple form of Western law with imagined 'custom'. Subsequent neglect by the state meant the courts were largely thrown back on their own social resources, resulting in a creative interpretation of both law and 'custom' that demonstrated the same flexibility and adaptability as traditional dispute management. They have not actually been applying 'custom' (i.e. a set of traditional rules). For several decades they have been skilfully negotiating the integration of simple legal principles with sociocentric local community understandings of what is fair and just. A contingency of this project is an ability to recognise the wider historical and social conflicts of which immediate disputes are frequently manifestations. In other words, illustrating Zorn's previously mentioned observation about Melanesia, village courts are realistically 'managing' disputes rather than 'settling' them. In this they also exemplify the analytical appropriateness of the abovementioned 'processual paradigm' mooted by Comaroff and Roberts. However, in the light of the anomalies of human rights discourse, initiatives like those of UNESCO and Australia's government-sanctioned development aid organisations appear to be increasing the regulation of village court practice in favour of a legalistic concern with human rights, reflecting state policy and practice (since the state is charged with implementing human rights initiatives) rather than values held by the diverse societies served by the courts.

Until now the effects of development aid interest in village courts have been limited by the ongoing state weakness and inadequate service delivery that aid organisations attempt to shore up or circumvent. While official reports of periodic reassessments and training programs delivered by external aid agencies imply positive achievements (see, for example, DFaT, 2015, 2016), the exercises do not in practice reach all of PNG's far-flung village courts. In areas that are infrastructurally ill-served, many village court officials have remained unpaid for long periods (see, for example, Gumar, 2020; The National, 2015a) and still do not receive the updated handbooks that are supposed to be distributed nationwide.[8] Where village courts manage to survive in these neglected areas, they continue to 'hold the sky up', in the best interests of their communities as a whole. In urban circumstances, and rural areas that are more accessible to training exercises and material support, there has been a steady increase in the impact of the legal and human rights models embedded in development aid practice (see, for example, Demian, 2014; DFaT, 2016; The National, 2015b).

If the efforts of development aid organisations eventually embrace all of PNG's village courts, it is inevitable that the drive to uniform practice in the courts would result in an emphasis on individual rights and a more rigid application of legal principles of individual responsibility and liability. Whether a development of this kind—obliging village courts to be less cognisant of the socio-historical context of cases—would lead to greater community acceptance of legal individualist principles is hard to predict. After all, juridical interventions, which date back to the early colonial period, have still not homogenised local community notions of justice in PNG. It is possible that, as magistrates are increasingly taught to adhere to a jurisprudence that is alien to the sociocentric understanding of justice that continues to prevail in Melanesian societies overall, the intimate relationship between the practice and deliberations of village courts and the sociality of the communities they serve will be weakened. In that case it is possible that villagers will increasingly turn to the unofficial courts I noted above, particularly in the current political and social climate where contemporary notions of 'custom' are being rhetorically championed in the interests of cultural preservation.

---

8   I can attest to the lack of payments and limited distribution of handbooks, uniforms, etcetera, from personal experience since my concentrated fieldwork on village courts in the 1990s (see Goddard, 2009): I retained computer file copies of English-language and lingua franca versions of an updated village court handbook produced in 2004, from which I printed copies to take with me on subsequent visits to PNG. I gave these to chairing magistrates in some areas I visited who went for lengthy periods without pay or administrative supplies. They remained dedicated to their job. As they were mostly aged and very experienced, the main practical worth of the handbooks to them was to provide updates on the maximum penalties they could impose for offences, and to be able to cite from the book when explaining penalties and the courts' jurisdictional limits to disputants, who commonly misunderstood the latter.

References

Abu-Lughod, L. (1991). Writing against culture. In R. Fox (ed.), *Recapturing anthropology* (pp. 137–162). School of American Research Press.

Amin, S. (1990). *Maldevelopment: Anatomy of a global failure.* Zed Books.

AusAID. (2007). *Papua New Guinea – Australia development cooperation strategy 2006–2010.* Australian Agency for International Development.

Belshaw, C. (1957). *The great village.* Routledge & Kegan Paul.

Berndt, R.M. (1962). *Excess and restraint: Social control among a New Guinea mountain people.* University of Chicago Press.

Bradley. C. (1998). Changing a 'bad old tradition': Wife-beating and the work of the Papua New Guinea law reform commission. In L. Zimmer-Tamakoshi (ed.), *Modern Papua New Guinea* (pp. 351–364). Thomas Jefferson University Press.

Brison, K.J. (1999). Imagining a nation in Kwanga village courts, East Sepik Province, Papua New Guinea. *Anthropological Quarterly, 72*(2), 74–94. doi.org/10.2307/3317965.

Brouwer, E., Harris, B., & Tanaka, S. (1998). *Gender analysis in Papua New Guinea.* World Bank Publications. doi.org/10.1596/0-8213-4394-7.

Burridge, K.O.L. (1957). Disputing in Tangu. *American Anthropologist, 59,* 763–778. doi.org/10.1525/aa.1957.59.5.02a00020.

Carothers, T. (ed.). (2006a). *Promoting the rule of law abroad: In search of knowledge.* Carnegie Endowment for International Peace.

Carothers, T. (2006b). The rule-of-law revival. In T. Carothers (ed.), *Promoting the rule of law abroad: In search of knowledge* (pp. 3–13). Carnegie Endowment for International Peace. doi.org/10.2307/j.ctt6wpk74.6.

Chanock, M. (1998). *Law, custom, and social order: The colonial experience in Malawi and Zambia.* Heinemann.

Comaroff, J.L., & Roberts, S. (1986). *Rules and processes: The cultural logic of dispute in an African context.* University of Chicago Press.

Curtis, L.J., & Greenwell, J.H. (1971). *Joint review of the lower courts systems.* Department of External Territories.

Demian, M. (2003). Custom in the courtroom, law in the village: Legal transformations in Papua New Guinea. *Journal of the Royal Anthropological Institute, 9*(1), 97–115. doi.org/10.1111/1467-9655.t01-2-00006.

Demian, M. (2014). *Innovation in Papua New Guinea's village courts: Exceeding jurisdiction or meeting local needs? Legal innovation: Part 1* (State, Society & Governance in Melanesia Program Briefing Paper No. 24). The Australian National University.

Department of Foreign Affairs and Trade [DFaT]. (2015). *Justice services and stability for development: An Australian investment to support law and justice in Papua New Guinea.* Australian Government.

Department of Foreign Affairs and Trade [DFaT]. (2016). *Papua New Guinea evaluation of village court officials' training: Summary of findings.* Australian Government.

Desailly, R.N., & Iramu, F. (1972). *Inquiry into the need for village courts and village constables* (mimeo.). Department of Attorney General Library (Papua New Guinea).

Dinnen, S., & Ley, A. (eds). (2000). *Reflections on violence in Melanesia.* Hawkins Press and Asia Pacific Press.

Eade, D. (2005). *Capacity-building: An approach to people-centred development.* Oxfam GB.

Epstein, A.L. (1972). Law, indigenous. In P. Ryan (ed.), *Encyclopaedia of Papua and New Guinea* (Vol. 2, pp. 631–634). Melbourne University Press and University of Papua New Guinea.

Eriksen, T. (2001). Between universalism and relativism: A critique of the UNESCO concept of culture. In J. Cowan, M. Dembour, & R. Wilson (eds), *Culture and rights: Anthropological perspectives* (pp. 127–148). Cambridge University Press. doi.org/10.1017/CBO9780511804687.008.

Errington, F., & Gewertz, D. (2007). Reconfiguring amity at Ramu Sugar Limited. In J. Barker (ed.), *The anthropology of morality in Melanesia and beyond* (pp. 93–109). Ashgate. doi.org/10.4324/9781315612454-8.

Evans, D., Goddard, M., & Patterson, D. (2011). *The hybrid courts of Melanesia: A comparative analysis of local courts of Solomon Islands, village courts of Papua New Guinea and island courts of Vanuatu* (World Bank Justice and Development Working Paper Series No. 13/2011). World Bank.

Fitzpatrick, P. (1980). *Law and state in Papua New Guinea.* Academic Press.

Garap, S. (2000). Struggles of women and girls—Simbu Province, Papua New Guinea. In S. Dinnen & A. Ley (eds), *Reflections on violence in Melanesia* (pp. 159–171). Hawkins Press/Asia Pacific Press.

Garap, S. (2004). Women caught in a 'big man' culture: Challenges for future democracy and governance. In N. Sullivan (ed.), *Governance challenges for PNG and the Pacific Islands* (pp. 157–163). DWU Press.

Garap, S. (2005). *Human rights in village courts: The challenges and opportunities of working with village courts*. Paper presented at Convention on Discrimination Against Women, Port Moresby, Papua New Guinea, 24 November 2005.

Goddard, M. (2005a). *The unseen city: Anthropological perspectives on Port Moresby, Papua New Guinea*. Pandanus Books.

Goddard, M. (2005b). Research and rhetoric on women in Papua New Guinea's village courts. *Oceania, 75*(3), 247–267. doi.org/10.1002/j.1834-4461.2005. tb02884.x.

Goddard, M. (2009). *Substantial justice: An anthropology of village courts in Papua New Guinea*. Berghahn Books.

Goddard, M. (2010). Heat and history: The Motu-Koita and Moresby. In M. Goddard (ed.), *Villagers and the city: Melanesian experiences of Port Moresby, Papua New Guinea* (pp. 19–46). Sean Kingston Press.

Goddard, M. (2011). Bramell's rules: Custom and law in contemporary land disputes among the Motu-Koita of Papua New Guinea. *Pacific Studies, 34*(2/3), 323–349.

Goddard, M. (2013). Liaisons dangereuses: les villageois urbains et le développement en Papouasie Nouvelle-Guinée. In D. Dussy & É. Wittersheim (eds), *Villes invisibles: Anthropologie urbaines du Pacifique* (pp. 163–191). L'Harmattan.

Golub, S. (2006). The legal empowerment alternative. In T. Carothers (ed.), *Promoting the rule of law abroad: In search of knowledge* (pp. 161–189). Carnegie Endowment for International Peace. doi.org/10.2307/j.ctt6wpk74.12.

Gordon, R., & Meggitt, M. (1985). *Law and order in the New Guinea Highlands: Encounters with Enga*. University Press of New England.

Gronemeyer, M. (1992). Helping. In W. Sachs (ed.), *The development dictionary* (pp. 53–69). Zed Books.

Gumar, P. (2020, 30 July). Village court officials undergo training. *PNG Post-Courier*. postcourier.com.pg/village-court-officials-undergo-training/ (accessed 31 July 2020).

Harper, E. (2011). *Customary justice: From program design to impact evaluation*. International Development Law Organization.

Hogbin, H.I. (1938). Social reaction to crime: Law and morals in the Schouten Islands, New Guinea. *Journal of the Royal Anthropological Institute 68*, 223–262. doi.org/10.2307/2843987.

Hogbin, I. (1947). Shame: A study of social conformity in a New Guinea village. *Oceania, 17*(4), 273–288. doi.org/10.1002/j.1834-4461.1947.tb00153.x.

Hviding, E. (1993). Indigenous essentialism? 'Simplifying' customary land ownership in New Georgia, Solomon Islands. *Bijdragen tot de Taal-, Land- en Volkenkunde, 149*(4), 802–824. doi.org/10.1163/22134379-90003114.

Independent State of Papua New Guinea [ISPNG]. (2010). *Papua New Guinea country report on the Convention on the Elimination of all forms of Discrimination against Women (CEDAW)*. United Nations.

Kaberry, P.M. (1942). Law and political organization in the Abelam tribe, New Guinea. *Oceania, 12*(4), 331–363. doi.org/10.1002/j.1834-4461.1942.tb00364.x.

Keesing, R.M., & Tonkinson, R. (eds). (1982). Reinventing traditional culture: The politics of kastom in island Melanesia [Special issue]. *Mankind, 13*.

Kuper, A. (1999). *Culture: The anthropologist's account.* Harvard University Press. doi.org/10.2307/j.ctv21hrh4p.

Kyed, H.M. (2011). Introduction to the special issue: Legal pluralism and international development interventions. *The Journal of Legal Pluralism and Unofficial Law, 43*, 1–23. doi.org/10.1080/07329113.2011.10756655.

Law Reform Commission of Papua New Guinea. (1977). *The role of customary law in the legal system*. Government Printer.

Lawrence, P. (1970). Law and anthropology: The need for collaboration. *Melanesian Law Journal, 1*(1), 40–50.

Leenhardt, M. (1998). *Do Kamo: La Personne et le Mythe dans le Monde Mélanésien.* Gallimard. (Original work published 1947.)

Lindstrom, L. (2010). *Settling and unsettling disputes: A village perspective.* Paper presented at USP Conference: Law and culture: Meaningful legal pluralism in the Pacific and beyond, Port Vila, Vanuatu, 30 August – 1 September 2010.

Llewellyn, K.N., & Hoebel, E.A. (1941). *The Cheyenne way: Conflict and case law in primitive jurisprudence.* University of Oklahoma Press.

Macintyre, M. (1998). The persistence of inequality. In L. Zimmer-Tamakoshi (ed.), *Modern Papua New Guinea* (pp. 211–228). Thomas Jefferson University Press.

Macintyre, M. (2005). Taking care of culture: Consultancy, anthropology, and gender issues. In P.J. Stewart & A. Strathern (eds), *Anthropology and consultancy: Issues and debates* (pp. 124–138). Berghahn Books.

Malinowski, B. (1959). *Crime and custom in savage society*. Littlefield, Adams & Co. (Original work published 1926.)

McLeod, A. (2005). Violence, women and the state in Papua New Guinea: A case note. *Development Bulletin, 67*, 115–118.

Merry, S.E. (1999). *Colonizing Hawai'i: The cultural power of law*. Princeton University Press. doi.org/10.1515/9780691221984.

Merry, S.E. (2003). Human rights law and the demonization of culture (and anthropology along the way). *Polar: Political and Legal Anthropology Review, 26*(1), 55–77. doi.org/10.1525/pol.2003.26.1.55.

Messer, E. (2002). Anthropologists in a world with and without human rights. In J. MacClancy (ed.), *Exotic no more: Anthropology on the front lines* (pp. 319–337). University of Chicago Press.

Moore, S.F. (1977). Individual interests and organisational structures: Dispute settlements as 'events of articulation'. In I. Hamnett (ed.), *Social anthropology and law* (pp. 159–188). Academic Press.

Nader, L. (2006). Promise or plunder? A past and future look at law and development. In *The World Bank legal review: Law, equity and development* (Vol. 2, pp. 87–111). The World Bank and Martinus Nijhoff. doi.org/10.1163/9789047411727_006.

The National. (2015a, 28 January). Court official waiting for pay. *The National* (PNG). www.thenational.com.pg/court-officials-waiting-for-pay/ (accessed 29 January 2015).

The National. (2015b, 17 August). Village court officials in workshop. *The National* (PNG). www.thenational.com.pg/village-court-officials-in-workshop/ (accessed 18 August 2015).

Neuhaus, J. (2009). Women in village courts in Papua New Guinea. *TSANTSA, 14*, 152–157.

O'Collins, M. (2000). *Law and order in Papua New Guinea: Perceptions and management strategies* (State, Society and Governance in Melanesia Project Working Paper 00/1). The Australian National University.

Oram, N.D. (n.d.). Towards a study of the London Missionary Society in Hula 1875–1968 [Pamphlet]. Michael Somare Library, University of Papua New Guinea.

Oram, N.D. (1979). Grass roots justice: Village courts in Papua New Guinea. In W. Clifford & S.D. Gorkhale (eds), *Innovations in criminal justice in Asia and the Pacific* (pp. 49–80). Australian Institute of Criminology.

Pacific Women Support Unit [PWSU]. (2018). *Pacific Women Papua New Guinea performance report 2017–2018*. Pacific Women Shaping Pacific Development, Australian Government Department of Foreign Affairs and Trade.

Pospisil, L. (1958). *Kapauku Papuans and their law*. Yale University Publications in Anthropology.

Pupu, N., & Wiessner, P. (2018). *The challenges of village courts and Operation Mekim Save among the Enga of Papua New Guinea today: A view from the inside* [DPA Discussion Paper 2018/1]. Department of Pacific Affairs, The Australian National University.

Read, K. (1955). Morality and the concept of the person among the Gahuku-Gama. *Oceania, 25*(4), 233–282. doi.org/10.1002/j.1834-4461.1955.tb00651.x.

Reay, M. (1974). Changing conventions of dispute settlement in the Minj area. In A.L. Epstein (ed.), *Contention and dispute: Aspects of law and social control in Melanesia* (pp. 199–239). The Australian National University Press.

Robbins, J. (2004). *Becoming sinners: Christianity and moral torment in a Papua New Guinea society*. University of California Press.

Sachs, W. (1992). Introduction. In W. Sachs (ed.), *The development dictionary* (pp. 1–5). Zed Books.

Sachs, W. (1993). Global ecology and the shadow of 'development'. In W. Sachs (ed.), *Global ecology: A new arena of political conflict* (pp. 3–21). Zed Books.

Sahlins, M. (1999). Two or three things that I know about culture. *Journal of the Royal Anthropological Institute, 5*(3), 399–421. doi.org/10.2307/2661275.

Scaglion, R. (1990). Legal adaptation in a Papua New Guinea village court. *Ethnology, 29*(1), 17–33. doi.org/10.2307/3773479.

Scaglion, R., & Whittingham, R. (1985). Female plaintiffs and sex-related disputes in rural Papua New Guinea. In S. Toft (ed.), *Domestic violence in Papua New Guinea* (pp. 12–33, Monograph No. 3). Law Reform Commission of Papua New Guinea.

Schwoerer, T. (2018). *Mipela makim gavman*: Unofficial village courts and local perceptions of order in the Eastern Highlands of Papua New Guinea. *Anthropological Forum, 28*(4), 342–358. doi.org/10.1080/00664677.2018.15 41786.

Strathern, M. (1972). *Official and unofficial courts: Legal assumptions and expectations in a Highlands community* (New Guinea Research Bulletin No. 47). New Guinea Research Unit, The Australian National University.

Strathern, M. (1988). *The gender of the gift*. University of California Press.

Talao, F. (2009). Papua New Guinea: Country report on human rights. *Victoria University of Wellington Law Review, 40*(1), 1–24. doi.org/10.26686/vuwlr.v40i1.5375.

Todd, J.A. (1936). Redress of wrongs in south-west New Britain. *Oceania, 6*(4), 401–440. doi.org/10.1002/j.1834-4461.1936.tb00203.x.

Topo, J. (2004). Equal representation and participation of women in decision-making positions in Papua New Guinea: Some dilemmas. In N. Sullivan (ed.), *Governance challenges for PNG and the Pacific Islands* (pp. 164–170). DWU Press.

Tuzin, D. (1997). *The cassowary's revenge: The life and death of masculinity in a New Guinea society.* University of Chicago Press.

United Nations. (1993). Vienna Declaration and programme of action. United Nations General Assembly: World Conference on Human Rights, Vienna, 14–25 June 1993. UN High Commission.

Vatnabar, M. (2003). Gender and development in Papua New Guinea. In D. Kavanamur, C. Yala, & Q. Clements (eds), *Building a nation in Papua New Guinea: Views of the post-independence generation* (pp. 269–282). Pandanus Books.

Village Court Secretariat. (1975). Selection of village court officials (Mimeo.). Village Court Secretariat.

Village Court Secretariat. (1976). Handbook for village court officials 1976 (Mimeo.). Village Court Secretariat.

Westermark, G. (1985). Family disputes and village courts in the Eastern Highlands. In S. Toft (ed.), *Domestic violence in Papua New Guinea* (pp. 104–119, Monograph No. 3). Law Reform Commission of Papua New Guinea.

Westermark, G. (1986). Court is an arrow: Legal pluralism in Papua New Guinea. *Ethnology, 25*, 131–149. doi.org/10.2307/3773665.

Wilson, R.A. (2007). Human rights. In D. Nugent & J. Vincent (eds), *A companion to the anthropology of politics* (pp. 231–247). Blackwell Publishing. doi.org/10.1002/9780470693681.ch15.

Young, D.W. (1992). Grassroots justice: Where the national justice system is the 'alternative': The village court system of Papua New Guinea. *Australian Dispute Resolution Journal, 3*(1), 31–46.

Zorn, J.G. (1990). Customary law in the Papua New Guinea village courts. *The Contemporary Pacific, 2*(2), 279–312.

Zorn, J.G. (1992). Graun bilong mipela: Local courts and the changing customary law of Papua New Guinea. *Pacific Studies, 15*(2), 1–38.

6

Collapsing the scales of law

Melissa Demian

What can be learned from the extremely common phenomenon of disputes brought to the village courts and even more informal disputing forums of Papua New Guinea that have no discernible or possible resolution? I have long been interested in these types of 'cases' (I deploy for the sake of convenience the legal term for a conflict being adjudicated or mediated although many such conflicts never reach a recognised legal forum) because of what they suggest about the legal consciousness of people in PNG.

Say the village courts of PNG and the myriad quasi-court disputing systems that can also be found across the country are a means of creating a public space for social and even political debate. Many of the kinds of cases that have no resolution, and even no status in law, may instead be regarded as techniques for discussing the most pressing issues of the day for a given community, whether that community is urban or rural. These discussions might range from reminding those present of the appropriate treatment of public and government resources, to considering the eruption of sorcery and witchcraft talk and its social consequences, to debating the nature of marriage in contemporary PNG. These issues, which can range from the intimate to the cosmological, are not ordinarily debated in everyday life— but they are in the village courts and in their related forums. What if, in other words, these forums are not so much about resolving disputes as they are a mode of local-level democracy at work, the creation of a truly public space for debate, however limited in time that space may exist?

I ask this question in order to consider, in this chapter, what the space of 'the local' means in PNG's multifarious forums for disputing and dispute management, especially when these forums make reference to national-level decisions and legislation. To speak of the localism of these forums always refers to other places both close by and far away, and other ways of reaching decisions, for as Strathern once reminded us of calling anything 'local':

> This is a relational epithet, for it points to specificities and thus to types of itself—you cannot imagine something local alone: it summons a field of other 'locals' of which any one must be only a part. (Strathern, 1995, p. 167)

And if we are to be serious about 'local-level' dispute management systems delivering justice, and are not simply paying lip-service to people finding their own reasons to take ownership of justice delivery systems that have been imposed or invented by central governments and their colonial precursors, then we must also ask how people find ways of collapsing the scale of such systems in order to encompass the authority of the centre within the various peripheries in which they are dwelling. In the case of PNG, this can mean rural contexts but also those of urban and peri-urban settlements, heterogeneous communities that have grown up around extractive industries such as mining and oil palm, and any other spaces where the relationship to the perceived sources of political and legal power is regarded as tenuous or remote.

If social relationships—which may include relationships with ancestral or spiritual interests—have had an injury done to them in many of these 'local' cases, and are the relationships whose moral state must be rectified (Demian, 2016; Robbins, 2009), the space of the local and the public in which the state of relationships is debated can indeed occur anywhere. Localism may refer to people conducting their affairs right here and right now, but there are always other people and other places in mind when they do so. Consider that in many parts of PNG the state's felt presence is very thin on the ground. And, as the informality of local systems such as the village court illustrates, it is sometimes hard to tell where a court ends and a mediation begins. There is not a great deal of 'law' on display at all times, but there is not necessarily a great deal of 'custom' either, and the latter is another category officially enshrined at the level of the state (for example, in the Constitution) in a way that does not always make sense at the local level, because the moral status of custom can be quite contentious.

Instead, people often attempt to serve the cause of relational justice by keeping cases *away* from processes of formal law. For example, following a 2015 village court case in Milne Bay Province about the destruction of a water pipeline, the primary magistrate who heard the case told me his aim had been to keep the young man on trial from going to the district court in Alotau. The lad was uneducated and wouldn't have stood a chance in a formal legal setting in the provincial capital, the magistrate told me. If the district court sent him to jail, his life would be derailed permanently. Better to keep him in the village, with moral correction for his misdeeds provided by the village court magistrates, by the pastor and by his own family. The court's decision in this case, to levy a fine and community service, self-consciously contained its own scale of action. Although the pipeline in question was strictly speaking government property, and therefore an interest of the state, the youthful offender's community decided in a public setting that he should be kept out of the system of state law.

The ways decisions of this kind are reached have their own, particular aesthetic. It has been my experience in observing village court cases in rural Milne Bay that, for instance, everyone present is entitled to have their say in the case at hand, multiple times if necessary. In particularly thorny cases involving several disputing families, such as those about adultery or land (although village courts are not permitted to hear land disputes, many putatively non-land cases have land as an underlying issue), magistrates often appear not to be mediating so much as exhausting their disputants into reaching an agreement with each other. These cases are also an opportunity for public oration on the topic under dispute, whereupon people sometimes joke that 'it's a village meeting now'—but this may in fact be an important function of the village court, rather than a distraction from its 'true' purpose. After 20 years of research on village courts in PNG, I have often suspected that the outcome of the case matters less than the performance of grievance in the public theatre provided by the court.

This, too, matters for any future considerations of what village courts are for. If their 'localness' can be defined by the way that they give ordinary people a platform from which to address each other, and an appropriate forum for the exercise of dramatic emotion in order to make the effects of others' actions known to the public of the court, there are implications here for how the courts are supposed to work. Sometimes they do their job best when they are not acting in the capacity of a court at all, or when other public forums start to take on the theatre of grievance aesthetic found in the village court, as actual village meetings to deal with public problems sometimes do. I have documented such theatrical meetings elsewhere (Demian, 2021, pp. 181–184), but wish to emphasise here that I characterise them as theatre not because people are performing sentiments they don't actually feel—they absolutely do feel them—but rather, because the forum of the court or the public meeting both legitimises and contains such sentiments and their dramatic expression, in order to reach a resolution for them.

The central theme of this chapter is to demonstrate the capacity of people in PNG to encompass the scale of the state within these intimate spaces at strategic moments and to consider some of the ways in which this can happen. Of importance for my purposes is to give attention to the means by which the presumed perspective of the state and its laws is only integrated or encompassed into intimate, 'local' spaces at key moments when particular actors are regarded as having brought it into these spaces.

The scales of law

In 2017 at a workshop in Port Moresby, the Director of the Office of Urbanisation had just finished speaking on what he saw as the primary challenges facing the growth of towns and cities in a country that, prior to the colonial era, had never had towns or cities. He touched on a number of familiar themes for urban PNG, such as the lack of sufficient and affordable formal housing and the lack of alienated land on which such housing could be built, given that most land in the country is still held under customary tenure. He concluded by saying he would like the government to enact new legislation, say, a National Urbanisation Management Act, to solve some of the problems he identified.

During the discussion following his presentation, a member of the audience at the workshop responded, 'There is an Act already.' She went on to mention the *Physical Planning Act 1989* and the *Land Act 1996*, both of which had the potential to be used by a creative local-level government council to institute urban planning offices of a kind PNG has never really had. 'The Act is there,' the workshop attendee said, 'it just has to be implemented.'

This interaction between a public servant and one of his constituents might have seemed a fairly pedestrian one. Indeed, one can imagine this sort of hair-splitting over legislation and its uses is fairly common among actors in the sphere of public policy in almost any national capital in the world. But it caught my attention because it was not the first time I had heard this type of conversation, nor would it be the last on the particular research project that brought me to that workshop. The project was not about land use per se, but about domestic violence in PNG's urban environments. At the time I was two months into the project and already intrigued by a phenomenon that had cropped up repeatedly when my co-researcher Zuabe Tinning and I met with women's groups or NGOs working to alleviate the effects of domestic violence. The recurring phenomenon was this: either one of our interlocutors or Zuabe would bring up two pieces of recent legislation, the *Lukautim Pikinini Act 2009* and the *Family Protection Act 2013*. These two Acts, invariably cited together, are aimed at child abuse or neglect and at domestic violence, respectively. I have long been interested in how the Parliament of PNG enacts 'social' legislation of this kind as an outward-looking exercise. That is, social legislation sometimes appears to emerge from a sense of national relationship to an international ecumene that periodically assesses PNG's ability to meet social indicators such as the Millennium Development Goals, which as Merry (2016, p. 16) has noted, form part of an 'ecology of indicators' that purport to measure 'progress' towards both overlapping and competing social and economic aims. There are both political and economic consequences to this exercise in social audit and scale-making. So parliament, with the assistance and advice of the Constitutional and Law Reform Commission, has spent over a decade enacting legislation that is aimed at addressing some of the social issues for which the country is routinely criticised by international development organisations and international media.

My aim in this chapter is not to assess the various reports that have come out in recent years, detailing the difficulty of being female or a child in PNG. Of course there are grave problems with the rapidly changing nature of family life that leave people in a state of uncertainty about their obligations to each other, but I do not see a need to add to the already significant noise being made about this issue by the international development sector. I am also concerned about presenting too cynical a view of PNG's parliament or suggesting that it only enacts social legislation in response to international pressure. That also is not my aim. Rather, one of the things that intrigued me on the recent project was the way that the presumed intentions of the PNG government are read by ordinary Papua New Guineans off the legislation it enacts. And it is not only educated, middle-class Papua New Guineans who do this; anyone with even a passing familiarity with changes in the country's legal landscape is interested in discussing how these changes might affect their daily lives.

There is more widespread familiarity with that landscape than one might expect. For example, in 2013 the *Sorcery Act 1971*, a piece of colonial legislation, was repealed. This was a somewhat fraught move, as it came in the wake of a series of gruesome and highly publicised vigilante executions stemming from accusations of sorcery or witchcraft. The ostensible reason for the repeal of the Sorcery Act was to disallow fear of sorcery as a defence in criminal law. The repeal of the Sorcery Act also went hand-in-hand with public assertions by then prime minister Peter O'Neill that capital punishment for murder would be back on the table as a sentencing option. This was largely a rhetorical move; PNG has not executed anyone and is unlikely to do so for a host of reasons both micro- and macropolitical in nature. But this pair of announcements at the level of government also generated a certain amount of anxiety among Papua New Guineans more widely: was the government now on the side of the witches and sorcerers? If not, why else would it remove the only legal recourse available to those who, in the view of some people, were defending their families and communities against malevolent beings and their powers?

I will return to the repeal of the Sorcery Act and its implications later in this chapter; for the moment my focus is on how Papua New Guineans bring Acts of parliament into their discussions of highly localised, even intimate issues of conflict. During the research I was pursuing in 2017, the Family Protection Act was the one discussed the most in the forums through which I was circulating. These included workshops of the kind described above, meetings with NGOs and with more informal modes of organisation at the community level such as church women's fellowships, neighbourhood associations and even looser groupings of women around efficacious personalities such as the village court magistrate or the *komiti*, a colonial-era role that, in its myriad postcolonial usages, often means a person acting as bailiff-cum-community-mediator for the landowners of an urban settlement (Forsyth et al., 2020). Persons who are efficacious enough to hold one such role often hold multiple ones, including more nebulous titles such as 'human rights defender' or 'chair of the women's association', where the women's association is often just themselves and a personal cohort of women from their settlement who may be co-ethnics, co-religionists or a mix of these and other forms of relationship-making in PNG's cities and towns (Hukula, 2017).

These various women's groups were keen to hear more about the Family Protection Act when Zuabe or a meeting participant from the NGO sector mentioned it. In particular, they were intrigued about the Act's provision that categorises intimate partner violence as a criminal offence, and that 'violence in marriage is not a private matter, but a social problem of public concern' (*Family Protection Act 2013*, section 4(c)). In some of our meetings, women told us it was the first time they had heard domestic violence was illegal, or had heard it definitively, that is, from someone presumed to be speaking from a position of access to an authoritative source of knowledge. This was despite the fact that the Constitutional and Law Reform Commission, the Family and Sexual Violence Action Committee and other national bodies had produced pamphlets on this very topic for years— preceding even the passage of the Act. But the pamphlets depended on a high degree of literacy in English, which many settlement women do not possess. Hearing information about laws and other policies directly from another person is often a far more effective method of dissemination in PNG than through a printed medium. But it is also a method that is highly contingent on particular actors coming together at particular moments and in the urban space: for example, an NGO worker accompanying an anthropologist on her research in order to 'take the temperature' of the local community's knowledge of available legal and medical resources. So while an authoritative person speaking about recent legislation has more impact, this is also a mode of dissemination that is ad hoc at best, and very unreliable at worst. Some women said that if I hadn't brought Zuabe or other support service representatives with me, they would never have encountered any of this information.

The refrain of knowledge revealed and brought into particular spaces by an authoritative source is one that came up repeatedly over the course of that project. A nurse at Port Moresby General Hospital, who runs its Family Support Centre for survivors of domestic violence, described the initiation of the centres in various urban hospitals around PNG in the following terms: 'MSF brought us to light and we learned it was wrong' (where 'it' refers to domestic violence). MSF of course is Médecins Sans Frontières, which took over the Family Support Centre program from Soroptimist International in 2007 and supported it until funding was withdrawn in 2013 and the program was passed on again, to the United Nations Children's Fund (UNICEF) and the PNG National Department of Health. The nurse's use of 'light' as a metaphor for revealed knowledge, especially moral knowledge, replicates almost exactly the use of this metaphor by the community in rural PNG with whom I had worked for 20 years, when they speak of the knowledge they gained from showing hospitality to missionaries towards the end of the nineteenth century. This nurse is now able to pass on what she learned in the course of her training by MSF and re-embody the moral alignment she acquired from MSF along with training in providing medical and psychiatric triage to the women who come to her clinic.

The nurse at the Family Support Centre can simultaneously 'stand for' the legislation whose provisions she is keen to make known to other women and the new moral order it appears to offer the whole of the population for whom she cares as well as the relational parameters of care itself (see also Street, 2014). It is worth noting that although most of our work was not with the men in these communities, men of course also spoke at the various meetings and mediations we attended, and their discussions of the new legislation ranged from the defensive to the analytical—often in terms of abstract categories of citizenship. As one village court magistrate told us gravely, 'I try to tell men that these days, the law of women is in the ascendant' (*lo blong ol meri i kam antap*). He went on to explain that he meant men had to be more vigilant about monitoring their own behaviour, because the law was on the women's side. There was also an implication in his words and tone that the law was no longer on the side of men, which Taylor (2008) has also documented for 'rights talk' in Vanuatu, and how the apparent gendering of rights as feminine raises questions for some ni-Vanuatu men about whether they have lost certain rights and entitlements in the process. But whether or not men and women interpret news of recent legislation as a redistribution of rights, the common refrain was that the legislation represented a shift, of at least a provisional kind, in the moral order. Even in our individual interviews with domestic violence survivors, some women appealed to Zuabe and myself as potential bearers of news about this shift. 'Is it all right for him to do that?' was a question we received on multiple occasions, and in various forms. In other words, our very presence as researchers was taken as evidence by some – particularly by the efficacious personalities – of the moral landscape of marriage and cohabitation having changed sufficiently that we showed up in their homes, churches and neighbourhoods, specifically in order to tell them about it.

Encompassing the metropole

Why should any of this matter? Why should Papua New Guinean women, or citizens categorised in any other way, see a particular value in being told by particular actors which legislation has been passed in recent years, and want furthermore to talk about it with those actors and with each other?

What kind of legal consciousness is being enacted when conversation at a village court in Milne Bay or a meeting with researchers in Port Moresby turns on questions of how recent legislation affects intimate relationships and how people are to resolve problems in those relationships?

The connections between levels of government, and between organisations that may have some connection to government bodies, do seem to be an object of interest for many people in contemporary PNG. One of the things that can be done with the interpretation of these relationships is to strategically remove relationships from the picture—sometimes literally. There is a diagram on the wall of an office in the Ahi Local-Level Government Council building in Lae (Plate 6.1). Ahi is the administrative district for Lae's closest suburban settlements. The diagram shows the putatively hierarchical relationship between the Ahi Council of Women and the National Council of Women, with some steps at the provincial and regional levels in between. But note that all other provinces, regions and local government councils have been removed to show a direct line of communication between Ahi and the national council.

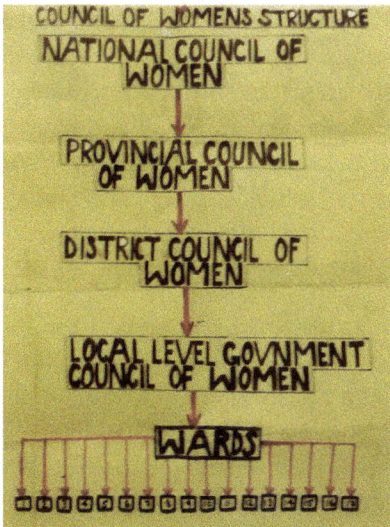

Plate 6.1. Ahi Council of Women diagram, Lae.

Source: Photograph by the author.

During my field trips to Lae in 2016, 2017 and 2019 I only ever met three people who identified themselves as members of the Ahi Council of Women, and they were its president, treasurer and secretary. All other members of this 'council' seemed provisional at best, imaginary at worst. I say 'at worst', but the aspirational nature of this entity can also be regarded as a creative act of collapsing the scale of the national into the local. The Ahi Council of Women has had no contact of which I am aware with any national or provincial body; the president of the Ahi council said that she saw a poster mentioning the national council in Lae and thought she ought to create a local branch of it. She and her co-councillors mustered the contacts they had through their multiple roles (as 'human rights defenders' and so on) to get an office in the Local-Level Government Council building, where they hold occasional meetings with women they are trying to help and attempt to extract funding for further activities from the local or district governments, since none is forthcoming from the National Council of Women.

I use this example of an attempt at bureaucratic scale collapse and the strategic removal of complicating relationships to ask whether a similar move is being made when my interlocutors in PNG spoke of knowledge about recent legislation as the primary mechanism for effecting changes in people's behaviour towards each other, or even as a form of social engineering. To be clear: the village courts are doing their usual job of interpreting the laws that are handed down to them. But it is the notion that *everyone* ought to be engaged in this activity that is of interest here. A term familiar to anyone who has worked in the public policy sphere in PNG—and possibly other places—is 'awareness', particularly the construction 'making an awareness' in the English usage of PNG. 'Making an awareness' was the mechanism by which many of my friends and research participants envisioned the transmission of recent Acts of parliament to the general populace. It couldn't be done with pamphlets, of course; it had to be done by means of face-to-face presentations and workshops through which people's 'mindset' (another inescapable item of NGO and church self-help language) would be transformed and they would then change their behaviour accordingly. 'Making an awareness' is itself a social form through which social relationships are imagined to adapt themselves to a moral order that has been reconfigured at the level of the country's parliament.

But does a shift in 'levels' actually concretise the abstracted kinds of persons found in, say, the Family Protection Act? I am mindful of Wastell's (2001) exhortation, when considering the law as a social system, not to presume that the migration of a legal object—such as an Act of Parliament—'between scales' will alter the nature or effects of that legal object. In Wastell's own words, echoing those from Strathern at the beginning of this chapter:

> Nothing is particularly 'local' unless it is measured against something 'bigger', less 'local' than itself—and here so many prejudices flee from analytical view, 'local' so often eliding notions of that which is smaller, more particular, concrete rather than abstract, substantial rather than ideational. The scale global:local depends upon a certain presumed but impossible metaposition which tells us that local really is more specific and atomistic than the impersonal

and all-encompassing global. The scale insists that we accept each manifestation of a local context as a constituent element of a global whole, each local perspective as a subjective position in an objective reality. (2001, p. 186)

Here, Wastell reminds us that framing local relationships in terms of those 'above' them on a scale generates a whole other cascade of assumptions about the social effects of migration between levels of the scale one has in mind. For her, the scale is global to local; for me, it is national to local, but with domestic violence legislation such as the Family Protection Act, there is little question that Papua New Guinean parliamentarians had the global in mind when they enacted this law. It was a moment of participation in what Lazarus-Black (2001) has called the 'pragmatics of inclusion', or a deliberate scaling of national law both 'out' into an international NGO-scape that has in the past decade done a great deal of work to recast human rights as the rights of women and girls and 'in' to inoculate or infuse the PNG legal landscape with this new language of rights. But where Lazarus-Black found that the introduction of comparable domestic violence legislation in Trinidad over 30 years ago appeared to offer women their first opportunity to act on domestic violence in particular ways now sanctioned by the law, at present, this legislation appears to offer Papua New Guineans the opportunity to talk about domestic violence in particular ways. Some village court magistrates in Lae, for example, have spoken of being harassed by police for attempting to remove a woman from the household she shared with a violent husband, rather than the police doing anything about the violence itself. So there is not yet a consensus even among actors in the legal landscape about what the new legislation may or may not oblige them to do. This is itself a kind of pragmatics of inclusion, where citizens can make strategic decisions about when a set of actions is even included in the rubric of the new laws.

But the adoption of 'the Act' as a potential tool for social engineering by some of my interlocutors does complicate some of the assumptions about what happens when any kind of scale is presumed to begin, such that legal objects might 'move' along that scale. Courts interpret laws made by parliaments and, in common law systems like that of PNG, they can even shift the nature and effects of a statute through the building of a body of case law and the creative application of precedent. How much more 'local' or 'concrete' does the law become by means of this process, though? And how much more local or concrete, again, does it become when nonlegal actors pick up a legal object and run with it, as it were?

Acts of parliament affect people personally but are made remotely in a fragmented metropole such as Port Moresby where one does not need to travel very far from the government district of Waigani to meet people whose lives might as well be happening on the other side of the country from the offices and chambers where laws are made. The sense of remoteness here is not necessarily spatial, in other words. In the words of Harms et al. (2014, p. 364), remoteness is 'not only determined by topography, but also topology, that is the level of connectedness experienced in cultural vocabulary'. The remoteness of a lawmaking body is precisely what makes it compelling in everyday discourse, and that discourse in turn makes use of the 'distance' of parliament from ordinary life precisely in order to lend discussions of Acts and their effects velocity and force.

I am arguing, in other words, that people would not wish to use Acts of parliament as tools for social experimentation and engineering if they were not considered to be remote in origin, with the creative work of connecting an Act to new social forms being taken up by ordinary citizens. The vernacularisation of laws such as the Family Protection Act *doesn't mean they become local*; precisely the opposite. Transforming a law understood to originate from 'far away' into something that is both intelligible and able to affect one's own life means that that law retains indices of remoteness, but its effectiveness is connected to the everyday practices in which people to play with the idea of distance as something that can either legitimise a legal instrument or actor or question the very grounds for legitimacy on which some people may act.

Take, for example, the elusive individual known as the 'bush lawyer'— an illegitimate actor in the eyes of legal professionals who is imagined to rely for his business on people whose remoteness from the legal metropole makes them unable to distinguish a real lawyer from a false one. During a 2012–15 team research project on village courts that I co-convened, only one project member documented the activities of persons who might fit the descriptions commonly offered for this category of person. I will not claim that bush lawyers do not exist, only that they remain known largely through the talk about them that circulates among legal professionals and police. They share this quality with sorcerers in PNG—also known largely through talk—and I am interested in extending the analogy to see what it might suggest about the anxieties manifested in the figure of the bush lawyer. The characteristics of the bush lawyer, insofar as I have been told about them, are as follows. He is not actually a lawyer (but is always a man). He may have little in the way of formal education, but possesses sufficient literacy, innate intelligence and charisma or confidence to convince other people he knows what he is talking about when it comes to legal matters, especially regarding the preparation of documents for presentation as evidence in the village court and even the district court. I was told by legal colleagues back in 2008 that I could find such persons propping up the bar at the Airways Hotel in Port Moresby, offering their services to the gullible and desperate. But the researcher on our project who had been working on village courts in Moresby found no sign of this character; instead, the bush lawyer seems to be appearing in rural areas or smaller provincial towns. Like the sorcerer, he is never quite where you think he is.

The sorcerer, too, is known to hire himself out to clients bent on revenge or the exercising of petty jealousies; both the sorcerer and the bush lawyer are imagined to act out of uncontrollable greed. Just as the law practised by the bush lawyer 'looks like' real law but isn't because the bush lawyer is not a real lawyer, the solution offered by the sorcerer isn't a real solution because the sorcerer is not a proper human being. In both cases, the generation of future trouble rather than any resolution of trouble in the present is anticipated to be the inevitable outcome. This is what I mean when I say the figure of the bush lawyer inspires anxiety. The counterfeit law of the bush lawyer, like the counterfeit humanity of the sorcerer, is a case study in negative mimesis. It is imitation with the destructive aim of inverting the appropriate order of things, rather than the productive and legitimate work of encompassing actual laws that emanate from actual legal sources within the ambit of everyday life.

Irregularities of this kind create category problems and further problems of scale. Spatially, sorcery is felt to happen at the peripheries—not just of the metropole, but also of certain modes of legal vision. The ideal of law is a regularised, not to say flat, topography and a means of maintaining standards from the centre outwards. Peripheral activities such as bush lawyering, sorcery and the vigilante actions against sorcery to which people sometimes resort all seem to indicate that the topography of law in PNG is far more uneven than any metropolitan perspective is currently willing to grant it. It is instead 'a scrunched-up "shadow map" of the world' (Saxer & Andersson, 2019, p. 141) upon which the flows and stoppages of social forms shaped by law are seen rarely to follow anything as orderly a path as they are imagined to do from the standpoint of the metropole. Arguably, too, the very ability of Papua New Guineans who are not legal professionals to imagine themselves or others as bearers of legal knowledge is itself the 'local effect' of the law. It is in these comparative moments that one is obliged to ask, with Wastell, how scale enters into an ethnographic understanding of lawmaking and law-using in the first place.

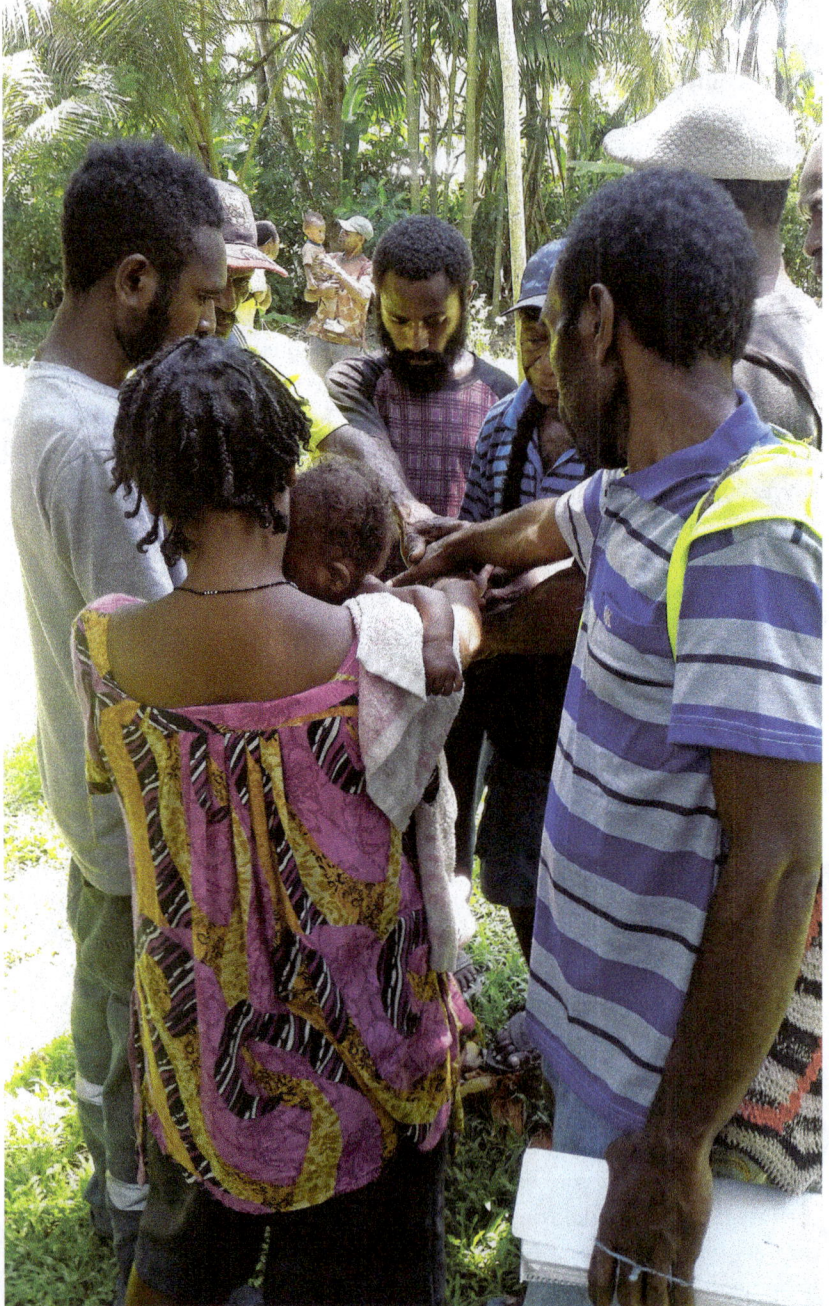

Plate 6.2. Saying sorry at the end of a *komiti* mediation between families, Lae.

Source: Photograph by the author.

Plate 6.2 shows two families in an effort of resolving a series of ongoing difficulties (*hevi*) between a young husband and his even younger wife, in a settlement in the suburban fringe of Lae. The problems encountered by this couple were multiple in nature and only at various points in their relationship—at least as recounted in the mediation conducted by their block *komiti*, which concluded in this public reconciliation—could they be described as 'domestic violence' as it is commonly understood in the law or the NGO-sphere. Nonetheless, the recent legislation was duly trotted out during the proceedings, in this case by the village court magistrate, who was not overseeing the mediation because it was not being held under the auspices of the court, but who was invited to participate as an informed observer. Both pieces of legislation—the Lukautim Pikinini Act and the Family Protection Act—were offered up as ingredients in the recipe of moral instruction that this youthful couple received over the course of the mediation to induce them to reflect more seriously on whatever they thought they were doing when they began cohabiting, having children and referring to each other as husband or wife.

On the one hand, the two Acts were indeed 'localised' in the mediation as they became components in the mix of moral, spiritual and legal sources of authority that could be marshalled to instruct the couple in how to behave like properly married adults. But apart from that enrolment of the Acts into the mix, not much about the Acts themselves was changed in terms of the abstractions they encode. The types of family members named in the Family Protection Act as being responsible for domestic violence, for example, does not include common perpetrators identified in our research such as co-wives or brothers-in-law and other *tambus*. Even the level of detail available in the Act is lost when it becomes a rubric for talking simply about husbands and wives or, worse, 'men and women'—abstract categories of persons that seldom have any real purchase on how Papua New Guineans might actually imagine a relationship in a state of conflict to be configured.

Gershon (2011) has reminded us that lawmaking is an attempt by legislatures to make differences within a citizenry intelligible, orderly and governable. She writes:

> In legislatures, differences are explicitly at stake in the construction of laws. From a legislative perspective, pluralism is imagined in terms of interest groups or competing agendas between lawmakers. Thus, laws are proleptic projects for legislators, produced out of agonistic discussions and through practices ideally transparent to a nation's citizenry … [but] the application of law to context is

itself a process in which the 'law' has to stand still for a moment, to be thought of as more monolithic. For court officials, laws are both acontextual and applicable to context, linked to particular circumstances through competing interpretations, and ideally an instantiation of an objective justice. (Gershon 2011, p. 167)

In this passage, Gershon is applying the issue of how legislatures make laws to how courts apply them. The differences being aggregated under the rubric of the law for a legislature are then applied by courts to the manifestations of those differences as they appear to them in a given case—the form of 'the case' is how they make the more abstract differences represented in a statute concrete in the manifestation of the disputing parties before them. I am interested here in how these abstract differences as represented in, say, parliamentary Acts, seem to escape the legal arena of the courts entirely and are taken up by ordinary citizens as objects of interpretation and 'agonistic discussions' of the kind Gershon finds among legislators. When I say 'abstract differences', I mean the cataloguing of persons in particular ways, such as between parents and children in the Lukautim Pikinini Act, or between husbands and wives in the Family Protection Act. Some of these categories can become even more abstracted once they become objects of discussion by people trying to work out what these Acts could mean for their everyday lives: husbands and wives, for example, become transmuted into the even vaguer men and women in urban Papua New Guinea, where the contracting of a marriage has become so informal and contingent in nature that cohabitation alone is now enough to claim conjugal rights and obligations in relation to another person (Goddard, 2010). Remaining to be seen as discussion of these Acts moves further into the Papua New Guinean public sphere is whether their non-mediation through the courts translates to the dramatic jumping of scales that it currently appears to be, or else to an obviation of any attempt to describe something identifiable as scales of law at all.

The 'local' again: Sorcery on trial in Milne Bay

In the final part of this chapter I return to the phenomenon that most commonly eludes any kind of scale-making project in PNG legal consciousness, because it has proven almost impossible to legislate, to contain or to control in any way within the lawmaking project. I refer of course to sorcery, and the way that this discourse continues to haunt the attempts of Papua New Guineans to manage it in their conflicts with one another and negotiate those conflicts at the local level.

For this purpose I leave behind my recent work in Lae and Port Moresby and turn to a compiled or normative account of how village courts on the Suau Coast of Milne Bay Province deal with the most difficult type of cases brought to them. The Suau-speaking region of Milne Bay was where I conducted fieldwork on and off for nearly 20 years, and that work continues to inform how I think not only about the way law has become vernacularised in PNG, but also about the way sorcery and village courts may be seen as versions of each other. When one is brought into the presence of the other, village court magistrates must take on an analogous perspective to that of the accused sorcerer and act as though they can perceive the state of relationships that are hidden from view. This is both what Suau sorcerers are understood to do when they use invisible forces to cause harm and what magistrates do when they elicit testimony from those attending their court that reveals not only the current state of relationships, but also their deep history.

Both the magistrates I have interviewed and some of the people involved in sorcery cases attest to their difficulty—indeed they seem to belong to an entirely different category from the normal round of adultery, damage to gardens or houses, and land boundary cases that are the village court's normal stock in trade. Category problems have been a recurring theme in this chapter and the type of case I discuss now also stands for category problems in the everyday lives of many Papua New Guineans, as well as for the law itself. These types of cases present a challenge to the very notion of a legal *system*—or rather, they offer possibilities for thinking about such a system 'in terms of communication and its binds [rather] than with interpreting systems in terms of functions and their failures' (Gershon, 2005, p. 100).

Sorcery cases on the Suau Coast normally follow on from at least one death and often more than one if they have occurred within the same matrilineage. They will proceed for many hours; magistrates reported to me cases that had gone on for a day or more without interruption. Emotions run high, so magistrates and peace officers must work hard to keep matters from getting out of hand. The accused person will invariably deny having caused these deaths. He—it is always he, since Suau witches can cause mischief of various kinds but do not kill people directly, and Suau sorcerers are by definition men—must be worn down with argumentation and any evidence that the accusers may be able to provide: marks on the body of their deceased relative, for example, or the sight or sound of an animal out of place, such as a diurnal bird calling in the middle of the night or a snake or crocodile appearing outside its normal habitat. Other known specialists in the magical technique in question may be brought in as 'expert witnesses' to assess the evidence of the accusers and to interrogate the accused. A forensic history (cf. Munn, 1990) must be built up in which the presumed grievance of the accused sorcerer or his lineage against the lineage of the dead person or persons is brought to light. The magistrates to whom I have spoken note their own worries that the decisions they make at the conclusion of such cases, in a physically and mentally exhausted state, may not bring about the reconciliation that is their aim and indeed may rebound on themselves in the future, with terrible consequences. At the *haus krai* for a woman my own age that I attended on a visit to the Suau Coast in 2015, other mourners noted pointedly to me that this was the third death in the family of the local village court chairman. Of course there could be no doubt as to what had caused these deaths; only the identity of the perpetrator was in question.

I would now like to step back from this sad scene and make a few fairly mundane remarks about the political and legal environment in which village courts such as the ones I have just described find themselves. As noted earlier in this chapter, in 2013 PNG repealed its Sorcery Act to both domestic and international acclaim (Siegel, 2013). Members of the legal profession in Port Moresby had already reported to me several years before the repeal of the Act that they felt it was no longer fit for purpose, as it appeared to make available a defence in criminal cases involving sorcery-related violence. Notwithstanding such a defence has almost never succeeded in court (Demian, 2011), the perception that it could potentially be used to exonerate murders was heightened throughout the country in the wake of several high-profile and gruesome killings related to sorcery accusations. Then Prime Minister O'Neill moved swiftly to have the Act repealed in parliament, along with introducing draconian penal measures such as the reinstatement of the death penalty. Human rights bodies such as Amnesty International were pulled in two directions and unable to mount a consistent response; they applauded the repeal of the Act and in the same breath denounced the return of capital punishment as a sentencing option (Amnesty International, 2013). It was a perfect illustration of how many international NGOs and donor agencies struggle to engage in a coherent fashion with PNG politics, which seem half of the time to be in accordance with the particular set of liberal humanistic values that these agencies promote and the other half of the time to be pointed in a direction that they cannot countenance. The religiously motivated destruction of traditional carvings in PNG's Parliament House was another example of this phenomenon, coming as it did directly on the heels of the repeal of the Sorcery Act and a national conversation about how to eradicate sorcery-related violence by means of eradicating sorcery itself (Santos da Costa, 2021; Schram, 2014). The debates about the destruction of the carvings, too, were dealing with categorical peripheries—a problem encountered by village courts when they confront sorcery cases.

However timely the repeal of the Act may have felt to some metropolitans in the legal professions, in practical terms this event was largely symbolic. Cases involving sorcery accusations rarely make it as far 'up' the scale of PNG's legal hierarchy as the national courts, where the repeal of this piece of legislation might actually be felt in terms of constraining the options available to defendants who have acted out of fear of sorcery. The majority of sorcery cases, instead, occur at the 'local' level of the village courts, particularly those in rural areas where concerns about sorcery are strongest, and indeed can be a matter of nearly daily conversation. For these courts, the repeal of the Sorcery Act has been functionally irrelevant. This is not, as I have already discussed, due to a lack of knowledge about Acts of parliament, but is instead due to a deep pragmatism on the part of magistrates combined with their obligations to the moral state of local relationships and their resolution, where 'local' can mean anywhere from a rural village to an urban settlement (Hukula, 2019).

There is also some evidence that even when rural people are aware of the repeal of the Act, this can be interpreted as evidence of indifference or even hostility on the part of Port Moresby elites to their concerns. The danger here is that people may move their sorcery-related conflicts out of the village courts entirely or strike them from the court records, for which there is ample evidence in the literature already (Goddard, 1998). In such instances, the risk of sorcery accusations escalating into violent conflict is compounded.

Violence stemming from sorcery accusations is rare in Milne Bay, although not unheard of. I make no claims to expertise on its various and appalling manifestations elsewhere, due to my primary research history in a province of PNG where sorcery is treated more as a social problem to be resolved than as a spiritual or existential threat to be confronted through the destruction of individual lives. But because I am interested in the legal scale of sorcery for the purposes of this chapter, I have paid attention to work on parts of the country where violence can be an outcome of sorcery narratives. It is worth mentioning briefly a frequent 'elephant in the room' or backgrounded feature in discussions about sorcery-related violence, which is that it appears consistently in communities where evangelical and neo-Pentecostal churches predominate rather than the older Christian denominations found throughout PNG. Some of the newer Pentecostal churches with connections to megachurches and their associated broadcast media empires based in Australia and the United States preach a doctrine of cosmological warfare against Satanic powers thought to be literally at work in the world and vigilance against these powers as a component of the embodied practice demanded of believers (Andersen, 2017; Coleman, 2020; Jorgensen, 2005). In PNG this set of ideas is sometimes taken up by groups of young men who translate the call for spiritual vigilance in their churches into actual vigilantism, as a means of seeking local renown and of speaking back to a state regarded as detached from or even hostile to the issues of pressing concern to themselves (Abrahams, 2000). Abrahams characterises vigilantism as a 'frontier phenomenon' (2000, p. 113), to indicate the way it tends to occur at social margins that can be geographical, economic or political in nature—again, no frontier is merely topographic in nature. Under conditions of perceived state withdrawal, and especially the seeming withdrawal of interest in sorcery signalled by the repeal of the Sorcery Act, an affective frontier emerges in which vigilante action against people accused of sorcery or witchcraft can be seen to flourish.

It does not flourish in Milne Bay, however, where sorcery cases instead continue to be brought to the village court, in the absence of any jurisdictional sanction for this to occur. The magistrates there have a job to do and, as one Suau magistrate insisted to me, 'We are the first court'—that is, the court where problems are taken first in order to prevent them from becoming even bigger problems. Sorcery is the biggest problem of all, to be handled by people who know properly about it rather than distant magistrates and judges in the provincial or national capital who may have no appreciation of how the sorcery of the Suau region works, or of how familial histories and futures are at stake in sorcery cases. To call the village court the 'first court' also inverts the normative hierarchy of PNG's courts, with the national court at the top, the district courts in the middle and the village courts at the bottom. As with other obviations of hierarchy, such as a local-level Council of Women that claims a direct relationship to the National Council of Women, placing the village court 'first' asserts the primacy of the local, especially when dealing with issues as intractable as sorcery.

In the examples I have offered here, the local is used to assess laws being made and unmade in the metropole of Port Moresby, and also to assess the relationship of 'local' people to that metropole and the ways in which it disseminates knowledge of what the laws are, what they are meant to do and to whose benefit they may appear and disappear from the legal landscape. These assessments can also be regarded as playing with scale in such a way that people distanced from the metropole, dwelling on physical or informational peripheries, can bring themselves back to the centre.

In order for a law to effect social change in this way, it has to remain remote in nature. If it becomes truly 'local'—that is, if it is seen to originate with a particular place and with the people using it—this would cause it to lose any power to have an effect on their lives. As a national court judge noted to me in 2008, the 'independence' of the common law and post-independence statutes enacted by parliament was what potentially made it appealing to many people in PNG, because it was not linked to any particular ethnic or regional group in the country (Demian, 2011, p. 66). 'It has a source', he said, and went on to explain that precisely because its source lay either with the formalities of parliamentary lawmaking or with the common law principles inherited from the United Kingdom, it was immune to manipulation by any particular group of interests within PNG. While this may seem like a piece of standard rhetoric about the impartiality of a functioning legal system, everything I have noted in this chapter suggests that this judge really did have his finger on what his fellow Papua New Guineans find valuable or interesting in laws such as Acts of parliament. Laws that are seen to come from elsewhere, from another scale of activity and experience, offer the beguiling prospect that one could, with enough imagination, make a conceptual jump to that other scale of experience in order to evaluate one's own actions as well as those of kin and other relations. It is critical that these laws come from somewhere identifiable, unlike the actions of sorcerers, bush lawyers and similar figures of illegitimacy who occupy an upside-down world of activities that stem from no place other than their own avarice. But if the somewhere from which national laws originate is deemed *both* part of the world that ordinary people inhabit *and* also sufficiently remote from the immediate cares and obligations of everyday life, the very foreignness of their origin is precisely what allows people to translate these laws into terms that infuse the everyday with new possibilities.

References

Abrahams, R. (2000). Vigilantism, state jurisdiction and community morality: Control of crime and 'undesirable' behaviour when the state 'fails'. In I. Pardo (ed.), *Morals of legitimacy: Between agency and the system* (pp. 107–126). Berghahn Books. doi.org/10.2307/j.ctv27tctfr.8.

Amnesty International. (2013, 28 May). Papua New Guinea repeals Sorcery Act while moving closer to executions. www.amnesty.org/en/latest/news/2013/05/papua-new-guinea-repeals-sorcery-act-while-moving-closer-executions/.

Andersen, B. (2017). Learning to believe in Papua New Guinea. In K. Rio, M. MacCarthy, & R. Blanes (eds), *Pentecostalism and witchcraft: Spiritual warfare in Africa and Melanesia* (pp. 235–255). Palgrave Macmillan. doi.org/10.1007/978-3-319-56068-7_10.

Coleman, S. (2020). Spiritual warfare in Pentecostalism: Metaphors and materialities. In V. Narayanan (ed.), *The Wiley Blackwell companion to religion and materiality* (pp. 171–186). John Wiley & Sons. doi.org/10.1002/9781118660072.ch8.

Demian, M. (2011). 'Hybrid custom' and legal description in Papua New Guinea. In J. Edwards & M. Petrović-Šteger (eds), *Recasting anthropological knowledge: Inspiration and social science* (pp. 49–69). Cambridge University Press. doi.org/10.1017/CBO9780511842092.004.

Demian, M. (2016). Court in between: The spaces of relational justice in Papua New Guinea. *Australian Feminist Law Journal, 42*(1), 13–30. doi.org/10.1080/13200968.2016.1191118.

Demian, M. (2021). *In memory of times to come: Ironies of history in Southeastern Papua New Guinea*. Berghahn Books. doi.org/10.2307/j.ctv2tsxj8h.

Family Protection Act 2013, No. 29 of 2013, Papua New Guinea. (2013). www.paclii.org/cgi-bin/sinodisp/pg/legis/num_act/fpa2013206/fpa2013206.html.

Forsyth, M., Dinnen, S., & Hukula, F. (2020). A case for a public Pacific criminology? In K. Henne & R. Shah (eds), *Routledge handbook of public criminologies* (pp. 163–178). Routledge. doi.org/10.4324/9781351066105-18.

Gershon, I. (2005). Seeing like a system: Luhmann for anthropologists. *Anthropological Theory, 5*(2), 99–116. doi.org/10.1177/1463499605053993.

Gershon, I. (2011). Studying cultural pluralism in courts versus legislatures. *PoLAR: Political and Legal Anthropology Review, 34*(1), 155–174. doi.org/10.1111/j.1555-2934.2011.01144.x.

Goddard, M. (1998). Off the record: Village court praxis and the politics of settlement life in Port Moresby, Papua New Guinea. *Canberra Anthropology, 21*(1), 41–62. doi.org/10.1080/03149099809508373.

Goddard, M. (2010). Making and unmaking marriage in Moresby. In M. Goddard (ed.), *Villagers and the city: Melanesian experiences of Port Moresby, Papua New Guinea* (pp. 110–136). Sean Kingston Publishing.

Harms, E., Hussain, S., & Shneiderman, S. (2014). Remote and edgy: New takes on old anthropological themes. *HAU: Journal of Ethnographic Theory, 4*(1), 361–381. doi.org/10.14318/hau4.1.020.

Hukula, F. (2017). Kinship and relatedness in urban Papua New Guinea. *Journal de la Société des Océanistes, 144/145*, 159–170. doi.org/10.4000/jso.7756.

Hukula, F. (2019). Morality and a Mosbi market. *Oceania, 89*(2), 168–181. doi.org/10.1002/ocea.5216.

Jorgensen, D. (2005). Third wave evangelism and the politics of the global in Papua New Guinea: Spiritual warfare and the recreation of place in Telefolmin. *Oceania, 75*(4), 444–461. doi.org/10.1002/j.1834-4461.2005.tb02902.x.

Lazarus-Black, M. (2001). Law and the pragmatics of inclusion: Governing domestic violence in Trinidad and Tobago. *American Ethnologist, 28*(2), 388–416. doi.org/10.1525/ae.2001.28.2.388.

Merry, S.E. (2016). *The seductions of quantification: Measuring human rights, gender violence, and sex trafficking.* University of Chicago Press. doi.org/10.7208/chicago/9780226261317.001.0001.

Munn, N. (1990). Constructing regional worlds in experience: Kula exchange, witchcraft and Gawan local events. *Man*, n.s., *25*(1), 1–17. doi.org/10.2307/2804106.

Robbins, J. (2009). Recognition, reciprocity, and justice: Melanesian reflections on the rights of relationships. In K.M. Clarke and M. Goodale (eds), *Mirrors of justice: Law and power in the post–Cold War era* (pp. 171–190). Cambridge University Press. doi.org/10.1017/CBO9780511657511.010.

Santos da Costa, P. (2021). Postcolonial nationalism and neo-Pentecostalism: A case from Papua New Guinea. *Nations and Nationalism, 27*(3), 1–15. doi.org/10.1111/nana.12731.

Saxer, M., & Andersson, R. (2019). The return of remoteness: Insecurity, isolation and connectivity in the new world disorder. *Social Anthropology/Anthropologie Sociale, 27*(2), 140–155. doi.org/10.1111/1469-8676.12652.

Schram, R. (2014, 9 February). A new government breaks with the past in the Papua New Guinea Parliament's 'haus tambaran'. *Material World* blog. materialworldblog.com/2014/02/a-new-government-breaks-with-the-past-in-the-papua-new-guinea-parliaments-haus-tambaran/.

Siegel, M. (2013, 29 May). Papua New Guinea acts to repeal sorcery law after strife. *New York Times*. www.nytimes.com/2013/05/30/world/asia/papua-new-guinea-moves-to-repeal-sorcery-act.html.

Strathern, M. (1995). The nice thing about culture is that everyone has it. In M. Strathern (ed.), *Shifting contexts: Transformations in anthropological knowledge* (pp. 153–176). Routledge. doi.org/10.4324/9780203450901_chapter_8.

Street, A. (2014). *Biomedicine in an unstable place: Infrastructure and personhood in a Papua New Guinean hospital*. Duke University Press. doi.org/10.1215/9780822376668.

Taylor, J.P. (2008). The social life of rights: 'Gender antagonism', modernity and *raet* in Vanuatu. *The Australian Journal of Anthropology, 19*(2), 165–178. doi.org/10.1111/j.1835-9310.2008.tb00120.x.

Wastell, S. (2001). Presuming scale, making diversity: On the mischiefs of measurement and the global: Local metonym in theories of law and culture. *Critique of Anthropology, 21*(2), 185–210. doi.org/10.1177/0308275X0102100204.

7

A system that allows people to say sorry: An interview with Fiona Hukula

Transcribed and edited by Camila F. Marinelli
and Melissa Demian

Dr Fiona Hukula has dedicated her career as a social scientist to the investigation of gender-based violence, community livelihoods and the pluralism of conflict resolution forums in urban Papua New Guinea. She worked at the National Research Institute (NRI) of PNG in Port Moresby for 23 years, culminating in the post of Senior Research Fellow and program leader for its Building Safer Communities Program. She is currently a Gender Specialist for the Pacific Islands Forum Secretariat in Suva, Fiji.

In this interview with Melissa Demian, Dr Hukula discusses some of the issues of pressing concern to the future of local-level legal developments in PNG. In particular, she offers a consideration of the relationship between formal and informal disputing systems, and the relationship of both to wider issues that affect conflicts in the urban communities in which she has worked. There is a caution here against overregulation of these systems, but also an exhortation to find a way to oversee informal modes of dispute resolution so that they actually serve the needs of all the people who resort to them. It is in these informal forums, argues Hukula, that the groundwork for a Papua New Guinean justice can be found—one in which people have the chance to make reparations to each other, rather than being cut off from their families and communities in a carceral model of punishment.

* * *

MD

Thank you so much for being up for this interview. I've talked to you over the years about your work both during and after the PhD, and what you've been doing since then at the NRI, and I feel like this is an opportunity for me to get to know what your thoughts are now about the state of all these systems you've been studying for years. So just to take us to the first question: can you talk a little about what gave rise to your interest in formal dispute resolution in PNG, and especially in Moresby, because that's something you've been working on forever.

FH

Yes, and thank you so much for this opportunity and this whole idea, Melissa. So really what gave rise to my interest was my PhD research in Morobe Blok in urban settlements here in Port Moresby, and I started observing an informal *komiti*, informal dispute resolution meetings, and that was what really gave rise to my interest. Because I had seen prior to living in the settlement these sort of ethnic groups gathering under trees all around Port Moresby, but I wasn't sure what it was. I just thought, 'There is some kind of trouble council going on.' But in fact, they were different forms of *komiti* happening.

MD

It is one thing to observe something is happening, right, you can do that all the time, but what was it in particular about that mode of resolving conflicts that seized your imagination? And so you said, 'Right, I want to study this.'

FH

Well, I think it was the fact that generally the people who were parties to the dispute seemed to come away happy with the outcome. So we are talking about a formal system of going through the police, going to courts, and here in Port Moresby people were essentially helping themselves to resolve disputes in their own way, within their own communities. And I think what was of interest also is that people knew that they have, or are aware that there are other options, meaning if they were unhappy with the *komiti* level then they could go to the village court or they could go to the police and look for other options for dispute resolution.

MD

And is it your impression that people, especially in Moresby and maybe in other urban settings—I've seen it a bit in Lae too—are inclined to go to the *komiti* first? Is it your impression that they're saying: 'We'll try this one first and then if this doesn't work out we'll try the village court or we'll try the formal legal system in some way.'

FH

Well, I would say my work is mainly in the urban settlements and with what can be classified as urban poor, even though that is in itself not exactly accurate, because you know all kinds of people live in settlements. But certainly, in the places that I've worked in Port Moresby, that is in Nine Mile, in Sabama, in Tokarara, I do see that people—especially people who are maybe not as educated or maybe not university degree-holders—that they tend to go to *komiti*-level dispute resolution options first. And I think it is also because they're part of a community, so having that community-level dispute resolution allows them all to engage in conversation about particular conflicts and how those have affected their community.

MD

That leads to my next question, which is about Moresby as a city. Every city has its own particular character; Moresby is no different. And Moresby has some unique features that have been written about over the years. You note that when people are particularly invested in the conflict being an issue of their community, Moresby really has communities in very particular ways, doesn't it? Because of the way it's all spread out and people are in very particular spaces. Do you have thoughts about how Moresby as an urban setting, both socially and in terms of its infrastructure, lends itself to these kinds of solutions?

FH

Yes, I think that Moresby—you know some people describe it as the big village, others describe it as this fast-modernising metropolis. But in terms of these kinds of solutions to conflict, Moresby still has that—in certain parts of the city that connection to dispute resolution that is also very rural or based on our ways of conflict resolution from the time before. You know, this idea of *bun na sindaun na toktok* [meet and discuss together], these kinds of things. Especially in communities where, as you mentioned, people are very vested in a certain area. So they want to make sure that things are okay, and they want to make sure that if there's a problem within, for example, different ethnic groups or *hauslain* [extended families], that it's sorted so we don't have paybacks or people don't feel uncertain to walk around in their own community.

MD

There's something about the kind of contained—I don't know how else to describe it—the contained nature of some settlement communities that makes people more inclined to say, 'This isn't just a dispute between my family and your family, or between me and you even, within our own households, but this affects all of us.'

FH

Yes, definitely, and in some settlements, and I would say in some suburbs, there's a whole investment in community through families, generations of families living in that one area. They get to know each other well, they call them *wanstrit* [shared street; neighbours], so people are quite relational. That is another aspect of urban kinship, based on that idea of place and belonging. Which all lends itself to this kind of conflict resolution: wanting to settle things among ourselves so that *bai mipla sindaun gut* [we will live together well] and have good relations within our community.

MD

And on that you've also documented not just dispute resolutions systems, but entire community groups, very local-level community groups in Moresby. I've seen you write about the Saraga Peace and Good Order Development Association, for example, out in Saraga. Do you have thoughts about how those groups in particular emerge?

FH

The Saraga Peace and Good Order Development Association—just to clarify: I haven't done any work there or written about them myself, but I do know that they are probably one of the very earliest kinds of peace and good order *komiti* that have come out within urban Port Moresby. And then you have other kinds of *komiti*. For example, in an urban settlement there's often a settlement chairman, and within that *komiti* there will be a law and order *komiti* or a peace and good order *komiti*. So this is the local-level community group that might also have a water *komiti*, and they emerge out of this idea of local governance. And of course it doesn't work all the time, but in many cases where people come to live together, either as an ethnic group or as any other kind of group, they form these *komiti* to start to see how they can self-regulate, and also deal with other issues around, you could say, development: how to get water into the settlements. The *komiti* that I know of that exist are often the peace and good order *komiti* and a water *komiti* or something like that.

MD

It's really interesting how the idea of infrastructure, like getting water into the community, and the idea of peace go together, or they seem to in the way that these groups form.

FH

When I was working on my PhD research at Morobe Blok, one of the things that one of my informants talked about was the link between water, violence against women and HIV. He was saying when there's no water and girls and women have to go to line up for the water tap, especially in the evenings, they leave themselves open to sexual harassment. Or if they go and wash, have to wash in somebody else's bathroom, or there's the outside bathroom, or when they have to move far away to get water. Those are all things that will affect them, they might be attacked, they might have sexual assault, there might be that risk of—if there's a sexual assault, maybe getting HIV or an STI [sexually transmitted infection]. And in the end when these kinds of things happen, conflict happens, and they will come back through that *komiti* process.

MD

So this is a way that the physical spaces people are living in and the kinds of access to the basic necessities of life in those spaces directly impact not only the potential for conflict, but how people think about resolving it.

FH

Yes, absolutely. And I would say water would be one.

MD

Are there others that spring to mind, other basic necessities that affect these interconnected issues?

FH

Having adequate lighting, so: electricity. That's a connection there. There's no electricity, so moving around after a certain time might not be as safe for people, like women and children especially, or even men, because there's a potential of being harassed or attacked. Or if a fight happens when people are drunk and there's no electricity, no lighting, people can't see what's going on, so those kinds of connections, and the potential for conflict is there.

MD

Have you heard of *komiti* systems of this kind happening in other urban situations in PNG or did they work differently? When I think of there being a 'Port Moresby model', because the communities there are so well organised—or some of them seem to be—do you think that that way of organising a community to get what it needs to prevent conflict from arising can work elsewhere in PNG? Or is that a uniquely Port Moresby thing?

FH

No, I think it can work elsewhere and I think it does work in other urban settings. I think that they have in Lae, I mean you'd know better, but I think in Lae they would have *komiti*. Or at least some kind of regulation where, especially in urban settlements, they would have some point of contact for people, community leaders especially. Those community leaders, the people that are recognised not only within the community but are known by police and other institutions of the state.

MD

And those people who are both respected in their communities and known to state actors, such as police—have you seen fruitful collaborations between these kinds of formal and informal actors in the community?

FH

Yes, I have. For example with Port Moresby, with the NCD [National Capital District], with the PNG Human Rights Defenders, a lot of them are village court officials. But they are also part of an association called the Human Rights Defenders, so they work together within the village court structure when they need to. They also work with communities and they work with the police, they work with the national entity FSVAC [Family and Sexual Violence Action Committee]. When I was doing work with the village courts at Kaugere, they seemed to also have a good working relationship with the police and other *komiti* or informal systems. But I have noted that there is some friction with these informal systems because, for example, the informal systems often use the same kinds of summons and all these kinds of things, but they are not officially recognised by the village courts. So they are running a parallel system; sometimes village court officials are involved, sometimes they're not. I have witnessed, when I was doing my PhD research, a very big *komiti* meeting where it was an informal meeting, a dispute resolution meeting, but they did invite the village court officials to observe.

MD

Sometimes the village court officials may be present but not involved; I've seen that too in Lae. And other times they may be acting as if it were a village court even when it isn't.

FH

Yes, because the village court—they are appointed because they are community leaders and then under the Village Courts Act they can mediate. So sometimes they have that dual role. And what I've noticed is that people say: 'Okay, we'll have a *komiti* meeting, if you're not happy with the decision of the *komiti*, you can take it to the village court.' And then they will take it to the court sitting on that day if they are not happy with the outcome.

MD

There's occasionally some concern at the level of the formal legal system. I'm thinking of conversations I've had over the years with people at the Village Courts Secretariat or with district court magistrates who are concerned that the village court system and the informal systems that feed into it, the ones that you've been describing, are doing things they shouldn't do, they're acting like courts when they're not courts and they need to be better regulated. That of course is the impulse of any state system of law, it's to regulate or govern informal approaches to dispute resolution. But for PNG, based on what you've seen, is that an approach you would recommend? Does there need to be more regulation of things like the *komiti*?

FH

I think that there needs to be some oversight. I've used the word regulation, but I certainly think that there needs to be some kind of oversight, so that we know that there are fair and just outcomes for those who are seeking assistance through this mechanism. Because, for example, in cases relating to gender-based violence there is a possibility that the wishes of the woman might be overlooked in the interest of harmony between families. I think there needs to be some kind of oversight in terms of how much they charge for fees, the table fees as they call them, and also how much they charge each party that comes to court. So I wouldn't use the word regulation, but I think there is need for some kind of oversight. But it is already working, it's there in the *komiti* work and so it's going to be hard to say: 'Nobody does *komiti*, and you will all go to the village courts.' Because obviously *komiti* has come about because people may not be happy with village courts, and so it is about finding that balance. It is also about making sure that both the work of *komiti* and also village courts reflects what people want in terms of dispute resolution at that very local level.

MD

Right. Perhaps the way forward, if there is going to be the kind of oversight you describe, is not to be too prescriptive about what the *komiti* does, but to make sure that everybody has equal access to it, in terms of things like table fees and in terms of outcomes.

FH

There's some standardisation, but not too much. You know that table fees are like this, it's 50 kina or it's 10 kina. And you don't turn up with your 10 kina and then someone says: 'Oh no, you're paying 50 kina.' Because I think sometimes *komiti* charge according to the kind of mediation that they're going to do.

MD

True, they change their fees from mediation to mediation.

FH

I've heard that. The ones that I've noticed, it's all the same. That requires a bit more research as well, to really understand how they come to this conclusion of how much to charge at the *komiti*.

MD

You've addressed this a bit already, but what are the risks involved in too much informality of *komiti* making things up as they go along versus the risk of overregulation?

FH

I think that the risk of too much informality is that we end up taking on cases that we're not supposed to. Really serious ones and ones that take advantage of vulnerable people; in many cases women and children and those who are not able to, for whatever reason, access the formal criminal justice system. And if we have too much regulation, then I think what will happen is that, with our already overburdened criminal justice system, we'll just keep not taking any of the very minor cases. Because all of these cases that happen in the communities, like drunk and disorderly behaviour and cases relating to domestic violence, should go through that formal system, but that has all these other challenges in itself. So, too much regulation will then have us in a system that is just overburdened and really not working. And the reason why we have this informal *komiti* system is that the system that we have is not working for the vast majority of people.

MD

People will find their own solutions, won't they, if they can't get things resolved with the system that is being handed to them or if that system, as you say, is so overburdened? There aren't enough magistrates and judges. There aren't enough police; police aren't paid properly; and the temptation is to say, well there aren't enough spaces in prisons, but there also aren't enough social workers, as in there aren't *any*.

FH

Yes, absolutely there is no space in prisons, that is so true. And there are not enough social workers. I think that the prison officers try really hard to work in a really tough environment. That is one place I'd really love to do more research, with the prisons.

MD

In the absence of enough formal criminal justice infrastructure to support them, people are going to look for the solutions that they can. In particular, I am curious to know if there are justice-seeking activities or justice-seeking circumstances that really shouldn't be part of the formal legal or criminal system. You mentioned that *komiti* meetings and mediations sometimes hear cases that they should not hear for all sorts of reasons. Are there conversely some types of cases that shouldn't go to the formal legal system?

FH

Oh yes, absolutely. I think for things like drunk and disorderly behaviour, especially for first-time offenders, stealing, you know—petty crimes. I think those kinds of crimes should be kept out of the formal legal system. To be honest, we also need to—we've already got the Family Protection Act—look at the way in which we deal with domestic violence. I'm not saying that it should be kept out of the formal legal system, but I think that where there is an opportunity for us to present other options, such as the possibilities for restorative justice or other kinds of dispute resolution between husbands and wives, there might be opportunities to look outside that formal justice-seeking pathway. The evidence is there, through the reviews of the FSVUs [Family and Sexual Violence Units at police stations]; the research that is being done in Lae by Michelle Rooney and colleagues is clearly speaking to us and saying that we've got the Family Protection Act, we've got everything in place in this referral pathway. But we are still failing, we are still hearing about women not wanting to go through that process.

So, how can we rethink how we deal with domestic violence? Cases of rape and cases relating to sorcery should go through the formal legal system, but I think that things other than those kinds of crimes can also be dealt with outside that system. That is my experience with working in settlements where I've seen violence occur because something has happened. For example, somebody was killed and the perpetrator was handed over to the police, but there was also a mediation between the two families or groups to ensure that there would be safe passage for members of the community to go and come. And this kind of *bel hevi* [troubling] stuff, because this person had killed another person—those are the kinds of things that I feel, guided with proper oversight, can be dealt with outside. Say, for example, if there was a case of rape or sorcery accusation-related violence that happened and then there was the payback that happened as a result of it.

MD

You mentioned restorative justice earlier and I've seen that come up as a thing that would be good to have. Again, this is more at the policy level or the more formal legal system–level colleagues to whom I've spoken in PNG. Is restorative justice now a system that can be taken around the world and offered to different communities as a way to do things? It's been tried in different ways in lots of different places. A question I often have, that I would love to pose to you, is: Is that not what is already happening at things like *komiti* meetings? Are they not already doing a form of restorative justice. Is it something that needs to be tailor-made for them or have they not already invented it for themselves?

FH

Certainly, yes. That's what they do, restoring peace within families and communities. But I think what we've done—and I'll come back to speaking about domestic violence—is that we pick and choose. We are restoring relations between communities for certain things and then for others we're told: 'Okay, you have to go through the formal system.' It's about finding that balance. That is what they do at *komiti* level, that's what they're doing at the village courts. It's finding a way to restore the harm or to restore the relations or repair the harm that's been done between two people, between the communities, between the families, so that's exactly what the *komiti* is, in my view.

MD

I've wondered about this for a while, as restorative justice often seems to be one of these models that's come from outside PNG and been offered as a solution. You can get a consultant to teach it or you can have a workshop or you can have an awareness—all those things that NGOs will bring with them. But I wondered to what extent that would be reinventing the wheel, in terms of: 'Here, let us tell you how to do something you're doing already.'

FH

The words 'restorative justice' like you hear people say, or like I just said, that's basically what they've been doing. The *komiti* has been practising restorative justice in its own way. And then you have, like you said, people coming in talking about this and putting a name to it or a description to it or a definition to it and then describing it as it is. But it's already in practice, being practised all the time. Did I make sense?

MD

Well, it makes sense to me, because I'm in agreement! I remain sceptical or agnostic about whether there is some kind of shiny new dispute resolution system that could be offered to PNG that they aren't already doing in some form.

FH

Yes!

MD

This book is about how people practice or seek justice in their everyday lives, and this leads me to a bigger question about what you think a contemporary Papua New Guinean theory of justice would look like. Because justice isn't only one thing and it's not the same thing to everyone everywhere. So, what does PNG justice look like, or should it look like, to you?

FH

PNG justice should look like a system that takes in both the *komiti*, a system that allows and accepts *komiti*, and village court–level dispute resolutions and things like that, that work at the very local level. But it also has that form of the introduced system, so they're working together in tandem; that is what a PNG contemporary theory of justice or justice system looks like to me. At present what it is, is that we talk about village courts, we talk about taking community ownership, but we also talk about this system that takes people away from their communities. The police come and take you away, they take you to the police cell and they take you to court, they take you to jail eventually, and then you have to come back into your community.

The system has to work for those kinds of crimes that need you to go away and be put into jail. But in those kinds of cases I just mentioned where there might be a first-time offender or a young person who stole a car or who stole a laptop to sell it to buy food and they end up going through this system and come out more hardened than how they were before? That's a kind of system that doesn't work for us. It should be a system that allows people to say sorry, to be held to account for their behaviour and also be integrated back into communities in a way that doesn't make them feel stigmatised and ostracised because of what they have done. That is one of the things that is always a cause of friction, because you're trying to align these different interests around people's motivations for wanting to say sorry, wanting to make sure that they are held accountable and also wanting to make sure that the families don't pay for what [the individual has] done. Because often, when somebody does something here, in Moresby and elsewhere, in other places, it's the families whose houses get burned down, they are chased out, things like that. So it should be a criminal justice system that allows us to take into consideration the ways in which we deal with conflict, but also have a succinct system that works. The introduced system we have now is saying: 'This is what we need to do, you need to go to the police, you need to be charged, you need to pay for the crime.'

MD

Maybe that is where a more systematised restorative justice approach might help?

FH

Yes.

MD

In terms of providing an alternative to just throwing somebody in jail or burning down their house.

FH

That's right. So that's where the *komiti*-level restorative justice is an organic thing that happens, and people say *yumi stretim hevi* [let's sort out the problem], but how do you institutionalise that in this introduced legal system? How do you hold people accountable, but also make sure that all the other things that can come with a crime that is committed are taken care of, so you don't have that kind of payback and houses being burned down or taken by force?

MD

Right, how do you prevent that escalation or how do you prevent conflicts from turning into other kinds of conflicts?

FH

Because it's never just an individual—'he did that to me'; it's always going to be about the community. And then when they don't turn up, especially if they are young boys, young people, there will be the threats on the family to make sure that this person turns up or else.

MD

And then it can become a harm not only caused by whoever perpetrated what, but also a harm done to the perpetrator's family.

FH

If that happens—for example, a house being burned down or a family being attacked and harassed—that is a crime in itself but it can be seen by the family of the victims [of the original crime] as justice. When I say oversight, these are the kinds of things where we need to make sure that there's a balance to ensure the perpetrator's family, where they are innocent, are not also victimised.

MD

Or even where it's not a question of innocence or guilt, but how far did the actions of a person ramify into the rest of his family and the rest of his community. You know, is his family going to be punished forever for something he's done?

FH

Exactly, yes. That's right.

MD

Looking at all these problems from the point of view of the NRI [National Research Institute], which has that huge social and policy remit as an institution, or from the point of view of the Constitutional and Law Reform Commission [CLRC], how do you think they have a role in this? My last question is twofold: Where could this be researched further at an institutional level in the country or whose job should it be to be investigating these alternative possibilities, and what should their priorities be?

FH

I think there's a role for academia, there's a role for the NRI in terms of policy advice, because we know from all the evidence the importance of community dispute resolution. That certainly is important research, it is important for policy. And then, the CLRC have an important role, which is to inform law and make sure that we have the kind of legal system or laws that are useful for people. Definitely for the CLRC there's a role in terms of legal research or around reforming laws. In academia, and in NGOs who work around gender-based violence and other areas, they're important in the kinds of work they do, especially researching programs that are in place to help women, to see whether this system that we have is actually working. And if we know that it's not working because of certain structural barriers or limitations, such as having not enough police, what are the kinds of things that we can do or advocate for to be able to make this a system that works for everybody. We've been talking about the urban setting, but the majority of our people are rural and so all of these kinds of dispute resolutions are their everyday life.

MD

And once you get to a rural community, at least from what I've seen in those contexts, there's even more improvisation going on, there's even more 'How do we make this work even though there's no police here'.

FH

Yes, certainly, and in the urban settings they have a choice. You can go to a *komiti*, you can go to village courts, but in our most remote rural areas, it's more like: 'Okay, well we have a problem, let's fix it.'

MD

Because it's just us.

FH

Yeah, that's it.

MD

Nobody else is going to come and sort this out, so we have to sort it out ourselves.

FH

Yes, and I know with sorcery accusation–related violence, especially in some parts of the Highlands, because of the terrain, it's just hard for the police to get there. It's just way too difficult.

MD

So you can disparage the police for not intervening in those cases, but then you have to ask questions again of how they are meant to get there, what resources do they have, what training do they have, what vehicles do they have.

FH

Yes.

MD

Final question! Where do you see your own research going with these topics that we've being talking about? If you had complete freedom to investigate any aspect of this stuff in the next few years, what would you like to be looking at in your own work?

FH

I would really like to look at, as I said, the prisons. But in terms of the *komiti*, the informal systems, I would like to look at that too. It's something that I've had in the background for some time, but looking at how all of these kinds of local dispute resolution and conflict resolution can work for domestic violence. Because I know from research I've done in the village courts, apart from *dinau moni* [debt]—and that is probably another thing that can be kept out of the formal system. *Disla liklik dinau moni go kam* [these small debts going back and forth], we find a way to sort that out. Apart from *dinau moni*, it is adultery or those kinds of domestic-related cases that come to the village courts. I would like to concentrate more on that area of work and see how that can be really built in to support the work of the Family Protection Act and provide more research or advice in that area.

MD

Well, I hope you get the opportunity to do it!

FH

Thank you.

Contributors

Dr Tomi Bartole is a researcher at the Slovenian Academy of Sciences and Arts. He is the co-curator of the exhibition 'Green Sky, Blue Grass: Colour Coding Worlds' at the Museum of World Cultures in Frankfurt, Germany.

Dr Melissa Demian is a Senior Lecturer in Social Anthropology at the University of St Andrews, Scotland. She is the author of *In memory of times to come: Ironies of history in Southeastern Papua New Guinea* (2021).

Dr Hiroki Fukagawa is an Associate Professor in the Graduate School of Intercultural Studies at Kobe University, Japan. He is the author of *Ethnography of the social body: Theories of personhood and sociality in New Guinea Highlands* (in Japanese; 2021).

Dr Michael Goddard is an Honorary Senior Research Fellow in the School of Social Sciences at Macquarie University, Australia. He is the author of *Substantial justice: An anthropology of village courts in Papua New Guinea* (2009).

Dr Eve Houghton is a Postdoctoral Researcher at the Royal Veterinary College, London. Her current work explores emergent zoonotic diseases in South Asia as a member of the One Health Poultry Hub.

Dr Fiona Hukula is a Gender Specialist for the Pacific Islands Forum Secretariat in Suva. Prior to this, she was a senior research fellow and program leader for the Papua New Guinea National Research Institute.

Dr Juliane Neuhaus is a Senior Lecturer in Social Anthropology at the University of Zürich, Switzerland. She is the author of *It takes more than a village court: Plural dispute management and Christian morality in rural Papua New Guinea* (2020).

Index

Note: page numbers in italics indicate a figure or illustration.

www.ingramcontent.com/pod-product-compliance
Lightning Source LLC
Chambersburg PA
CBHW070328270326
41926CB00017B/3809